From Alpha to Omega

Ancillary Exercises

ISBN 0-941051-61-7

10 9 8 7 6 5 4 3

From Alpha to Omega

Ancillary Exercises

Jon Bruss

Focus Publishing
R. Pullins Company
Newburyport MA 01950

For My Students at Bethany Lutheran College

Foreword

These exercises and the accompanying key have been designed as an ancilla to Anne H. Groton's *From Alpha to Omega: A Beginning Course in Classical Greek*. *Ancillary Exercises* has fifty lessons corresponding to the fifty lessons in Groton's text. Exercises for each of the fifty lessons focus specifically, though not exclusively, on the grammatical, syntactical and vocabulary content of the corresponding lesson in *A Beginning Course*. Each of the fifty lessons in *Ancillary Exercises* is accompanied by a complete key so that students may check their work immediately.

The volume arose out of my own experiences in the classroom, both as a student and as a teacher—experiences I believe I share with many of my colleagues. For starters, the exercises are modeled on the "Self-Tutorial Exercises" in *Wheelock's Latin*, which many students, including myself, have used to great profit.

Secondly, as a teacher I have been perennially frustrated by, among other things: (a) students' bewilderment in reading and learning from a text about something so arcane as ancient Greek; and (b) the lack of introductory Greek texts on the market with adequate drills to reinforce grammatical and syntactical knowledge and an operational vocabulary. This volume of *Ancillary Exercises* addresses these areas of frustration; that is, it asks the kinds of questions which will lead students not only to read more slowly and carefully, but to come away from *A Beginning Course* actually understanding what they have read; and it supplies adequate drills ranging from simple to complex for reinforcing the basics of Greek grammar, syntax, and vocabulary.

The applications for this volume are manifold. Above all, these exercises have been designed to enhance students' independence—hence their satisfaction, hence their tenacity—in learning classical Greek. The self-taught student should find *A Beginning Course*, coupled with the following exercises, sufficient to the task of mastering Greek grammar, syntax and basic vocabulary at an introductory level. College Greek courses taught on a three-day-per-week schedule will be able to make use of these exercises in out-of-class and in-class drill sessions, if not also as out-of-class assigned work. Closer to my own experience in teaching an introductory college-level Greek course five days per week, I have found that assigning the exercises for a given lesson on the day students are to read the lesson in *A Beginning Course* helps to focus their reading and my lectures and give structure to class drills. In many cases, the *Ancillary Exercises* provide for such a careful study of *A Beginning Course* that the need for lecturing is obviated. In any case, those more generously endowed with the teaching genius than I will find more and perhaps better uses for this volume.

I wish to express thanks to Anne H. Groton, a most encouraging teacher and friend, and to my students who willingly or unwillingly allowed themselves to be guinea pigs over the last two years. Among the latter, special thanks goes to Mr. Aaron Ferkenstad, whose eagle eye, effeciency and computer expertise have made timely publication of this work possible.

Table of Contents

ANCILLARY EXERCISES

ANSWER KEY TO ANCILLARY EXERCISES

Ancillary Exercises

Lesson 1

1. For the following, write in Greek both the upper-case and lower-case forms of the letter.

   (1) beta
   (2) phi
   (3) alpha
   (4) mu
   (5) zeta
   (6) gamma
   (7) sigma
   (8) epsilon
   (9) psi
   (10) rho
   (11) kappa
   (12) upsilon
   (13) xi
   (14) omega
   (15) lambda
   (16) theta
   (17) pi
   (18) delta
   (19) tau
   (20) chi
   (21) iota
   (22) eta
   (23) omicron

2. Say aloud the letters of the Greek alphabet, in order, from beginning to end.

3. For each letter of the Greek alphabet, give the sound it makes, along with an English example of the sound.

4. What is a diphthong?

5. (a) What two types of diphthong does the Greek language have? (b) What are the short and long vowels in Greek?

6. List all of the Greek diphthongs, giving in English their equivalent sound.

7. Explain the difference between the iota subscript and the iota adscript.

8. (a) When does one use a breathing mark in classical Greek? (b) What symbols indicate a breathing and what does each mean? (c) Where is the breathing mark placed? (d) Which letters found at the beginning of a word always take a rough breathing mark?

9. List all consonantal stops in the Greek language.

10. Of the consonantal stops in the Greek language, which are: (a) labials; (b) dentals; (c) palatals?

11. If a γ is followed by another palatal, how is it pronounced?

12. Of the remaining consonants in the Greek language, which are: (a) nasals; (b) double consonants; (c) sibilants?

13. (a) Explain in your own words the rules that govern whether a cluster of consonants is pronounced together or separately. (b) Indicate whether the consonants in the following consonant clusters should be pronounced together or separately: βδ, μβ, φθ, τρ, τμ, λπ, χθ, λλ, κτ.

14. How can one determine how many syllables a Greek word has?

15. How does one break into syllables a Greek word whose vowels/diphthongs are separated by a consonant or a consonant cluster?

16. Below is a list of Greek words. (a) rewrite each word in Greek on a separate piece of paper; (b) say the word aloud in Greek several times, placing emphasis on the accented syllable, until you can read the word smoothly; (c) identify how many syllables the word has; (d) rewrite the word in Greek, this time separating properly between its syllables.

(1)	κάμηλος	(11)	ἐγχειρίδιον
(2)	ἄγγελος	(12)	διεφθαρμένη
(3)	ἀεί	(13)	ἀποστροφή
(4)	ἔπληξεν	(14)	ἀποκολοκύντωσις
(5)	ῥᾴων	(15)	οὐρανός
(6)	ἐπίλογος	(16)	τραγῳδία
(7)	ῥητορικός	(17)	τάττω
(8)	συμβουλεύειν	(18)	ὑπείροχον
(9)	τράπεζα	(19)	χαμαί
(10)	ἀθανάτων	(20)	ἀποβδέλυγμα

Lesson 2

1. How many different types of accent are there in ancient Greek, and what are they?

2. Originally, what did the various Greek accents indicate, and how are they conventionally used today?

3. When placing an accent mark on a lower-case vowel that also has a breathing mark, where is the accent placed? Give examples that illustrate the possibilities.

4. When placing accent marks on upper-case individual vowels or improper diphthongs whose first vowel is upper-case, where is the accent placed? Give examples that illustrate the possibilities.

5. When placing an accent over a proper diphthong, where is the accent placed? Give examples that illustrate the possibilities.

6. How many accents may most Greek words receive?

7. Which syllables in a Greek word may receive an accent? What are these syllables conventionally called?

8. Below is a list of Greek words. Identify the syllable asked for in the parentheses that follow each. Example:

κάμηλος (ultima)   Answer: λος

    (1) θεασαμένη (antepenult)   (6) πρός (penult)
    (2) ἀγανακτήσας (ultima)   (7) μέρος (antepenult)
    (3) ἐπιθυμεῖ (penult)   (8) ἀρκεῖται (ultima)
    (4) κέρασιν (antepenult)   (9) ἀγαλλόμενον (penult)
    (5) στερούμενοι (ultima)   (10) καί (antepenult)

9. On which of the three accentable syllables may the following accents appear: (a) acute; (b) grave; (c) circumflex? Searching over Groton Lesson 1.A, give a correct example for each.

10. What do we mean when we say a syllable is: (a) short; (b) long by nature; (c) long by position?

11. There follows a list of Greek words. Give the length of the syllable asked for in the parentheses after each.

    (1) θεασαμένη (penult)   (6) πρός (ultima)
    (2) ἀγανακτήσας (penult)   (7) μέρος (ultima)
    (3) ἐπιθυμεῖ (ultima)   (8) ἀρκεῖται (ultima)
    (4) κέρασιν (antepenult)   (9) ἄλλοι (penult)
    (5) στερούμενοι (antepenult)   (10) καί (ultima)

12. There follows a list of Greek words. Give the length of the syllable that is bold-face in each.

    (1) **θε**ασαμένη   (6) **πρό**ς
    (2) αὐ**τῆς**   (7) **μέ**ρος
    (3) ἐπιθυ**μεῖ**   (8) ἀρ**κεῖ**ται
    (4) **ὤ**των   (9) ἄλ**λοι**
    (5) στερού**με**νοι   (10) πλεονεξ**ί**αν

13. Give the two general principles of accenting, in your own words.

14. Below are several sets of three words. Each is accented, but of the three, only one is correctly accented. (a) Select from the three the correctly accented form. Then, (b) rewrite the word in Greek, splitting it correctly into syllables.

	A	B	C
(1)	ἀγγελός	ἄγγελος	ἀγγελος
(2)	δίεφθαρμενη	διεφθάρμενη	διεφθαρμένη
(3)	σταύρον	σταῦρων	σταυρον
(4)	ἔτυμων	ἐτύμων	ἐτύμων
(5)	παράγγελμασιν	πάραγγελμασιν	παραγγέλμασιν
(6)	ἀνάρσιος	ἆναρσιος	ἀναρσιός
(7)	γυναικός	γυναικὸς	γύναικων
(8)	θεοὺς	θεὲους	θεους
(9)	δὲκατου	δέκατου	δεκάτου
(10)	κέκομμένος	κεκόμμενος	κεκομμένος

Lesson 3

1. List the parts of speech in Greek.

2. When one encounters a verb in a Greek sentence, what does the verb indicate?

3. What are the various properties that a Greek verb has?

4. When we speak of "person" associated with a Greek verb, what do we mean?

5. When we speak of "number" associated with a Greek verb, what do we mean?

6. When we speak of "voice" associated with a Greek verb, what do we mean?

7. When we speak of the terms "transitive" and "intransitive" associated with a Greek verb, what do we mean?

8. How many moods does the Greek verb have, and what does each indicate about the verb?

9. (a) How many tenses may the Greek verb be found in, and what are they? (b) What do we mean when we speak of primary and secondary tenses?

10. When we speak of the term "aspect" associated with a Greek verb, what do we mean?

11. Tease all the implications out of the phrase that describes the conjugations you are learning in the present lesson: (a) present active indicative; (b) present active imperative.

12. How does one determine the present stem of the Greek –ω verb?

13. How does one form (a) the present active indicative, (b) the present active imperative, and (c) the present active infinitive of the –ω verb?

14. What type of accent does the Greek verb have, and what does this imply as to its accentuation?

15. Below are several verb endings for the present active. For each, give what it indicates as far as the verb's mood, number, and person.

    (1) -ω   (6) -ειν
    (2) -ουσι(ν)   (7) -ετε
    (3) -ει   (8) -ομεν
    (4) -έτω   (9) -όντων
    (5) -εις   (10) -ε

16. Conjugate the following verbs in the demanded forms; say aloud each verb you conjugate; give translations of each.

    (1) ἐθέλω, present active infinitive
    (2) γράφω, present active indicative
    (3) σπεύδω, present active imperative
    (4) κλέπτω, present active indicative and infinitive
    (5) φυλάττω, present active imperative
    (6) θύω, present active imperative and infinitive

17. Explain the function of the ν-movable.

18. Translate the following sentences from English into Greek (1) Write and don't steal. (2) We are both offering sacrifice and standing guard. (3) Let him not steal! They are teaching. (4) Are you willing to write? (5) Let them hasten to stand guard. (6) We are not hastening to steal. (7) Don't

4

be willing to steal. (8) Both write and sacrifice! (9) We are not willing to hasten. (10) Be eager to stand guard; they are willing to steal.

19. For extra practice, turn to the key for Lesson 3, **18.**, and translate those Greek sentences into English.

Lesson 4

1. What is a noun? Give examples in English.

2. We have seen that the Greek verb changes form in order to reflect how it is being used in a sentence. Does a Greek noun do the same?

3. (a) What are the genders of a Greek noun? (b) What does "gender" mean?

4. Does a noun's gender ever change?

5. How many different numbers may a Greek noun have?

6. How does one determine the function of a noun in an English sentence? Give examples.

7. How does one determine the function of a noun in a Greek sentence?

8. What do the following cases in Greek signify about the function of a noun: (a) genitive; (b) vocative; (c) dative; (d) accusative; (e) nominative?

9. (a) Generally speaking, what kind of accent can one say that the noun has? (Hint: think about what kind of accent we say that the verb has, generally speaking.) (b) What are the implications of the accent being of this type?

10. Give the two oddities of feminine first declension accentuation.

11. Why do some feminine first declension nouns prefer α endings to η endings in the singular forms?

12. What is the feminine article in Greek? Give its full declension.

13. Decline the following nouns, along with their articles.
    (1) ἡ ἀγορά
    (2) ἡ ἐπιστολή
    (3) ἡ ἡσυχία
    (4) ἡ χώρα

14. Explain how one expresses the indirect object of a Greek verb.

15. Translate the following sentences from English into Greek: (1) I am sending the letter. (2) I am sending, o goddess, the letter. (3) I am sending the letter, o goddess, into the marketplace. (4) Let the goddess send tranquility out of the tent. (5) Write letters in the marketplace! (6) The goddesses of peace are hastening to offer sacrifice. (7) We are sacrificing to the goddess. (8) We are sacrificing letters to the goddess. (9) Do you wish to educate the goddesses in the tent and in the marketplace? (10) Let them be eager to steal the letters out of the tents.

16. For extra practice, turn to the key for Lesson 4, **15.**, and translate those Greek sentences into English.

Lesson 5

1. There are two types of short α feminine first declension nouns. (a) First of all, in general, describe how both of these differ from the feminine first declension nouns you have already learned; and (b) secondly, describe how these two types of short α feminine first declension nouns differ one from the other.

2. In what ways are the feminine first declension short α nouns similar in their declension to the feminine first declension long α nouns?

3. What is the reflexive use of the definite article? Give an appropriate Greek example of your own invention, along with your translation of it.

4. Conjugate the verbs below in the forms demanded.

    (1) βλάπτω, present active indicative
    (2) ἀκούω, present active imperative
    (3) κελεύω, present active infinitive

5. Give the case of the direct object of the following verbs.

    (1) θύω   (5) πέμπω
    (2) βλάπτω   (6) κελεύω
    (3) ἀκούω   (7) παιδεύω
    (4) κλέπτω   (8) γράφω

6. Decline the following nouns in the singular and plural, together with their article. Then say them aloud, first looking at your work, then with your eyes closed. Make sure you stress the appropriate syllable (the accented syllable).

    (1) θεά, -ᾶς, ἡ   (4) δέσποινα, -ης, ἡ
    (2) μοῖρα, -ας, ἡ   (5) θεράπαινα, -ης, ἡ
    (3) κλίνη, -ης, ἡ   (6) θάλαττα, -ης, ἡ

7. Translate the following sentences from English into Greek.

    (1) Let the mistress command her maids to write letters. (2) Are you (*pl.*) listening to the goddess? (3) When they hear the sea, they write letters to their mistress. (4) It is time to teach. (5) It is time for the maids to teach in the marketplace. (6) Since it is time to write letters, let the mistresses not harm their maids. (7) Continue to listen! We are teaching and writing letters. (8) The goddess is commanding the mistress and her servants to hasten out of their beds and into the marketplace. (9) Because we are hearing the sea, we are offering sacrifice to our Fate. (10) Don't command the maids to harm their mistress!

8. For extra practice, turn to the key for Lesson 5, **7.**, and translate those Greek sentences into English.

Lesson 6

1. What **aspect** does the future active indicative have?

2. From which principal part of the Greek verb is the future active indicative formed?

3. Why is it important to memorize not only the first, but also the second principal part of the Greek verb?

4. What is the standard stem-change that takes place in forming the future active indicative? Supply with an example.

5. The standard addition of σ to the present stem to form the future active indicative stem becomes more complex with verbs whose stem ends in a consonant. Below, there are listed several consonants. Supposing that these consonants were to come at the end of the present stem of a verb, when combined with σ, what would they yield?

   (1) πτ   (7) δ
   (2) β   (8) τ
   (3) ττ   (9) γ
   (4) θ   (10) φ
   (5) χ   (11) π
   (6) κ

6. Deciphering what the present stem, and hence the first principal part of a verb, might be from a future active indicative form can be difficult at times. However, arriving at the present stem is not simply guess-work. Below are several future stem-endings. Give the possible present stem-endings which the future stem-endings might represent.

   (1) ψ
   (2) σ
   (3) ξ

7. Below are several regularly formed second principal parts of various verbs. For each, list the possible first principal parts on which these may be based.

   (1) λύσω   (6) διώξω
   (2) πλήξω   (7) βουλεύσω
   (3) μεταπέμψω   (8) λείψω
   (4) πείσω   (9) σείσω
   (5) τάξω   (10) σπεύσω

8. Give the two principal parts of the following verbs that you already know or that have been introduced to you in this lesson.

   (1) guard   (9) steal
   (2) pursue   (10) have
   (3) hear   (11) command
   (4) sacrifice   (12) educate, teach
   (5) be about [to] (13) change
   (6) harm   (14) hasten
   (7) wish   (15) send
   (8) write

9. Conjugate the following verbs in the future active indicative and infinitive.

   (1) μέλλω
   (2) διώκω
   (3) θύω

10. Discuss the syntactial properties of μέλλω.

11. Describe the Greek practice of elision.

12. Translate the following sentences from English into Greek.

(1) No longer hesitate to educate the girl in the house! (2) O goddess, do you intend to change the girl into a mistress? (3) The maidservant is not pursuing her fate, but Lady Fate is pursuing the girls. (4) Do you (s.) possess a house? Are you (s.) able to guard your house? (5) When we shall send the letters to the lady, she will hesitate to chase her maidservants. (6) You (pl.) will no longer offer sacrifice to the goddesses, but you will command your servants to offer sacrifice. (7) The maid is stealing the letter! I shall steal my letter back out of the house! (8) Since you are hesitating to teach the girls, I intend to write letters in the house. (9) O goddesses, shall we change the mistresses back into girls? (10) She will wish to hear both the girl and the sea again.

13. For extra practice, turn to the key for Lesson 6, **12.**, and translate those Greek sentences into English.

Lesson 7

1. List the case endings for the second declension masculine.

2. In what ways do the second declension masculine and the first declension feminine differ from one another in form?

3. In what ways are the second declension masculine and the first declension feminine similar to one another?

4. Decline the masculine article in the singular and plural.

5. Decline the following nouns in the singular and plural, together with their article.

    (1) ἵππος, -ου, ὁ
    (2) ἀδελφός, -οῦ, ὁ
    (3) ἀδελφή, -ῆς, ἡ
    (4) ἄνθρωπος, -ου, ὁ

6. Give the gender and declension of the following nouns:

    (1) ἀδελφή   (4) ὁδός
    (2) ἄνθρωπος   (5) λίθος
    (3) θεός   (6) χαρά

7. Explain in your own words the dative of manner and the dative of means.

8. Conjugate the verb χαίρω, χαιρήσω in the following forms:

    (1) future active infinitive and present active infinitive
    (2) future active indicative
    (3) present active imperative
    (4) present active indicative.

9. Translate the following sentences from English into Greek.

(1) Do not harm the horse! (2) Do not harm the horse with stones! (3) Does the human being intend to hasten? (4) Will the human being hesitate to hasten away from the river? (5) Hello, brother! Rejoice in your pain, since the gods will send joys. (6) Both the brother and the sister will take delight in their journey. (7) Let the horses chase the women out of the river and into the road. (8) Fate will not send joys, but let the woman take joy in her pains. (9) Can the gods change a horse into a human

being? Can they also change a human being into a rock? Let them not be willing to harm humankind. (10) O god, o fate, o humankind, I shall rejoice in my joy and I shall intend to sacrifice to the gods.

10. For extra practice, turn to the key for Lesson 7, **9.**, and translate those Greek sentences into English.

Lesson 8

1. (a) Give points of similarity between the forms of second declension neuter nouns and the forms of second declension masculines. (b) Give points of dissimilarity between the two.

2. List the case endings for the neuter second declension in the singular and plural.

3. (a) Decline the neuter article in the singular and plural. (b) Decline the feminine article in the singular and plural. (c) Decline the masculine article in the singular and plural.

4. Below are several articles. Please indicate for each the number, case, and gender of the noun it might go with.

   (1) τά   (9) τοῖς
   (2) τόν   (10) τό
   (3) ὁ   (11) τῶν
   (4) τοῦ   (12) τῷ
   (5) τῇ   (13) ταῖς
   (6) ἡ   (14) οἱ
   (7) τούς   (15) τάς
   (8) τῆς

5. When a neuter nominative plural is the subject of a sentence, indicate what happens to the verb it governs. Supply your answer with an example that illustrates your point; give a contrasting example.

6. What gender are adjectives?

7. (a) In what ways must an adjective agree with the noun it modifies? (b) What does this mean about an adjective's form in relation to the verb?

8. When one encounters an adjective in the vocabulary of *From Alpha to Omega*, how is one able to predict what forms it will assume in the various numbers, genders, and cases?

9. Below are several definite article/noun phrases. For each, place the adjective listed alongside them between the article and the noun in the appropriate form. Example:

   τῷ φυτῷ / καλός, -ή, όν   τῷ καλῷ φυτῷ
   (1) τῆς δεσποίνης / ἀγαθός, -ή, -όν
   (2) ὦ ἄνθρωπε / καλός, -ή, -όν
   (3) τὰ τέκνα / ἄξιος, -α, -ον
   (4) ταῖς ὁδοῖς / ἀγαθός, -ή, -όν
   (5) τὴν θεάν / καλός, -ή, -όν
   (6) τὴν θεόν / ἀγαθός, -ή, -όν
   (7) τὸν θεόν / ἄξιος, -α, -ον

(8) τῶν ἡσυχιῶν / καλός, -ή, -όν
(9) τῇ χώρᾳ / ἀγαθός, -ή, -όν
(10) τὴν σκηνήν / ἄξιος, -α, -ον

10. (a) Give examples of the various ways to put an adjective in the attributive position in Greek. (b) Give examples illustrating the predicate position of an adjective in Greek.

11. Translate the following phrases into English:

(1) ἡ καλὴ θεά
(2) καλὴ ἡ θεά
(3) θεά ἡ καλή
(4) ἡ θεά καλή
(5) ἡ θεὰ ἡ καλή

12. How is the attributive position occupied with a noun that has no definite article?

13. Decline the adjective ἀγαθός, -ή, -όν.

14. Conjugate the following verbs in the forms indicated.

(1) λείπω, future active indicative and infinitive
(2) εὑρίσκω, present active imperative and infinitive
(3) ἀπολείπω, present active indicative

15. Give the two principal parts you know for the following verbs:

(1) abandon
(2) find
(3) leave

16. Translate the following sentences from English into Greek.

(1) O Mistress Fate, shall I abandon my good life? (2) The mistress is worthy of the handsome gift. (3) We shall find our good work. (4) The beautiful horses are finding the worthy country. (5) The children are abandoning the beautiful plants. (6) The children will harm the beautiful house with stones. (7) They will chase the good girls with worthy horses. (8) Since I am going to abandon my good life, do not leave behind your worthy works. (9) Let them no longer steal beautiful gifts from the worthy treasury! (10) Let the children no longer steal beautiful gifts from the worthy treasury! (11) Let the humans no longer steal beautiful gifts from the worthy treasury! (12) Are you (pl.) eager to discover beautiful plants? It is time to send the servants into the countryside upon horses. The countryside is still beautiful. Let the servants not delay to find plants, but let them intend to leave behind their works.

17. For extra practice, turn to the key for Lesson 8, **16.**, and translate those Greek sentences into English.

Lesson 9

1. In addition to the feminine α and η stem nouns of the first declension, what other first declension nouns are there?

2. In the masculine first declension, when should one expect the endings of the various cases to be primarily α endings, and when should one expect them to be primarily η endings?

3. If one encounters a masculine first declension noun in the vocabulary, what clues give it away as belonging to this category of noun?

4. Below are several nouns given in the form of their lexical entry. For each, give its declension and gender.

   (1) εὑρετής, -ου, ὁ   (4) θεωρία, -ης, ἡ
   (2) κόσμος, -ου, ὁ   (5) θεῖον, -ου, τό
   (3) Ἱππίας, -ου, ὁ   (6) ἄνθρωπος, -ου, ἡ

5. Decline the following noun along with its article.

   (1) δεσπότης, -ου, ὁ
   (2) νεανίας, -ου, ὁ

6. Decline the following article/adjective/noun phrases in the singular and plural.

   (1) ὁ ἐλεύθερος μαθητής
   (2) ὁ καλὸς οἰκέτης
   (3) ἡ ἀξία θεός
   (4) ἀγαθὸς νεανίας

7. Give several similarities and several differences between first declension feminine and first declension masculine nouns.

8. Explain in your own words what a substantive is in Greek.

9. Below are several article/adjective [phrase]/noun or article/adjective [phrase] phrases. (a) Rewrite the whole expression, underlining the adjective or adjective phrase. (b) Label each as to whether the adjective or adjective phrase is functioning as a substantive or not. (c) For each, supply a translation.

   (1) οἱ ἐν τῇ ἀγορᾷ ἄνθρωποι   (7) τὰ ἐν τῇ ἀγορᾷ
   (2) αἱ καλαί   (8) αἱ ἀθάνατοι θεαί
   (3) τῷ ἐν τῇ οἰκίᾳ δεσπότῃ   (9) τῇ ἐν τῇ οἰκίᾳ
   (4) τῶν ἀθανάτων   (10) τῶν θεῶν τῶν ἀθανάτων
   (5) τὰ ἀγαθὰ ἔργα   (11) τὰ ἀγαθά
   (6) τοῦ ἐν τῇ καλῇ οἰκίᾳ δώρου   (12) τοῦ καλοῦ

10. When used in an adjectival phrase, what is the implication of μή; of οὐ?

11. Using ἡ σκηνή in the nominative and ὁ ἄνθρωπος in the genitive, demonstrate the various ways in which the genitive of possession may be phrased in Greek. Supply each of your examples with a translation.

12. Translate the following sentences from English into Greek.

    (1) The enslaved in the house will serve the master. (2) Those in the house will serve the master. (3) The [women] in the house serve the master. (4) Let the family member send a letter to the unworthy student. (5) Let the enslaved family member send a letter to the unworthy servants. (6) Let the free [ones] no longer serve the youths. (7) Let the free [women] no longer serve the immortal goddesses. (8) Since you (s.) are abandoning your former master, do you intend to find and serve an unworthy mistress? (9) Leave (pl.) the ugly things in the marketplace, and chase the beautiful youths into their tents. (10) Do we wish to serve the ugly and unworthy [woman]? (11) Do we wish to serve the ugly and unworthy [men]? (12) Do you (pl). wish to chase the horses with rocks away from the river? (13) Do you (s.) wish to chase the handsome students away from their master [who is] in the house? (14) Are the children free from

pains? Let them no longer serve their pains, but serve joy. (15) We will find the unworthy master's ugly house in the marketplace.

13. For extra practice, turn to the key for Lesson 9, **12.**, and translate those Greek sentences into English.

Lesson 10

1. From which principal part of the Greek verb is the imperfect active indicative formed?

2. Dissect the phrase **imperfect active indicative**. What does it mean as concerns mood, tense, aspect, and voice?

3. Explain in your own words how one forms the imperfect active indicative from the first principal part of the verb.

4. What happens to the following vowels and diphthongs when augmented by ε?

(1)	ει	(6)	ε
(2)	α	(7)	οι
(3)	ευ	(8)	αυ
(4)	ο	(9)	ι
(5)	υ	(10)	αι

5. What happens to a word which begins with a prefixed preposition when adding the ε augment to it to form the imperfect?

6. What does the ε augment always indicate in Greek?

7. What kind of accent does the imperfect active indicative always have in Greek?

8. (a) Conjugate the following verbs in the imperfect active indicative. (b) Give all possible translations of the second person singular form.

(1)	διώκω	(5)	λέγω
(2)	ἐθέλω	(6)	φεύγω
(3)	θύω	(7)	πράττω
(4)	δουλεύω	(8)	ἀπολείπω

9. What happens to the verb ἔχω when augmented in the imperfect active indicative? Conjugate it in the imperfect active indicative.

10. (a) When μέν appears in a clause not followed by δέ, what does it mean? (b) When δέ appears in a clause not preceded by a clause beginning with μέν, what does it mean? (c) When μέν and δέ appear, in that order, in successive clauses, how do they function?

11. What do we mean when we say μέν and δέ are **postpositives**? Give an example in Greek of your own devising.

12. When the article precedes μέν and δέ, not followed by a noun, how should one translate it? Give two examples, one using the singular article, one using the plural article.

13. Translate the following sentences from English into Greek.

(1) This one is dear to the students, that one is not. (2) Some are dear to unworthy students, others are not. (3) I was in truth pursuing the horse, since it was fleeing the servants. (4) On the one hand, let the masters speak; on the other hand, let the household servants not speak. (5) Were you (pl.) therefore leaving behind your life? (6) Were you (s.) doing good works? I was not doing good works. Let the slaves, therefore, do good works. (7) On the one hand, we were fleeing both death and danger; on the other hand, they were chasing their dear fate. (8) The horse, on the one hand, is dear to the handsome youth; the girl, on the other hand, is truly not dear to the youth. (9) Some [women] were writing letters, others [women] were not. (10) Some [men] were writing letters, others [men] were sacrificing to the goddesses of fate. (11) We were saying some things; they were saying other things. Can we find the truth? (12) I do not flee my friends, but I shall speak the truth. (13) The master is indeed dear to his mistress. (14) The students were teaching the master, but the master was not able to teach the students. (15) We kept on writing letters to the girls, but they continued not to speak the truth. (16) The immortals used to chase humans, but humans are free from the gods.

14. For extra practice, turn to the key for Lesson 10, **13.**, and translate those Greek sentences into English.

Lesson 11

1. Distinguish between the active, middle, and passive voices in Greek. Supply your distinction with examples in English that illustrate your point.

2. In this chapter we are learning middle/passive forms and middle forms. For each of the following tenses, indicate whether the forms we are learning arc middle/passive or simply middle: future, imperfect, present.

3. From which principal part are the following formed:

    (1)   present middle/passive indicative
    (2)   imperfect middle/passive indicative
    (3)   present middle/passive imperative
    (4)   future middle indicative and infinitive
    (5)   present middle/passive infinitive?

4. Explain how to form: (a) the present middle/passive indicative, imperative and infinitive from the first principal part; (b) the future middle indicative and infinitive from the second principal part; and (c) the imperfect middle/passive indicative from the first principal part.

5. Below is a list of verbs in English. For each, give in Greek the forms demanded. Translate the third person singular for each. For infinitives, give the translation of the infinitive.

    (1)   chase, future middle indicative
    (2)   sacrifice, future middle infinitive
    (3)   say, imperfect middle/passive indicative
    (4)   wish, imperfect middle/passive indicative
    (5)   flee, present middle/passive imperative
    (6)   act, present middle/passive indicative
    (7)   serve, present middle/passive infinitive
    (8)   persuade, imperfect middle/passive imperative
    (9)   turn, imperfect middle/passive infinitive

6. How does one express the agent of a passive verb in Greek?

7. When one encounters either a present or imperfect middle/passive, what are some clues as to whether the verb is in the middle or the passive voice? Supply with examples of your own devising.

8. Give in Greek the present middle/passive indicative, third person plural, for the following list of verbs in English. Supply a translation.

   (1) change   (4) teach
   (2) guard   (5) persuade
   (3) write   (6) turn

9. What case do the direct objects of the following verbs go in?

   (1) ἀλλάττομαι
   (2) πείθομαι

10. What **aspect** do the following verb forms have?

    (1) present middle/passive indicative
    (2) present middle/passive imperative
    (3) imperfect middle/passive indicative
    (4) future middle indicative

11. Translate the following short sentences from English into Greek.

    (1) I shall persuade. (2) I shall obey. (3) You (*s.*) are obeying. (4) You (*s.*) were persuading. (5) He is turning the horse. (6) She is betaking herself into the house. (7) We were changing the girl into a mare. (8) We were exchanging the girl for a mare. (9) You (*pl.*) will have the children taught. (10) You (*pl.*) will teach the children. (11) I was guarding against the evil. (12) I was standing guard in the tent. (13) You (*s.*) will indict the servants. (14) You (*s.*) will write a letter for yourself. (15) You (*s.*) will write a letter. (16) I shall flee. (17) We shall hear. (18) We are being heard. (19) Let the gift be left behind. (20) Let the stones be found! (21) You (*pl.*) were being hurt by the mistress. (22) You (*pl.*) were hurting the mistress [for yourselves].

12. For extra practice, turn to the key for Lesson 11, **11.**, and translate those Greek sentences into English.

13. Explain how the cases work, in general, for a preposition that may take three cases.

14. Translate the following sentences from English into Greek.

    (1) Do not betake yourself under the wagon, evil slave! (2) When the master speaks, he persuades his students; shall we obey the master? (3) Some were being heard by the students, others were being harmed by the children. (4) Can the master's character be changed by the gods? (5) I am guarding against my fate under the tent. (6) Let them betake themselves with a wagon far away from the little ugly lake and the marketplace. (7) You (pl.), on the one hand, were chasing the children from under the tent into an ugly place; the horses, on the other hand, were being guarded by the maidservants in a beautiful place. (8) The treasure in the wagon is being left far away in a marsh. (9) We, on the one hand, will have our children taught; the students, on the other hand, are being taught by the noble master. (10) Obey (s.) your Fate, o man!

15. For extra practice, turn to the key for Lesson 11, **14.**, and translate those Greek sentences into English.

Lesson 12

1. Conjugate εἰμί in the present active indicative.

2. Conjugate εἰμί in the imperfect active indicative.

3. Conjugate εἰμί in the future active indicative.

4. Give the present and future active infinitives of εἰμί.

5. Conjugate εἰμί in the present active imperative.

6. Translate the following forms of εἰμί.

   (1) εἰσί(ν)   (10) εἶ
   (2) ἔσται   (11) ἔσεσθε
   (3) ἴσθι   (12) ἔστε
   (4) ἦσαν   (13) ἦστε
   (5) ἔσεσθαι   (14) ἐστέ
   (6) ἐσμέν   (15) ἔσονται
   (7) ἔσομαι   (16) ἔστω
   (8) ἔστων   (17) εἶναι
   (9) ἦσθα   (18) ἦν

7. Which forms of εἰμί are enclitic?

8. What kind of accent does εἰμί bear in the present active indicative, second person singular, present active imperative and infinitive, future active indicative and infinitive, and imperfect active indicative?

9. What do we mean when we say that word has an enclitic accent?

10. Explain what happens to the accent in the following descriptions of phrases. Each description refers to a "preceding word" and an "enclitic". It is assumed that the enclitic will follow the "preceding word." Give your own examples illustrating your explanations.

    (1) The preceding word has an acute on the penult; the enclitic is two syllables long.
    (2) The preceding word is a proclitic.
    (3) The preceding word has an acute on the antepenult.
    (4) The preceding word has a circumflex on the ultima.
    (5) The preceding word has a circumflex on the penult.
    (6) The preceding word has a grave on the ultima.
    (7) The preceding word has an acute on the penult; the enclitic is one syllable long
    (8) The preceding word has been elided, and the accent was on the elided syllable.
    (9) The preceding word is another enclitic.

11. When we use the term **deponent** to speak of the Greek verb, what do we mean?

12. Which Greek verbs have we so far encountered that are deponent in the future?

13. Translate the following short sentences, the first five into Greek, the second five into English.

(1) I am fleeing the horse. (2) I shall flee the horse. (3) You are in the marketplace. (4) Will you be in the marketplace? (5) We are being heard by the despot. (6) τοῦ δεσπότου ἀκουσόμεθα. (7) τοῦ δεσπότου ἀκουόμεθα. (8) τοῦ δεσπότου ἀκούομεν. (9) φεύξει τὸν ἵππον. (10) φεύγει τὸν ἵππον.

14. Under what conditions is ἐστί accented not as an enclitic, but as a normally accented verb with recessive accent? What impact may this have on its meaning?

15. Give the basic meaning of εἰμί; what special third person meaning may it have?

16. Translate the following sentences from English into Greek.

(1) Since it is possible for war to destroy the countryside, let the goddess send her peace. (2) In [the] beginning was the Word. (3) We shall flee our enemy [in war], since they were destroying houses. (4) Since we had war, at least we had a good despot. (5) The man is hateful to his students. Let the master have the students taught far away from the man! (6) Peace is a beautiful thing. (7) Peace and tranquility are beautiful things. (8) The mistress was saying a word hateful to her maids. (9) Throughout the marketplace there was peace, since the goddess was pursuing the war far away. (10) On account of the servant's bad speech, let there be war [on the one hand] and not peace [on the other].

17. For extra practice, turn to the key for Lesson 12, **16.**, and translate those Greek sentences into English.

Lesson 13

1. Describe the difference between the positioning of a standard adjective and a demonstrative adjective.

2. Detail the difference in use between the demonstrative as adjective and the demonstrative as pronoun.

3. List the three demonstrative adjectives you have learned in this chapter, including their masculine, feminine, and neuter nominative singular forms.

4. Describe the formation of the demonstrative ὅδε, ἥδε, τόδε.

5. In what ways is the declension of ἐκεῖνος, ἐκείνη, ἐκεῖνο similar to and different from the declension of a standard first/second declension adjective such as ἀγαθός, ή, όν.

6. Unlike many adjectives, the stem of the demonstrative οὗτος undergoes many changes. Below, list as many of those changes as you can, and under what circumstances they occur in the declension of this demonstrative.

7. Below, translate each item, and give the number, case, and gender along with the syntactical use of the case.

(1) οὗτος	(7) ἐκείνων	(13) τῷδε	(19) τήνδε
(2) ἐκεῖναι	(8) ταύταις	(14) τοῦτο	(20) ταῦτα
(3) τάσδε	(9) τῆσδε	(15) ταῖσδε	(21) αὗται
(4) ἐκεῖνος	(10) ἐκεῖνον	(16) ἐκεῖνο	(22) ἐκεῖνα
(5) ἐκείνη	(11) ἐκείνη	(17) αὕτη	(23) ταῦτα
(6) τούτων	(12) τούτῳ	(18) τῇδε	(24) ἐκείνοις

8. Translate the following phrases and sentences, representing their correct case, into correct classical Greek.

(1) this human (nom.)   (6) of this human   (11) of that human
(2) This is a human.   (7) for those trees   (12) those trees (acc.)
(3) these trees (nom.)   (8) this servant (acc.)   (13) to this good servant
(4) to those fates   (9) of that river   (14) into this marketplace
(5) That is a tree.   (10) This is a servant.

9. Write and say aloud the demanded form of the verb βλέπω; give the meaning in English.

      (1) first person singular, present indicative active
      (2) first person singular, future indicative middle
      (3) second person singular, present indicative active
      (4) second person singular, present imperative active
      (5) second person singular, present indicative passive
      (6) second person singular, present imperative passive
      (7) third person plural, present imperative active
      (8) third person singular, present imperative middle
      (9) third person plural, present imperative passive
     (10) second person plural, future indicative middle
     (11) second person plural, present imperative passive

10. Translate the following sentences from English into Greek.

(1) This philosophy is not wise. (2) This wise philosophy is truly wisdom. (3) This philosopher will destroy this argument. (4) That unworthy philosopher will offer sacrifice for himself to these goddesses. (5) This mistress is looking at the philosophy of that wise woman. (6) While I see this thing now, I shall see that thing then. (7) For those wise maidservants will destroy this long argument for themselves. (8) When this child will betake itself into that marketplace, then s/he will see this beautiful girl [here]. (9) This woman is indeed not wise, but this man is wise. Are you wise? (10) That [man] was a philosopher; this [woman] is a philosopher; these [women] will be both wise and philosophical.

11. For extra practice, turn to the key for Lesson 13, **10.**, and translate those Greek sentences into English.

Lesson 14

1. Explain classical Greek conventions regarding the third person personal pronoun.

2. (a) What are the singular and plural first person personal pronouns in classical Greek? (b) Decline each.

3. (a) Identify the singular and plural second person personal pronouns in classical Greek. (b) Decline each.

4. Explain the difference in meaning between αὐτός, –ή, –ό in the predicate position and αὐτός, –ή, –ό in the attributive position.

5. When αὐτός, –ή, –ό stands alone in a sentence (does not modify a noun in either predicate or attributive position), how does it function?

6. Explain the dative of possession.

7. Translate the following:

    (1) I was striking.
    (2) He is striking.
    (3) He will strike them for himself.
    (4) They are being struck by us.
    (5) They (fem.) are carrying the book.
    (6) The cloak was carried by you (pl.).
    (7) I shall carry the cloak.
    (8) You (pl.) were carrying the cloak.
    (9) We shall carry the book [for ourselves].
    (10) We were carried.
    (11) I was striking you.
    (12) He was striking them for himself.
    (13) He was being struck by you.
    (14) She herself is carrying the book.
    (15) The book is being carried by them (fem.).
    (16) The cloak is being carried by you (sing.).
    (17) You (sing.) shall carry the cloak.
    (18) We carry the book [for ourselves].
    (19) We were carrying the book [for ourselves].
    (20) We are being carried.

8. Translate the following sentences twice, once with ἔχω and once with the dative of possession.

    (1) The child has a cloak.   (6) They have horses.
    (2) The children have these books.   (7) She has books.
    (3) You (*pl.*) have a beautiful horse.   (8) We have horses.
    (4) You (*sing.*) have a beautiful horse.   (9) I have wagons.
    (5) The mare has a wagon.

9. Identify and translate each of the following.

    (1) ὑμεῖς   (6) αὐτοί   (11) οὗτοι   (16) σύ
    (2) αὐταί   (7) αὗται   (12) αὕτη   (17) αὐτή
    (3) τοῦτο   (8) αὐτό   (13) ὑμῖν   (18) ἡμῖν
    (4) ἡμεῖς   (9) ἡμῶν   (14) μου   (19) μοῦ
    (5) σοῦ   (10) ὑμῶν   (15) αὐτός   (20) οὗτος

10. Translate the following sentences from English into Greek:

(1) I shall strike the same book. (2) I shall strike the book itself. (3) I was striking this book with rocks. (4) These same books were being struck by us. (5) We were striking these books. (6) You have both the books and the cloaks. (7) Do not rebuke me! (8) The wagon is upon this cloak. (9) I, at any rate, shall not carry the cloak. (10) You yourself were not striking [for yourself] the horses themselves.

11. For extra practice, turn to the key for Lesson 14, **10.**, and translate those Greek sentences into English.

Lesson 15

1. Define "contract verb."

2. Do all Greek verbs have contract forms? Explain.

3. Explain the "vowel food-chain" as it applies to contract verbs.

4. Below are several forms of various contract verbs. Indicate what each contract form represents prior to contraction.

    e.g.   φιλεῖται = φιλέεται

    (1) τιμώντων   (5) δηλούμεθα
    (2) τιμᾷς   (6) δηλοῦτε
    (3) φιλοῦ   (7) δηλοῖ
    (4) φιλεῖσθαι

5. Give the form indicated below in Greek.

    (1) I help, I laugh, I explain.
    (2) I am being helped, I am being honoured, I am being shown.
    (3) I was helping, I was laughing, I was explaining.
    (4) I was helping (for myself), I was honouring (for myself), I was showing (for myself).
    (5) You (s.) help, you (s.) laugh, you (s.) explain.
    (6) You (s.) are being helped, you (s.) are being honoured, you (s.) are being shown.
    (7) You (s.) were helping, you (s.) were laughing, you (s.) were explaining.
    (8) You (s.) were being helped, you (s.) were being honoured, you (s.) were being shown.
    (9) Help! Laugh! Explain!
    (10) Get helped! Be honoured! Be shown!
    (11) She kisses, she makes clear, she laughs.
    (12) She is being kissed, she is being made clear, she is being honoured.
    (13) She was kissing, she was making clear, she was laughing.
    (14) She was being kissed, she was being made clear, she was being honoured.
    (15) Let her kiss! Let her explain! Let her laugh!
    (16) Let her get kissed! Let her be made clear! Let her be honoured!

6. Give the form indicated below in Greek.

    (1) Let them love, let them honour, let them explain.
    (2) Let them be loved, let them be honoured, let them be explained.
    (3) They were being loved, they were being honoured, they were being explained.
    (4) They were kissing, they were honouring, they were explaining.
    (5) They are being loved, they are being honoured, they are being explained.
    (6) They kiss, they honour, they explain.
    (7) Kiss! Honour! Explain!
    (8) Be kissed! Be honoured! Be explained!
    (9) You were being kissed, you were being honoured, you were being explained.
    (10) You were kissing, you were honouring, you were explaining.
    (11) You are being kissed, you are being honoured, you are being explained.
    (12) You are kissing, you are honouring, you are explaining.
    (13) We were being honoured, we were being kissed, we were being explained.
    (14) We were honouring, we were kissing, we were explaining.

19

(15) We are being honoured, we are being kissed, we are being explained.

(16) We are honouring, we are kissing, we are explaining.

7. The verbs in the following exercise all have futures that in some way differ from their present. For the following: (a) translate into Greek each verb form; (b) articulate how the future differs from the present.

(1) You (*s.*) are laughing; you will laugh.
(2) They carry. They will carry.
(3) You (*pl.*) hear; you will hear.
(4) She says; she will say.
(5) We throw; we shall throw.
(6) I am; I shall be.
(7) They are fleeing; they will flee.
(8) You (*s.*) behold; you (*s.*) will behold.
(9) I bear (for myself); I shall bear (for myself).

8. Translate the following sentences from English into Greek.

(1) I shall both sieze the servants and ridicule their masters. (2) Is the character of these ones apparent to you? I shall demonstrate it to you. (3) Some were hitting the horses with stones, but others will truly hit the former with the same things. (4) Will the philosophers exchange truth for honour? (5) Don't laugh, evil child, since good people will laugh at you. (6) These same people both were helped by the gods at that time and are being helped by them now. (7) I shall escort the philosopher through the marketplace, for then he will acquire honour from the people. (8) The youth says the following, "I am fond of kissing the girl;" but will the same girl say the following, "I am fond of being kissed by him"? (9) The masters do not yet honour [for themselves] that wisdom of this philosopher. Let them [the masters] not be honoured by their servants!

9. For extra practice, turn to the key for Lesson 15, **8.**, and translate those Greek sentences into English.

Lesson 16

1. What gender is a third-declension noun?

2. How does one identify the stem of: (a) a first declension noun? (b) a second declension noun? (c) a third declension noun?

3. Explain the accentuation conventions regarding third declension nouns.

4. (a) Generally speaking, must an adjective modifying a noun share with the noun it modifies its ending? (b) More specifically, must a noun of the third declension be modified by an adjective with third declension endings?

5. Give the lexical entry in Greek for each word below, then identify the stem of each.

(1)	shield	(5)	speaker
(2)	guard, guardian	(6)	lion
(3)	grace, favour, gratitude	(7)	name
(4)	thief	(8)	contest, competition

6. Give the demanded form, along with the article, below.
    Example: favour, accusative plural   τὰς χάριτας

    > (1)   shield, dative plural
    > (2)   shield, vocative singular
    > (3)   guard, accusative singular
    > (4)   guard, genitive plural
    > (5)   favour, nominative plural
    > (6)   favour, accusative singular
    > (7)   thief, genitive plural
    > (8)   thief, vocative plural
    > (9)   speaker, dative singular
    > (10) speaker, dative plural
    > (11) lion, nominative plural
    > (12) lion, nominative singular
    > (13) name, nominative or accusative singular
    > (14) name, genitive plural
    > (15) contest, dative plural
    > (16) contest, accusative singular

7. Translate the following sentences from English into Greek.

    (1) He is chasing the guard. (2) The evil lion is chasing the guard. (3) The evil lion is chasing the guard for the sake of the worthy child. (4) The speaker will say the following [things], "I saw both the thieves and the shields, but the guards were not eager to pursue the former and they did not wish to seize the latter." (5) I shall either put on a contest or show the lions. (6) When the thieves will snatch the horses from the countryside, let both the handsome guards make shields and the noble speakers make long speeches against them. (7) The speaker was thankful to the wise philosophers, but the people would laugh at those same philosophers. (8) I shall hit the lion with rocks, but I shall guard the noble children with beautiful shields.

8. For extra practice, turn to the key for Lesson 16, **7.**, and translate those Greek sentences into English.

Lesson 17

1. The endings of sigma-stem third-declension nouns are confusing if you are unfamiliar with the rules of vocalic contraction and the typical third-declension endings. In order to become better acquainted with how the contraction works, please: (a) identify the form of the following nouns; and (b) describe the formation of the following forms of nouns.

(1)	τειχῶν	(6)	αἰδῶ
(2)	γέρως	(7)	τείχη
(3)	γέρα	(8)	γέρα
(4)	Σωκράτους	(9)	τριήρεις
(5)	τριήρη		

2. How many sets of endings does the third-declension adjective have? Explain.

3. Must a third-declension noun be modified by a third-declension adjective? Explain.

4. What is the gender of a third declension noun? Explain.

5. Explain the various meanings of the preposition πρός. How many other three-way prepositions have you learned so far? List them.

6. Please supply the form demanded below, along with the article, where appropriate.

(1) wall, dative singular	(7) Socrates, vocative singular
(2) trireme, genitive singular	(8) trireme, dative plural
(3) shame, nominative singular	(9) shame, dative singular
(4) prize, accusative singular	(10) prize, accusative plural
(5) divine being, nominative singular	(11) divine being, genitive singular
(6) true, accusative M/F plural	(12) happy, accusative neuter plural

7. Conjugate the verb προσβάλλω in the future active indicative and the imperfect middle/passive indicative.

8. Conjugate the verb προσποιέω in the present active imperative, the present middle/passive imperative, and the imperfect active indicative.

9. What are the two basic meanings of προσποιέω, and how does a user of Greek distinguish between the one and the other?

10. Translate the following short sentences from English into Greek.

(1) Socrates is faring well. (2) Socrates is faring badly. (3) Socrates was pretending to fare badly. (4) True shame is good. (5) Let the enemy attack the wall. (6) The long trireme was near the marsh. (7) You shall acquire a prize, but I shall acquire honour. (8) Socrates is speaking to his guardian spirit. (9) Is the happy [one] faring well? Let him do good deeds! (10) By the gods, I shall have true privileges!

11. Translate the following sentences from English into Greek.

(1) Let not the guards attack the good speaker with shields. (2) Socrates, on the one hand, is eager to stand guard against the trireme; his students, on the other, are badly pretending to do the same thing. (3) Life is good for the prosperous, for they themselves found the true prize. (4) Don't snatch the shields from the wall, for they were sent to me from the noble despot. (5) We ourselves shall pretend to attack the wall, while you yourselves will really attack the triremes. (6) In the contests we shall acquire either prizes and honours or shame and evils. (7) By the gods, take the prizes from the trireme and to the happy Socrates. (8) These people do not have shame, for they used to laugh at the true words of the speaker. (9) Let not the gods send pains to us, but a happy life. (10) These things were being said by Socrates: "These wise people are truly sincere."

12. For extra practice, turn to the key for Lesson 17, **11.**, and translate those Greek sentences into English.

Lesson 18

1. In your own words, explain how "aspect" and "time" work in regard to the aorist tense.

2. Identify the features of the formation of the first aorist similar to and distinct from (a) the future, (b) the present, and (c) the imperfect.

3. Off of which principal part of the verb are the following tenses built:

     (1) present active, middle, and passive
     (2) future active and middle
     (3) imperfect active, middle, and passive
     (4) aorist active and middle.

4. Explain in your own words the genitive of value.

5. Give the three principal parts you know so far for the Greek verbs expressed by the English below:

(1) make	(10) intend, hesitate	(19) send
(2) harm	(11) hear	(20) laugh
(3) reveal, make clear	(12) persuade	(21) hasten
(4) destroy	(13) wish	(22) help
(5) turn	(14) pursue	(23) change
(6) honour	(15) serve	(24) sacrifice
(7) seize	(16) write	(25) steal
(8) guard	(17) see	(26) command
(9) carry	(18) love	

6. (a) Identify which forms of πολύς, πολλή, πολύ do not have the stem πολλ–. (b) Decline the adjective πολύς, πολλή, πολύ.

7. Conjugate the following verbs in the demanded forms.

     (1) ἐρωτάω, first aorist active indicative
     (2) πωλέω, first aorist middle imperative
     (3) χαίρω, first aorist active infinitive
     (4) φυλάττω, first aorist active imperative
     (5) ἀγγέλλω, first aorist middle indicative
     (6) γράφω, first aorist middle infinitive

8. Translate the following sentences from Greek into English.

(1) ὁ μὲν ἄγγελος πολλ᾽ ἤγγειλεν, ὁ δὲ ῥήτωρ οὔ. (2) ἀγγελεῖ ὁ φύλαξ ταῦτα; (3) ὁ λόγος τοῦ ῥήτορος οὔκ ἐστιν ἄξιος πολλῶν δραχμῶν, ἀλλ᾽ ὀλίγων. (4) ἠρώτησαν οἱ φύλακες τάδε· οἱ ἄγγελοι τὸν πόλεμον ἀγγέλλουσιν, ἢ μέλλομεν αὐτὸν ἡμεῖς ἀγγελεῖν; (5) τὰ μὲν γέρα πολλῶν δραχμῶν ἐπώλησεν, τὰς δ᾽ ἀσπίδας ὀλίγων. (6) ὀλίγοι μὲν ἄνθρωποι τοῖς ῥήτορσιν ἐπείσαντο, πολλοὶ δὲ τοῖς φιλοσόφοις. (7) ἐγὼ μόνος περὶ ταύτης τῆς κακῆς τριήρους ἠρώτησα; τοῖς οὖν πολλοῖς οὔκ εἰσι τρόποι ἄξιοι. (8) οὐ μόνον ἐπώλησαν οὗτοι ταύτας τὰς ἀσπίδας τοῖς κλωψίν, ἀλλὰ καὶ ἤγγειλαν οἱ κλῶπες τάδε· πωλησάτω ὁ Σωκράτης ἡμῖν τὴν ἀσπίδα ὀλίγων ὀβολῶν. (9) τὸν ἄγγελον περὶ τοῦ τείχους μὴ μόνον ἐρώτησον, ἀλλὰ καὶ λέγε αὐτῷ· μὴ λυσάντων τὰ τείχη οἱ πολέμιοι. (10) ἀγγειλάτω ὁ κλὼψ τάδε· τὰ τέκνα οὔκ ἔκλεψα, ἐκεῖνα γὰρ κακά.

9. Translate the following sentences from English into Greek.

(1) Let him not steal the drachmas! (*use aorist imperative*) (2) The people are not wise; the philosophers are. (3) I shall not sell my prizes for only a few obols. (4) The messengers honoured their guards much. (5) Let him not only honour the girl, but let him also kiss her! (*use aorist imperative*) (6) Do not move into the marketplace! (*use aorist imperative*) (7) I was not eager to write a letter to the people. (8) Let them have their children taught only in their homes, not in the marketplace. (*use aorist imperative*) (9) Let them exchange their many obols for a few drachmas. (10) You there, help me turn my wagon out of the river! (*use aorist imperative*)

10. For extra practice, turn to the key for Lesson 18, **9.**, and translate those Greek sentences into English.

Lesson 19

1. List the personal endings used in the second aorist for the indicative, imperative, and infinitive, active and middle; next to them, place the personal endings used for the equivalent forms in the imperfect and first aorist.

2. (a) Explain in your own words what a reflexive pronoun is and how it functions. (b) Why does it make sense that there is no such thing as a nominative reflexive pronoun?

3. Explain in your own words the difference in meaning and usage between the reflexive pronoun and: (a) the personal pronoun and (b) the intensive adjective.

4. The following verbs have irregular accentuation in the second aorist: λέγω, εὑρίσκω, λαμβάνω. (a) Identify the forms in which the accent is irregular and (b) indicate which type of accent one would normally expect on those forms.

5. Write a brief paragraph describing the difference in the position occupied by the personal pronoun, reflexive pronoun, and demonstrative pronoun when using each to show possession. Give your own examples.

6. Give the three principal parts you know so far for the following verbs:

   (1) throw   (6) say
   (2) receive   (7) have
   (3) find   (8) flee
   (4) remain, await (9) leave
   (5) collect   (10) carry, bear

7. Give the following forms of the reflexive and personal pronoun. Translate each.
   example: first person singular accusative =
              ἐμαυτὸν or ἐμαυτήν, ἐμέ = myself, me
   (1) first person plural genitive
   (2) second person singular dative
   (3) third person plural accusative
   (4) second person plural accusative
   (5) first person plural nominative
   (6) third person singular dative
   (7) second person plural nominative
   (8) first person singular dative
   (9) second person singular genitive
   (10) third person plural dative
   (11) third person singular nominative
   (12) first person plural accusative

8. Give the demanded form of each of the following

   (1) βάλλω, second person singular, aorist imperative active
   (2) βάλλω, second person singular, present imperative active
   (3) λέγω, third person plural, imperfect indicative middle/passive
   (4) λέγω, third person plural, aorist indicative active
   (5) λέγω, third person plural, aorist imperative active

(6) λέγω, third person plural, future indicative active
(7) εὑρίσκω, first person singular, future indicative middle
(8) εὑρίσκω, first person singular, aorist indicative middle
(9) βάλλω, future active infinitive
(10) βάλλω, aorist active infinitive
(11) βάλλω, aorist middle infinitive
(12) βάλλω future middle infinitive
(13) λαμβάνω, third person singular, future indicative
(14) λαμβάνω, third person singular, aorist indicative active
(15) λαμβάνω, second person plural, present imperative middle
(16) λαμβάνω, second person plural, aorist imperative middle
(17) φέρω, first person plural, imperfect indicative middle
(18) φερώ, first person plural, future indicative middle
(19) φερώ, first person plural, aorist indicative middle

9. Translate the following short sentences from English into Greek.

(1) He loved her. (2) She loved him. (3) He loved himself. (4) She loved herself. (5) She loved her own name. (6) He loved her name. (7) He loved his own name. (8) They awaited us. (9) They themselves awaited us. (10) We ourselved awaited them. (11) You (*pl.*) sent the letter. (12) You (*pl.*) sent the letter to yourselves. (13) You (*s.*) hit (*use aorist*) him. (14) You (*s.*) hit (*use aorist*) yourself. (15) I shall find myself. (16) I myself shall find him. (17) Did he carry his own book? (18) Did he carry his book? (19) Did he carry our book? (20) Did we carry our own book? (21) Did the master flee his own servants? (22) Did the master flee them? (23) Did they flee their own master? (24) Did they flee her master?

10. For extra practice, turn to the key for Lesson 19, **9.**, and translate those Greek sentences into English.

Lesson 20

1. In your own words, describe the following terms as they apply to the Greek verb: (a) perfect; and (b) pluperfect.

2. Speak to the matter of "time" and "aspect" as they come to bear on the perfect and pluperfect of the Greek verb.

3. Give the distinguishing features of the following forms of the Greek verb: (a) present; (b) future; (c) imperfect; (d) aorist; (e) perfect; and (f) pluperfect.

4. Give the similarities that exist between: (a) the perfect and pluperfect; and (b) the pluperfect and aorist and imperfect.

5. Which principal part is needed to derive the following forms of the Greek verb: (a) perfect; (b) present; (c) future; (d) imperfect; (e) pluperfect; and (f) aorist.

6. The following terms describe various forms in which the Greek verb may be found: active, middle, passive, infinitive, indicative, imperative. Indicate in which of the foregoing forms a verb in one of the following specified tenses you have learned so far may be found: (a) present; (b) imperfect; (c) future; (d) aorist; (e) perfect; (f) pluperfect.

7. Articulate the differences and similarities between the first perfect and the second perfect.

8. Give the four principal parts you know as of now of the following Greek verbs.

(1)	hurl	(14)	carry
(2)	guard	(15)	do, make
(3)	attack	(16)	write
(4)	steal	(17)	do, act
(5)	turn	(18)	announce
(6)	command	(19)	see
(7)	send	(20)	leave
(8)	gather	(21)	rejoice
(9)	honour	(22)	hear
(10)	harm	(23)	flee
(11)	abandon	(24)	change
(12)	persuade	(25)	pursue
(13)	strike	(26)	rebuke

9. Give the first principal part, indentify and translate the following forms:

(1)	δεδίωχας	(14)	γεγραφέναι
(2)	ἐδεδιώχης	(15)	ἐγεγράφημεν
(3)	ἐδίωξας	(16)	ἐγράψαμεν
(4)	ἐδίωκες	(17)	ἠρώτησαν
(5)	ἐπεποιήκεσαν	(18)	ἠρωτήκασι
(6)	πεποιηκέναι	(19)	ἠρωτήκεσαν
(7)	πεποίηκας	(20)	ἠρωτηκέναι
(8)	ἐπιπέπληγε	(21)	ἠκούσατε
(9)	ἐπεπλήγει	(22)	ἀκούσατε
(10)	ἐπεπεπλήγει	(23)	ἀκηκόατε
(11)	ἐπέπληξε	(24)	ἠκηκόετε
(12)	ἔπληττε	(25)	ἀκούσεσθε
(13)	γεγράφαμεν	(26)	ἀκούετε

10. Translate the following sentences from English into Greek.

(1) The god had thrown Fate down from heaven. (2) The Greek has hurled a rock. (3) The Greek hurled a rock. (4) The Greek had hurled a rock. (5) We are seeking the Greek land. (6) We had sought the Greek land. (7) The messenger had reported the following: "When the Greeks had cast aside their shields, they sought to flee into big trees." (8) Socrates has spoken on our behalf, for we had honoured him and had held contests for him and had offered sacrifice to the immortal gods on his behalf. (9) Socrates is said to have brought the truth of philosophy down from the heaven itself. (10) Since we had sought to pursue our enemy by sea, they moved by land upon horses.

11. Translate the following sentences from English into Greek.

(1) Since the philosopher had sought the truth, the people have thrown him down from the [city] walls. (2) The guard said the following, "We have turned the wagon across the river, for our enemy had sought to throw it into it." (3) The master asked us the following, "Have you stolen my treasure? O evil servants, I had received it from Socrates and I had added to it from the treasure of the thieves." (4) We are seeking our land, Greece. (5) The man is said to have said the following when he had changed the ground into a treasure, "I have found it! I have changed the ground into true treasure!" (6) The evil one has persuaded the servants to carry his own prizes into the house, and they have trusted him. But

they were not wise and the evil man destroyed them when they had carried his prizes into the house. (7) The wise ones have sold their garments for many obols. (8) The girl wrote the following letter to the handsome youth: "O handsome and noble youth, I have loved you much and I have persuaded my servants to bring this letter to you. Will you love me? Then betake yourself to me. I have awaited you." (9) Don't help that woman! The speaker has already helped her much. (10) On the one hand, the few have not trusted the evil speaker; on the other hand, the crowd have both trusted him and honoured him much.

12. For extra practice, turn to the key for Lesson 20, **10.**, and translate those Greek sentences into English.

13. For extra practice, turn to the key for Lesson 20, **11.**, and translate those Greek sentences into English.

Lesson 21

1. What distinguishes the interrogative pronoun/adjective from the indefinite pronoun/adjective?

2. Give both the uncontracted and contracted forms of the genitive and dative singular of the interrogative pronoun/adjective τίς.

3. Give both the uncontracted and contracted forms of the genitive and dative singular of the indefinite pronoun/adjective τις.

4. Give the alternate forms of the neuter plural nominative and accusative indefinite pronoun/adjective.

5. Decline the Greek interrogative pronoun/adjective in both genders and numbers.

6. Decline the Greek indefinite pronoun/adjective in both genders and numbers.

7. Discuss the positioning of the indefinite adjective.

8. Discuss the positioning and form of the possesive adjective in Greek and compare and contrast it with the positioning and form of the demonstrative, personal and reflexive pronouns used to show possession.

9. Translate the following sentences from English into Greek.

   (1) I'm afraid; someone will kill me! (2) Socrates died when the Greeks killed him on account of his philosophy. (3) I have much fear, for many about me are dying. (4) That shield is mine, not yours! (5) That shield is ours, not yours! (6) That shield is hers, not theirs! (7) Why have you stolen the Greeks' trireme? (8) Whom has Socrates harmed? (9) To whom do you intend to send this letter? (10) Whose children have you stolen? They will truly die in your house. (11) Do not scare me! I fear many things. (12) Socrates exchanged something for those obols. (13) A certain guard told me the following: "Some guards had fled away from the walls, others moved over them."

10. For extra practice, turn to the key for Lesson 21, **9.**, and translate those Greek sentences into English.

Lesson 22

1. Identify the principal part of the Greek verb off of which each of the following is built:

(1) present indicative active
(2) future middle
(3) perfect passive
(4) imperfect passive
(5) imperfect active
(6) present middle imperative
(7) aorist middle infinitive
(8) pluperfect active
(9) pluperfect middle
(10) perfect active

2. Discuss the general formation of the perfect/pluperfect middle/passive of verbs whose basic stem ends in a vowel. How does one identify which verbs those are?

3. Explain what happens in general terms when forming the perfect/pluperfect middle/passive of verbs whose basic stem ends in a consonant.

4. Below, demonstrate what happens to the consonants when the given stem consonant combines with the given personal ending consonant. Please also indicate which other stem consonants operate in the same fashion under the same circumstances.

Stem Consonant + Personal Ending Consonant = ? Other Stem Endings

π	σ
κ	σθ
λ	τ
χ	μ
ρ	σ
δ	σθ
ν	any ending
ζ	τ
ν	μ
β	σ
θ	τ

5. Give the five principal parts you know for each of the following verbs.

(1) lead
(2) throw
(3) persuade
(4) write
(5) guard
(6) abandon
(7) steal
(8) teach
(9) attack
(10) strike
(11) change
(12) receive
(13) do
(14) carry
(15) announce
(16) speak
(17) turn
(18) rejoice
(19) find
(20) cast aside
(21) pursue
(22) snatch, seize
(23) reproach
(24) gather
(25) leave
(26) send

6. Conjugate the following verbs in the perfect and pluperfect middle/passive indicative and in the perfect middle/passive infinitive. For the first person singular of both the perfect and pluperfect, give the translation of the passive; translate also the perfect passive infinitive.

(1) lead
(2) persuade
(3) strike
(4) destroy
(5) leave
(6) attack
(7) gather
(8) announce

7. Explain in your own terms the dative of personal agency, making note of when it is and is not used.

8. Translate the following sentences from English into Greek.

    (1) You have been struck by me. (2) I have been struck by you. (3) He had harmed her much. (4) She had been harmed much by him. (5) We shall lead a prosperous life. (6) We have led a prosperous life. (7) We were leading a prosperous life. (8) A propserous life has been led by us. (9) A prosperous life had been led by us. (10) The master has sent us this law. (11) This law has been sent to us from the master. (12) Both the customs and the character of the Greeks had persuaded them to seek a noble life. (13) Take my livelihood, but do not take my life! (14) Neither had I killed them, nor had they died. (15) You have been reproached by the politicians, while others have fled far away. (16) You (*pl.*) had been both persuaded and commanded to attack the trireme. Why did you hesitate? (17) Contrary to their own customs and character, the Greeks fled when they had been attacked. (18) It is possible to sacrifice a human, but it is contrary to law. It is both possible to sacrifice an animal, and it is in accord with law. (19) Neither say nor wish to say the following: "The master shall die." (20) He had neither been pursued nor been found when he died.

9. For extra practice, turn to the key for Lesson 22, **8.**, and translate those Greek sentences into English.

Lesson 23

1. Explain in your own words what a relative pronoun is.

2. Explain how one determines the appropriate number, case, and gender for a particular relative pronoun.

3. What are the different senses of the Greek word πᾶς, and how does one derive those different senses from context?

4. What is the meaning of a time expression used in: (a) the dative case? (b) the accusative case? (c) the genitive case? For each, make up a sentence in Greek and translate it into English.

5. Give the following forms of the relative pronoun.

    (1) masculine accusative singular   (6) neuter dative plural
    (2) feminine dative singular   (7) masculine accusative plural
    (3) feminine accusative plural   (8) neuter accusative singular
    (4) feminine genitive singular   (9) masculine genitive plural
    (5) neuter genitive singular

6. Give the following forms of πᾶς.

    (1) masculine accusative singular   (6) neuter dative plural
    (2) feminine dative singular   (7) masculine accusative plural
    (3) feminine accusative plural   (8) neuter accusative singular
    (4) feminine genitive singular   (9) masculine genitive plural
    (5) neuter genitive singular

7. Give the following five forms of the words ἔτος, ἡμέρα, and νύξ:

(a) dative singular; (b) dative plural; (c) accusative singular; (d) nominative plural; (e) accusative plural.

8. Translate the following sentences from English into Greek.

(1) I saw the girl who is beautiful. (2) I saw the girl whose treasure is much. (3) I saw the girls to whom I sent letters. (4) I saw the girls whom the master loved. (5) I saw the speaker who is happy. (6) I shall see the speaker whose argument was good. (7) The speaker whom the people rebuked has appeared. (8) She has seen all the children whom the philosopher had gathered around himself. (9) They were looking at all the children whose animals had been stolen by thieves. (10) The whole trireme had been destroyed by thieves while we were attacking the enemy's walls. (11) The thieves betook themselves daily into the marketplace of the enemy who had much treasure. (12) My guardian spirit has appeared to me the whole day. (13) Within only a few days we sold all the shields which we had stolen from the guards. (14) Let them not destroy the treasure which the speaker's children have gathered for many years.

9. For extra practice, turn to the key for Lesson 23, **8.**, and translate those Greek sentences into English.

Lesson 24

1. Explain in your own words what one means by the grammatical term "participle."

2. Inasmuch as the participle is an adjective, what properties should one expect of it?

3. Inasmuch as the participle is a verb, what properties should one expect of it?

4. What two positions may a participle occupy and how is a distinction between the two made?

5. What is the force of a participle in the: (a) present; (b) aorist; (c) perfect; (d) future?

6. Give the following participial forms for the indicated verb.

    (1) εἰμί, present masculine dative singular
    (2) ἁρπάζω, perfect active feminine dative plural
    (3) λείπω, aorist active neuter genitive singular
    (4) πλήττω, future active masculine nominative singular
    (5) λαμβάνω, perfect active feminine dative singular
    (6) φεύγω, aorist active neuter accusative singular
    (7) πέμπω, aorist active neuter accusative plural
    (8) ῥίπτω, present active masculine nominative plural
    (9) ἀποκτείνω, future active feminine accusative plural
  (10) βλέπω, perfect active neuter genitive plural

7. Give the following participial forms for the indicated verb. For contract-verb participles, see Groton, pp. 478–479. To review rules of contraction, see Groton §92.

(1) ὠφελέω Present active masculine genitive plural

present active feminine genitive plural
present active neuter dative plural

(2) γελάω present active masculine accusative singular
present active feminine nominative singular
present active neuter nominative singular

(3) δηλόω present active masculine accusative plural
present active feminine dative plural
present active neuter genitive singular

8. Give the active participle in both numbers, all cases, and all genders for the following tenses of the verb καλέω: (a) present; (b) future; (c) aorist; (d) perfect

9. (a) Translate the following sentences from Greek into English. (b) For each one, identify any participles as either attributive or circumstantial.

(1) τοῦτο πέμπω τῷ φύλακι τῷ φιλοῦντι τὴν κόρην. (2) τοῦτο πέμπω τῷ φύλακι φιλῶν τὴν κόρην. (3) τοῦτο πέμπω τῷ φύλακι καίπερ φιλοῦντι τὴν κόρην μου. (4) ἐλάβομεν δῶρα πολλὰ παρὰ τῆς ἡμᾶς ἐπὶ δεῖπνον καλεσάσης δεσποίνης. (5) ἐλάβομεν δῶρα πολλὰ παρὰ τῆς δεσποίνης καλέσασαι τὴν πᾶσαν οἰκίαν ἐπὶ δεῖπνον. (6) ἐχαίρησε τὸ τέκνον τῇ ξενίᾳ τῇ ἀγαθῇ. (7) ἐχαίρησε τὸ τὸν θησαυρὸν εὑρὸν τέκνον τῇ ξενίᾳ τῇ ἀγαθῇ. (8) ἐχαίρησε τὸ τέκνον τῇ ξενίᾳ τῇ ἀγαθῇ τὸν τῆς φιλίας θησαυρὸν εὑρηκός. (9) ἐχαίρησαν οἱ ῥήτορες τῇ μοίρᾳ καίπερ τὸν θάνατον εὑρόντες. (10) ἐχαίρησαν οἱ τὴν ἐλπίδα εὑρόντες ῥήτορες τῇ μοίρᾳ. (11) ἄνευ φόβου οὐκ ἐλπίς. (12) τὴν θεράπαιναν ὡς πλήξων αὐτὴν πρὸς τὴν θύραν ἐκάλεσα. (13) ὡς ὑμᾶς τιμήσων κεκόμικεν ὑμῖν ὁ ξένος δῶρα πολλοῦ ἄξια.

10. For extra practice, turn to the key for Lesson 24, **9.**, and translate those English sentences into Greek.

Lesson 25

1. Describe in your own words the distinctive features of the following middle/passive participles: (a) future middle; (b) first aorist middle; (c) perfect middle/passive; (d) second aorist middle.

2. Indicate from which principal part the following middle/passive participles are formed. Give examples. (a) present middle/passive; (b) future middle; (c) aorist middle; (d) perfect middle/passive.

3. (a) Explain in your own terms the supplementary use of the participle. (b) Illustrate with examples.

4. Give the genitive singular participle in all genders for the verb λύω in the following forms:

   (1) present active, present middle/passive
   (2) future active, future middle
   (3) aorist active, aorist middle
   (4) perfect active
   (5) perfect middle/passive

5. Give the masculine dative singular and feminine accusative plural for both the aorist active and aorist middle participles of the following verbs:

 (1) λέγω   (6) ἀποκτείνω
 (2) ἀγγέλλω   (7) εὑρίσκω
 (3) διδάσκω   (8) πείθω
 (4) συλλαμβάνω   (9) ἀπολείπω
 (5) φέρω

6. Give the neuter accusative plural and the feminine accusative singular for both the perfect active and perfect middle/passive participles of the following verbs:

 (1) λέγω   (6) ἀποκτείνω
 (2) ἀγγέλλω   (7) εὑρίσκω
 (3) διδάσκω   (8) πείθω
 (4) συλλαμβάνω   (9) ἀπολείπω
 (5) φέρω

7. Translate the following sentences from English into Greek.

(1) I did not stop teaching. (2) I did not stop teaching my students. (3) I did not stop teaching my students who now have been well educated. (4) I did not stop teaching my students because they had been well-educated. (5) I did not stop the teachers from speaking although they had bad opinions. (6) You stopped the evil teachers from turning the good laws into bad ones. (7) The children enjoyed drawing the bodies of their teachers. (8) Being rebuked by this unworthy orator often, we shall indict him for the sake of our own glory. (9) The ones who will acquire the great prizes in the contests will put on both many and great dinners in the marketplace. (10) With the avowed intention of gathering together all the Greeks, the orator hastened by land and sea, commanding the people–though they were unwilling—to betake themselves to Greece.

8. For extra practice, turn to the key for Lesson 25, **7.**, and translate those Greek sentences into English.

Lesson 26

1. Explain the difference between a direct and indirect question.

2. When converting a direct question into an indirect question in Greek, what seven principles should be borne in mind?

3. Give the following direct interrogative adverbs in Greek. Follow them with their indefinite and indirect interrogative forms.

 (1) whence?
 (2) whither?
 (3) how?
 (4) where?
 (5) when?

4. Translate the indefinite forms of the words above in **3.** into English.

5. Give the following forms of the indirect interrogative in Greek. Translate each into English.

 (1) masculine dative singular

    (2) feminine dative singular
    (3) neuter accusative plural
    (4) neuter accusative singular
    (5) feminine accusative plural
    (6) feminine genitive singular
    (7) masculine accusative plural
    (8) neuter genitive plural
    (9) feminine dative plural
    (10) masculine dative plural
    (11) masculine nominative singular
    (12) feminine nominative singular

6. There are two forms of negation in a Greek question. What are they, and what impact does each have on the meaning of the question in which it is found?

7. Below are sentences containing direct questions. (a) Translate the sentence into English. (b) Convert the Greek sentence into one containing an indirect question. (c) Translate the converted sentence.

(1) ἠρώτησέν με ὁ ῥήτωρ, Εἶ σὺ διδάσκαλος; (2) ἐρωτησάτω ἡ θεράπαινα τὴν δέσποιναν, Πότερον ἐθέλεις τρέψασθαι εἰς τὴν ἀγορὰν ἢ μεῖναι ἐν τῇ οἰκίᾳ; (3) ἔπαυσα αὐτὰς ἐρωτώσας, Ποῦ εἰσὶν οἱ παῖδες ἡμῶν; (4) ἠρωτήσατε τὴν ἀναξίαν διδάσκαλον, Τίνας δόξας κακὰς τοὺς παῖδας τήμερον διδάξεις;

8. (a) Translate the following sentences into Greek. (b) Convert the Greek sentence into one containing an indirect question. (c) Translate the converted sentence into English.

(1) Some have already asked us, "The fate of the body after death is not evil, is it?" and others, "Isn't the fate of the soul in this life evil?" (2) Socrates used to ask his students, "Whither will the soul of a philosopher flee when it is often pursued (*use participle*) by unworthy [ones]?" (3) The teacher will ask us, "Which great books have you seen, or have you not seen any?" (4) The master seized the thieves, asking them, "Didn't you want to steal also my children?" (5) Gazing at his treasure with his eyes, the prosperous [one] would often ask himself, "By whose great favour did I receive these things?"

Lesson 27

1. How many principal parts does a normal Greek verb have?

2. What forms are derivable from the following principal parts of the Greek verb: (a) first; (b) second; (c) third; (d) fourth; (e) fifth; and (f) sixth?

3. Explain in your own words the features that mark the aorist passive.

4. When we speak of a second aorist passive, what do we mean? Give several examples.

5. There are three verbs you know whose stems end in a vowel and yet receive a σ on the end of their stem before suffixing the first aorist passive θ. What are they?

6. What happens in the first aorist passive to the stem of a verb whose final consonant is: (a) a labial; (b) a dental; (c) a palatal?

7. What happens in the aorist passive to the stem of a contract verb?

8. Using the verb λύω, give the following forms of the aorist passive: (a) indicative; (b) participle (full); (c) imperative; and (d) infinitive.

9. Give the sixth principal part of the following verbs:

(1)	ἀνοίγω	(15)	διώκω
(2)	ἀποκρίνω	(16)	ἀλλάττω
(3)	ἀκούω	(17)	πράττω
(4)	δηλόω	(18)	πλήττω
(5)	κρίνω	(19)	ἐπιπλήττω
(6)	χαίρω	(20)	φυλάττω
(7)	γελάω	(21)	φέρω
(8)	ζητέω	(22)	ἄγω
(9)	κλέπτω	(23)	τρέπω
(10)	λαμβάνω	(24)	βλέπω
(11)	γράφω	(25)	ἀγγέλλω
(12)	καλέω	(26)	πείθω
(13)	βάλλω	(27)	κομίζω
(14)	βλάπτω		

10. Translate the following sentences from English into Greek.

(1) I asked her whether her son was of age. (2) The blind man who was struck by the gods (*use participial phrase*) responded to them saying, "You, o immortals, are evil!" (3) I asked my master long ago whether he had already judged the contest. (4) The ancient [woman], with the avowed intention of exchanging her robe for a drachma, asked the speaker whether he would sell her robe. (5) Let the door be opened and let the evil be separated from the good! (6) The old men have already decided many cases long ago; the young men just now will decide a recent case.

11. Translate the following sentences from Greek into English.

(1) ἠρώτησεν ὁ νέος ῥήτωρ τοῦτον τὸν παλαιὸν τυφλὸν εἰ ποτ' ἔβλεψεν. (2) ἠρωτήθημεν ὑπὸ τῶν τὰς αἰτίας κρινάντων οὕστινας φύλακας ἐν τῇ λίμνῃ εἴδομεν τὴν ἅμαξαν εἰς τὴν ἀγορὰν τρέψαντες. (3) ἄρτι τοῖς ἡμᾶς βεβλαφόσιν ἀπεκρινάμεθα τάδε· μὴ βλάψετε ἡμᾶς. (4) ἀνεῴχθησαν οἱ τοῦ τυφλοῦ ὀφθαλμοὶ ὑπὸ τῆς ἀθανάτου. (5) ὁ φύλαξ, τῷ κλωπὶ ἐπιπλήττων, τὰς θύρας τὰς οὐκ ἀνοιχθείσας λίθοις ἔβαλεν. (6) ἐχάρησε μὲν γράφων ὁ ἄνθρωπος οὐκ ἔχων ποτε βλέπειν· ἐπαύσατο δὲ λόγους ποιῶν ὁ παλαιὸς ῥήτωρ ὡς μήκετι ἐρῶν τοῖς πολλοῖς.

12. For extra practice, turn to the key for Lesson 27, **10.**, and translate those Greek sentences into English.

13. For extra practice, turn to the key for Lesson 27, **11.**, and translate those English sentences into Greek.

Lesson 28

1. Explain in your own words the formation of the future passive.

2. Give the complete future passive (indicative, infinitive, and participle [masculine, feminine, and neuter nominative singular]) of the verbs: (a) ἁμαρτάνω and (b) γεννάω.

3. Give the following forms of οἶδα, along with their translation into English:

    (1) second person singular, perfect active indicative
    (2) second person singular, pluperfect active indicative
    (3) third person plural, perfect active indicative
    (4) second person plural, pluperfect active indicative
    (5) first person singular, pluperfect active indicative
    (6) first person plural, perfect active indicative;
    (7) first person singular, future perfect deponent indicative
    (8) third person plural, future perfect deponent indicative
    (9) second person plural, future perfect deponent indicative
    (10) the full conjungation of the imperative
    (11) perfect active infinitive
    (12) perfect active participle, masculine genitive singular
    (13) perfect active participle, feminine dative plural
    (14) perfect active participle, neuter dative plural.

4. Give the six principal parts in Greek of the following English verbs: (a) believe; (b) make a mistake; (c) beget; and (d) know.

5. Translate the following short Greek sentences into English.

(1) τὸν ἵππον ἠγαγόμην. (2) ἤχθην ὑπὸ τοῦ ἵππου. (3) παιδεύσῃ τὰ τέκνα; (4) παιδευθήσῃ μόνον βιβλίοις; (5) ἁμαρτησόμεθα τῆς ὁδοῦ; (6) ἡ ὁδὸς ἁμαρτηθήσεται; (7) πιστευθήσονται οἱ ῥήτορες. (8) πιστεύσονται οἱ ῥήτορες. (9) ἐφοβήθη ὁ κλὼψ ὡς λυθησόμενος. (10) μῶν μέλλεις τὰς δραχμὰς ὀλίγων ὀβολῶν ἀλλάξεσθαι; (11) μῶν μέλλουσιν αἱ δραχμαὶ ὀλίγων ὀβολῶν ἀλλαχθήσεσθαι; (12) ἴσασιν οἱ κακοὶ ὁδοὺς λῦσαι. (13) ἴσθι τὰ τοῖς σοφοῖς εἰρημένα. (14) ἴστω τὰ ὑπὸ τῶν σοφῶν λεχθέντα. (15) ἴστων τὰ ὑπὸ τῶν σοφῶν λεχθησόμενα. (16) συλλήψονται τοῦ βίου οἱ εὐδαίμονες θησαυρὸν μέγαν. (17) συλληφθήσεται τοῦ βίου θησαυρὸς μέγας ὑπὸ τῶν εὐδαιμόνων.

6. Translate the following English sentences into Greek.

(1) The Lord said to me, "You are my son, today I have begotten you." (*Psalm 2.7, LXX, adapted*) (2) I shall never miss out on these contests. (3) These contests will never be missed out on by me. (4) You (*pl.*) did not make a mistake, did you? (5) We shall know all our sins, because they will be made obvious to us by the master. (6) She asked whether all things in the world would be made plain to her, or whether she would know only a few things. (7) Never seek to beget children, for they are animals. (8) When did the mistress give birth to you? (9) On account of this we shall never know whether the gods have truly been born, since Socrates commanded us not to believe in them. (10) On account of this, I shall beget many children [for myself], because I myself was born. (11) In this household, the master has authority because to him belong all the slaves. (12) Let the mistress not yet release her maidservants, for they themselves have sinned greatly. (13) The thieves, knowing both their sin and their fate, have slain themselves. (14) Let the speakers never have authority; indeed, they do not yet know how to honour the laws of the ancients. (15) We shan't be chosen masters, shall we? We don't know whether we shall be trusted.

7. For extra practice, turn to the key for Lesson 28, **5.**, and translate those English sentences into Greek.

8. For extra practice, turn to the key for Lesson 28, **6.**, and translate those Greek sentences into English.

Lesson 29

1. Decline ἡ πόλις, pointing out which forms differ from standard third-declension nouns.

2. Decline ἡ μήτηρ, pointing out oddities in the declension.

3. Decline in the singular and plural: τὸ ἄστυ, ὁ βασιλεύς, ἡ θυγάτηρ, and ὁ πατήρ.

4. Translate the following sentences from English into Greek.

   (1) The prytanis asked whether the generals had attacked the city. (2) The father of this prytanis, although he was once king of the city, now has a house far away in the countryside. (3) The city is walls and houses and a marketplace; the city-state is human beings–kings, mothers, fathers, daughters, sons, generals, orators, mistresses and slaves–and laws. (4) Throughout the evening we were looking at the evil sky, asking whether our fate would move upon us. (5) The generals and their guards, as if to stop the people from making an uproar, hastened together with the prytanises into the marketplace. (6) Only the generals and their guards knew how to stop the people from making an uproar in the marketplace. (7) Generals, will you attack many cities, or will you really only pretend to be enemies to other city-states? (8) I do not know whether the generals will attack many cities or whether they will really only pretend to be enemies of other city-states. (9) Turning your cart into the city, you will miss out on the great confusion near the sea. (10) The king whom everyone loved was born in this city. (11) The king who loved all was born in this little city which has not been seen by many people. (12) The king, having been born in this city, loved his city-state greatly. (13) In the evening, my father betook himself to our house and found his bed. (14) For the whole day, my mother had sought to sell both shields and clothing made by her in the marketplace. (15) You haven't seen the young king who was just born, have you? We do not know how to find him or where he is.

5. For extra practice, turn to the key for Lesson 29, **4.**, and translate those Greek sentences into English.

Lesson 30

1. We have already learned a number of verbs in Greek that are partially or "semi-" deponent. List those verbs, giving their first and second principal parts, translating both of them.

2. When we use the term "deponent" to describe a Greek verb, what do we mean?

3. Fully deponent verbs fall into two basic categories: middle deponent and passive deponent. What distinguishes the two?

4. Identify whether the following verbs are either semi-deponent, fully deponent middle, or fully deponent passive.

   (1) μάχομαι, μαχοῦμαι, ἐμαχεσάμην, _____, μεμάχημαι, _____.
   (2) ἀκούω, ἀκούσομαι, ἤκουσα, ἀκήκοα, _____, ἠκούσθην.

(3) βούλομαι, βουλήσομαι, _____, _____, βεβούλημαι, ἐβουλήθην.

(4) ἀφικνέομαι, ἀφίξομαι, ἀφικόμην, _____, ἀφῖγμαι, _____.

(5) φεύγω, φεύξομαι, ἔφυγον, πέφευγα, _____, _____.

(6) αἰσθάνομαι, αἰσθήσομαι, ᾐσθόμην, _____, ᾔσθημαι, _____.

5. Translate the following sentences from English into Greek.

(1) Today, I fled away from my house; this night, I shall flee away from my city. (2) They arrived during the night, but you shall arrive during the evening. (3) He did not want to flee his master, while she intends even to ridicule him. (4) Having arrived into the marketplace, now we shall want to sell our shields. (5) You (*pl.*) aren't coming to the assembly, are you? We wish to flee the prytanises. (6) Arriving at the council, the prytanises asked whether the assembly had wished to hear their plan.

6. Explain in your own words the genitive absolute.

7. Following are English sentences, each containing a phrase that may be represented in Greek with a genitive absolute. Translate each sentence below into Greek.

(1) With the horse having been hit with rocks, the cart was turned into the river. (2) The assembly having fled, the orators stopped speaking. (3) The girls loved no one, no worthy man having been found. (4) The heralds summoned the people with one voice, the uproar being very great. (5) Do you know whither the Greeks have fled, their homeland having been destroyed?

8. The sentences above have been slightly rewritten below so that a genitive absolute phrase cannot be used to express the circumstantial participles in them. Translate the following into Greek. Once you have done this, refer back to the original sentences above, and make note of how both the Greek and English differ from 7. to 8.

(1) The horse, having been hit by rocks, turned the cart into the river. (2) The rhetors stopped speaking to the assembly after it had fled. (3) The girls, having found no man to love them, loved no one. (4) The heralds summoned the people with one voice through the uproar, because it was very great. (5) Do you know whither the Greeks have fled from their homeland, since it had been destroyed?

9. Decline the Greek word εἷς in the masculine, feminine, and neuter.

10. Decline the Greek word οὐδείς in the masculine, feminine, and neuter.

11. Decline the Greek word μηδείς in the masculine, feminine, and neuter.

12. Greek sentences may have more than one negative in them. When do those negatives cancel one another out?

13. Translate the following sentences into English.

(1) οὐδεὶς εἰς τὴν ἀγορὰν οὐκ ἀφίκετο. (2) οὐκ ἀφίκετο οὐδεὶς εἰς τὴν ἀγοράν. (3) μὴ ἴστω μηδεμία τοῦτο. (4) μηδεμία μὴ ἴστω τοῦτο. (5) οὐδέν μοι ἔπεμψεν οὐδείς. (6) οὐκ ἔπεμψέ μοί τις οὐδέν. (7) οὐδέν μοι οὐκ ἔπεμψεν.

14. Translate the following sentences from English into Greek.

(1) Since there are many things common to both the laws and wisdom,

much will be taught us by both rhetors and philosophers. (2) Neither did the messengers bring this counsel nor did the prytanises receive it, although the assembly had wished to command the generals to attack their enemy. (3) The assembly was added to one by one. (4) While I heard not one sound, I shall ask the others whether they heard something or not. (5) With the generals about to destroy the fatherland, we arrived at the sea and, having betaken ourselves into the triremes, commanded our slaves and mothers, sons and daughters, to come into them. (6) There being not even one real man in our fatherland, whence shall we get guards? (7) Although the sound of the din has not yet been feared by the children, neither mothers nor fathers wish to betake themselves into their beds on account of their own fear.

15. For extra practice, turn to the key for Lesson 29, **5.**, **7.**, **8.**, **13.**, and **14**, and translate those sentences back into Greek or English.

Lesson 31

1. In your own words, explain what an adverb of manner is. Give examples of English sentences using such an adverb.

2. In English our standard way of making an adverb of manner is simply to add –ly to the end of a word (e.g., severe (adj.) becomes severely (adverb)). However, some adverbs in other languages are often difficult to express in English with a single word ending in -ly. How can one circumvent this problem in English?

3. Explain the two ways in which adjectives may become adverbs of manner in Greek.

4. For the following adjectives, give the adverbial form[s].

(1) κακός	(8) ἄξιος	(15) ἀληθής
(2) καλός	(9) ἀγαθός	(16) εὐδαίμων
(3) δῆλος	(10) ἐχθρός	(17) μόνος
(4) μέγας	(11) κοινός	(18) πρότερος
(5) ὅδε	(12) μικρός	(19) πᾶς
(6) οὗτος	(13) μακρός	(20) φιλόσοφος
(7) ἀθάνατος	(14) ὀλίγος	(21) πολέμιος

5. Translate the following sentences into Greek.

(1) She undeservedly received the prize. (2) You attacked me in a hostile manner. (3) This book was written philosophically. (4) He spoke thus. (5) Do not arrive blindly! (6) Will you obey your mistress in a slavish manner? (7) I have been well taught. (8) We shall search for the truth like Greeks (in Greek manner). (9) This letter was written beautifully, while that book was not written in this very way. (10) He led life prosperously.

6. What is a result clause?

7. What are the similarities and differences in formation between the natural and actual result clauses, and how do they differ in meaning?

8. Translate the following sentences from English into Greek.

(1) He lived so shamefully that you would not believe [it]. (2) We have been taught by so many teachers that we now know everything. (3) This

deed is so easy that even a child might perform it. (4) She performed her work so easily that she will be able to come to her home this very hour. (5) Won't the immortals live forever? (6) He lived so shamefully that he also died shamefully. (7) We've been taught by so many teachers that we might know everything. (8) This deed was so easy that a child performed it. (9) She performed her work easily so as to come home in this very hour. (10) The unworthy thieves won't live forever, will they, so that they would be inimical to our children? (11) With the council having heard the prytanises, the herald reported the plan to the assembly so that there was a great commotion. (12) This is my husband, whom, while I live, I shall love. (13) How shamefully these people who have not been educated by philosophers live! They live so shamefully as to turn even the gods away from themselves! (14) Although no speaker spoke not truthfully, the assembly hesitated to believe their speeches. (15) The sound was so great that it opened the very doors of the house.

9. For extra practice, turn to the key for Lesson 31, **8.**, and translate those Greek sentences into English.

Lesson 32

1. What is the typical ending in Greek for the comparative adjective?

2. What is the typical ending in Greek for the superlative adjective?

3. Speak to the formation of the typical comparative adverb in Greek.

4. Speak to the formation of the typical superlative adverb in Greek.

5. How are the comparative and superlative adjectives of καινός formed? The adverbs?

6. How are the comparative and superlative adjectives of φίλος formed? The adverbs?

7. How are the comparative and superlative adjectives of Ἑλληνικός formed? The adverbs?

8. How are the comparative and superlative adjectives of εὐδαίμων formed? The adverbs?

9. Give the following forms in Greek:

   (1) σοφός, comparative, feminine accusative plural
   (2) φιλόσοφος, comparative, feminine genitive singular
   (3) ἀθάνατος, superlative, masculine genitive plural
   (4) ἐλεύθερος, superlative, neuter accusative singular
   (5) νέος, comparative, feminine dative plural
   (6) δοῦλος, superlative, masculine dative singular
   (7) αἴτιος, comparative, masculine nominative plural
   (8) ἀληθής, superlative, neuter dative plural
   (9) πολέμιος, comparative, neuter genitive singular

10. Translate the following short sentences into Greek.

    (1) She is wiser than he. (2) They lived as Greek as possible. (3) Who can be more immortal than the gods? (4) My friends are most dear to

me. (5) You (*pl.*) are very guilty of this sin. (6) They responded in a most unworthy fashion. (7) The prytanis spoke clearly; the rhetor, more clearly; the herald, most clearly. (8) This road is longer than that [one]. (9) Socrates is wiser than all the most ancient philosophers. (10) Friend, live rather prosperously and most sincerely.

11. Give the following forms of the verb γίγνομαι, with a translation beside each.

   (1) present indicative, second person singular
   (2) aorist participle, neuter dative singular
   (3) pluperfect middle/passive, first person plural
   (4) future infinitive
   (5) perfect active participle, feminine genitive singular
   (6) perfect middle/passive participle, masculine accusative singular
   (7) aorist imperative, third person plural
   (8) present imperative, third person singular

12. Give the following forms of the verb σῴζω, with a translation beside each.

   (1) present active indicative, second person plural
   (2) aorist active participle, feminine genitive singular
   (3) perfect middle/passive, third person singular
   (4) aorist passive infinitive
   (5) pluperfect active indicative, third person plural
   (6) perfect active participle, neuter dative plural
   (7) aorist passive imperative, second person singular
   (8) aorist active imperative, second person singular

13. Translate the following sentences from English into Greek.

(1) The evil mistress asked me in the most unworthy manner possible whether I had sought to save the children rather than the animals. (2) And yet, she herself was most guilty of their death. (3) In the future, this young man, the most clever of all the rather recent prytanises, will become despot of our city. (4) The herald with a great voice, on the pretext of saying most true things, shamefully told the people unworthy things. (5) But yet, the most sought for treasure was saved from the thieves so as to become our city's prize. (6) Let not the king become guilty of such a great sin that he become happier than the immortal gods. (7) That evening with the daughter of the despot was dearer to me than my own mother and father. (8) The speaker, having arrested his enemies, said, "You, my city, shall become as free as possible from all griefs." (9) As for the rest, not one of the most slavish household servants spoke the truth to me. (10) Save our city from its enemies, o immortal gods, and seek in a most sincere fashion to send us a very prosperous life.

14. For extra practice, turn to the key for Lesson 32, **13.**, and translate those Greek sentences into English.

Lesson 33

1. Give in Greek the masculine nominative singular of the positive, comparative, and superlative of the following adjectives:

      (1) much, many   (9)   good [in ability/worth]
      (2) shameful   (10) great, large
      (3) easy   (11) good [in might]
      (4) [morally] good   (12) little, few
      (5) bad [in might]   (13) bad [in ability/worth]
      (6) beautiful   (14) small
      (7) [morally] bad   (15) hostile
      (8) sweet

2. Give in Greek the adverbial forms of the positive, comparative and superlative of the following adjectives:

      (1) much, many   (9)   good [in ability/worth]
      (2) shameful   (10) great, large
      (3) easy   (11) good [in might]
      (4) [morally] good   (12) little, few
      (5) bad [in might]   (13) bad [in ability/worth]
      (6) beautiful   (14) small
      (7) [morally] bad   (15) hostile
      (8) sweet

3. Decline the comparatives πλείων and καλλίων in the masculine, feminine, and neuter singular and plural.

4. Give in Greek the demanded form in the positive, comparative, and superlative of each of the adjectives below:

      (1) great, neuter genitive singular
      (2) small, masculine dative singular
      (3) [morally] good, neuter accusative plural
      (4) bad [in worth], feminine nominative singular
      (5) good [in might], masculine vocative singular
      (6) [morally] bad, feminine nominative plural
      (7) good [in worth], feminine accusative plural
      (8) bad [in might], neuter dative plural
      (9) sweet, neuter genitive plural

5. Decline ἡδύς in the masculine, feminine, and neuter in the singular and plural.

6. When a comparison is made in Greek, how may one indicate the degree of difference? Illustrate with examples.

7. Translate the following sentences from English into Greek.

   (1) This general will become a very evil king. (2) He will be much more evil than the earlier kings. (3) The quite beautiful girl speaks sweetly. (4) And yet, she is better [in might] than many other girls. (5) The terrible herald spoke as shamefully as possible so that the people would not hear him. (6) Whose voice is sweeter than that of philosophy? (7) They became much more hostile to me. (8) While the speech of the orator was taught to her rather easily, the wisdom of the philsopher was not easily taught to me. (9) And yet, I was most easily taught of all students. (10) The orator has more treasure than I, but the best general collected the most.

8. For extra practice, turn to the key for Lesson 33, **7.**, and translate those Greek sentences into English.

Lesson 34

1. We use three terms to distinguish various types of numerical expression: cardinal numeral, ordinal numeral, and numerical adverb. How are these distinct from one another? Give examples in English and Greek.

2. Certain cardinal numerals are declinable in Greek. Which are they?

3. Decline the following cardinals:
   - (1) τέτταρες
   - (2) δύο
   - (3) τρεῖς
   - (4) εἷς

4. Give in Greek the cardinal resulting from each computation below (in the masculine nominative, when needed), along with the masculine nominative of its ordinal, as well as its numerical adverb.

   (a) 10-9
   7+8
   17+3
   19-11
   12+1

   (b) 22+18
   45+45
   75-45
   32+38
   107-57

   (c) 20 x 100
   1,000 x 10
   200 x 100

5. Explain in your own terms the partitive genitive. Give an example.

6. Translate the following sentences from English into Greek.

   (1) Twenty-five of the hundred triremes were destroyed. (2) The generals attacked the city eight times, while one thousand of the men of the city sought to kill their enemy (*use gen. abs.*). (3) Having sought for eight days to see that handsome man, on the eighth I did, in fact, see him. (4) I've told you this four times: four children had four horses from their four fathers. (5) One of the six beautiful maidens was much more beautiful and worthy and good than the other five, so that nine out of the ten youths would have easily loved her. (6) Having added our five hundred triremes to the other city's two hundred triremes, we were able to bring the greatest possible grief against our enemy. (7) The first king was the best; the second was a little worse; the third was the worst by much. Is their any hope of having a better king? (8) I have written eleven thousand letters to my daughter who has received not even one of them. (9) There are nineteen shields in the house, but there are thirty-two men. Which thirteen of them do not wish to have shields? (10) The king added so much to the treasury that it now has one hundred thousand drachmas.

7. For extra practice, turn to the key for Lesson 34, **6.**, and translate those Greek sentences into English.

Lesson 35

1. Generally speaking, what is indicated by the subjunctive mood?

2. How many tenses can the subjunctive be formed in, and what are they? Which are most common?

3. What is the difference in meaning between the present subjunctive and the aorist subjunctive?

4. Give the characteristics of formation of the following subjunctive forms: (a) aorist passive; (b) present active; (c) aorist active; (d) present middle/passive; (e) aorist middle.

5. Conjugate the following in the demanded form:

    (1) βούλομαι, aorist passive subjunctive
    (2) ἀφικνέομαι, aorist middle subjunctive
    (3) εὑρίσκω, aorist active subjunctive
    (4) σῴζω, present active subjunctive
    (5) φέρω, present middle/passive subjunctive
    (6) συλλαμβάνω, future middle subjunctive

6. Conjugate the following in the demanded form:

    (1) ὠφελέω, present passive subjunctive
    (2) γελάω, present middle subjunctive
    (3) δηλόω, present active subjunctive
    (4) δηλόω, present passive subjunctive
    (5) ζητέω, present active subjunctive
    (6) γελάω, present active subjunctive

7. (a) Give the six principal parts of the verb μάχομαι. (b) Give the following forms of the verb μάχομαι.

    (1) present indicative, second person singular
    (2) present subjunctive, second person singular
    (3) present imperative, second person singular
    (4) imperfect indicative, second person singular
    (5) future indicative, third person plural
    (6) future indicative, second person plural
    (7) aorist subjunctive, third person singular
    (8) aorist indicative, third person singular
    (9) aorist imperative, third person singular
    (10) aorist infinitive
    (11) perfect indicative, first person plural
    (12) pluperfect indicative, first person plural
    (13) perfect infinitive

8. Give the six principal parts of the verb φαίνω.

9. What are the three independent uses of the subjunctive? Write them down and explain each.

10. Translate the following sentences from English into Greek.

    (1) One of the goddesses is asking the others whether they ought to appear to both the best and the worst of the people. (2) Should we fight against the enemy city, or should we prepare to seek peace? (3) Don't let the preparation for war be stopped! (4) Don't let there be a battle concerning gold and

silver! (5) Don't call our allies now, for we have not yet made preparations for war. (6) Let us be allied to the city which has more triremes than the city which has only twenty! (7) Should we be allied to the city which has more triremes than the city which has only twenty? (8) We are allied to the city which has more triremes than the city which has only twenty. (9) Let me seek to steal the possessions of that very evil despot, who has most shamefully collected so much gold and so much silver that he now appears to be the most prosperous as possible. (10) With our enemy having fought more battles than we, the generals of our city made preparations longer ago than our allies. (11) Destroy the philosopher, but don't destroy his philosophy! (12) This thing is most terrible! Should we tell all the prytanises about it, or only one of them?

11. For extra practice, turn to the key for Lesson 35, **10.**, and translate those Greek sentences into English.

Lesson 36

1. Generally speaking, what does a verb in the optative mood in Greek imply?

2. In which tenses is the Greek optative mood found, and what is implied by each of these tenses?

3. Conjugate the following verbs in the forms demanded:

   (1) μάχομαι, aorist middle optative
   (2) λύω, present active optative
   (3) κλέπτω, aorist passive optative
   (4) εἰμί, future optative
   (5) γίγνομαι, imperfect middle optative
   (6) συλλαμβάνω, future middle optative
   (7) λαμβάνω, aorist active optative
   (8) παρασκευάζω, future passive optative
   (9) γράφω, future active optative
   (10) θύω, present mid./pass. optative

4. Conjugate the following verbs in the forms demanded:

   (1) ποιέω, present active optative
   (2) γελάω, present passive optative
   (3) δηλόω, present middle optative
   (4) ἐρωτάω, present active optative
   (5) ὠφελέω, present middle optative
   (6) δηλόω, present active optative
   (7) εἰμί, present optative

5. Name the two independent uses of the optative, explain each, and supply with examples.

6. Translate the following sentences into Greek.

   (1) The youths may chase the horse. (2) May the youths chase the horse! (3) The youths might not chase the horse. (4) Would that my daughters might be honoured by all men! (5) May no man not continue to honour my daughters! (6) My daughters might not be honoured by all men. (7) If only all men might honour my daughters. (8) If only the philosophers might go on making clear all faults. (9) The philosophers might not go on making all faults clear. (10) May the philosophers not go on making all faults clear.

7. List from memory the six principal parts of the verb χράομαι.

8. Conjugate the verb χράομαι in the: (a) present indicative; (b) present subjunctive; (c) present optative.

9. Translate the following sentences from English into Greek.

(1) If only the army might be ready to fight a battle against the enemy army. (2) The first soldier and the second soldier might be a little more useful to us than the third and the fourth. (3) The king might, on the one hand, use all his possessions in doing good things for the people; on the other, may he not go on using his gold and silver in acquiring more slaves! (4) Might our army be sufficient to appear as terrible as possible to the enemy? (5) Although possessions are useful and silver more useful, gold is most useful of all. (6) May our city-state experience sweet peace, and may our generals continue to experience sweeter victory. (7) While the camp was used by the soldiers who had arrived by land (*use gen. abs.*), the city was used by those from the triremes who had arrived by sea. (8) If only books might be written by generals about camps, soldiers, and armies! (9) May the best man have the victory! (10) General, should we prepare to use our shields? (11) Don't say this: "May the very evil speaker be chosen king." (12) Let us all ask with one voice, "Might you, o victory, go on experiencing rather long and prosperous life among us?"

10. For extra practice, turn to the key for Lesson 36, **9.**, and translate those Greek sentences into English.

Lesson 37

1. In your own words, describe what a conditional sentence is.

2. What are the technical terms for the two clauses that comprise a Greek conditional sentence?

3. How many different *basic* types of Greek conditions are there, and what are they?

4. How many different types of Greek conditions are there, and what are they?

5. It's easiest to learn the Greek conditions by memorising for each both its formula in Greek and a formula for its translation in English. Below, for each condition, give both its Greek formula and a formula for its translation into English.

Example:	Protasis	Apodosis
Present Simple Particular	εἰ + present indicative,	present indicative
	If x is _____ing,	y is _____ing.
	or	
	If x _____ s,	y _____s.

(1) Future less vivid
(2) Past simple particular
(3) Past general
(4) Future most vivid
(5) Present general
(6) Past contrary-to-fact
(7) Future more vivid
(8) Present contrary-to-fact

6. List all the conditions that have ἄν or ἐάν in them, and give their Greek formulas and English translation formulas.

7. List all the conditions that have the optative mood in them, and give their Greek formulas and English translation formulas.

8. List all the conditions that have only indicatives, and give their Greek formulas and English translation formulas.

9. List all the conditions that have the subjunctive mood in them, and give their Greek formulas and their English translation formulas.

10. Below are several sentences in English. You will not be required to render them into Greek. However, were you to render them into Greek, what type of condition would each demand in Greek?

   (1) If Frank was watering his lawn, it was getting wet on his neighbour's yard as well. (2) You would have harmed the children, if you had thrown them too high into the air. (3) If no one ate watermelon, the watermelon was ruined. (4) Socrates will not fight in a trireme, if the general will not command him to fight. (5) If ever the teacher speaks, she has brilliant things to say. (6) The ground is getting progressively more dry if it is not raining outside. (7) If the river should overflow its banks, our house would be ruined. (8) If ever the river overflowed its banks, the fields were inundated with bounteous and fertile silt. (9) If the candle burns out, we shall be left in the dark. (10) If you were eating watermelon rind, your tummy would certainly ache.

11. Translate the following sentences from English into Greek.

   (1) If you should win unjustly, you would injure the laws of the city-state. (2) Might he corrupt the youth by teaching them unjust things? (3) If Athenian justice had been the best, the Athenians would not have killed Socrates. (4) If ever they do wrong to you, you are free from the penalty. (5) If our nature was ever better, all humans loved the others equally. (6) I will corrupt all justice, if you will not punish the evil despot. (7) If they injure many people, will you seek to guard the injured? (8) If only the evil king would die! (9) If there is a din in the city, the enemy are attacking the walls. (10) You would be listening to your teacher now if you were not seeking to corrupt the other students. (11) If the general died, his army also died.

12. For extra practice, turn to the key for Lesson 37, **11.**, and translate those Greek sentences into English.

Lesson 38

1. Give two examples in English which illustrate the use of the relative pronoun as definite and indefinite; explain your examples.

2. If a relative clause is indefinite in nature, how is it to be regarded in Greek? Give analogous examples illustrating this in English and Greek.

3. Below are several pairs of short conditional sentences. The first of each pair is a "straight" condition; the second of each pair is a closely related relative condition. Translate them into Greek.

(1) (a) If we should speak, we would corrupt the youth. (b) Whenever we should speak, we would corrupt the youth. (2) (a) If (ever) the teacher taught opinions, they were not true. (b) Whichever opinions the teacher (ever) taught were not true. (3) (a) If you had corrupted the youth, you would have been destroyed. (b) Whoever had corrupted the youth would have been destroyed. (4) (a) If they were corrupting the youth, they would be being destroyed. (b) Whomever they were corrupting, they would be being destroyed.

4. Give the Greek equivalent(s) for each of the following conditional relative expressions in English:

(1)	whoever	(6)	whenever
(2)	whosever	(7)	howsoever
(3)	whomever	(8)	whencever
(4)	to/for whomever	(9)	wherever
(5)	whithersoever		

5. Translate the following sentences from English into Greek.

(1) Whithersoever he had betaken himself, he would have found pain and not joy. (2) Whoever will be chosen archon will rule the Athenians well. (3) Whencever you should arrive in our city, you would find it a much better place than all others. (4) Whosesoever cloak she is wearing, she is prettier than all the other girls. (5) Toward whomever you are well disposed, she will use great goodwill toward you as well. (6) To whomever your spirit desired to send letters, they would receive them most eagerly. (7) Whenever that man was chosen archon, he ruled the people with equal and just laws. (8) Howsoever he seeks to speak with passion, let us not be persuaded by his words. (9) Wherever they had abandoned their children, they would have found them.

6. For extra practice, turn to the key for Lesson 38, **5.**, and translate those Greek sentences into English.

Lesson 39

1. Express in your own words the difference in meaning between the natural result clause, the actual result clause, and the purpose clause.

2. Result clauses and purposes clauses follow certain formulae as they are created in Greek. Give the formulae for the natural result clause, actual result clause, and purpose clause, taking into account the following: introductory conjunction; verb form; negation; case of subject.

3. The purpose clause may use either subjunctive or optative as the mood of its verb. Please explain under what circumstances one or the other is used.

4. Since deciding whether a purpose clause should use the subjunctive or the optative depends on whether the main verb is in primary or secondary tense, please explain which verb forms belong to the primary, which to the secondary tenses.

5. Give the six principal parts of the following verbs: γαμέω, ἕπομαι, and βοάω.

6. Give the demanded forms of the following verbs:

      (1) γαμέω, present active optative
      (2) βοάω, imperfect active
      (3) ἕπομαι, imperfect
      (4) βοάω, present active subjunctive
      (5) ἕπομαι, aorist middle optative
      (6) γαμέω, aorist active optative

7.   When the verb of the main clause introducing an indirect question is in the secondary tense, what form should the verb of the indirect question be in? What is the force of following one option or another?

8.   Translate the following sentences from English into Greek.

(1) If I should choose to marry this woman, would my mother and father stop crying out against me? (2) I am following the horse in order to find the house of its master. (3) I followed the horse in order to find the house of its master. (4) Should I follow the horse in order to find the house of its master? (5) Stay down now and betake yourself up the ladder later in order that the child not cry out. (6) The men asked their wives whether they had followed strange men into the marketplace. (7) The women will ask their husbands how they intend to discover their error. (8) The archon invited all the prytanises to his house in order to hold a wedding for his daughter and the man who would be her husband. (9) The general moved up and down in his trireme in order to command his soldiers to fight the best possible. (10) The troops will listen to their general in order to win a victory and so that there might be a great shout when they arrive back in their city.

9.   For extra practice, turn to the key for Lesson 39, **8.**, and translate those Greek sentences into English.

Lesson 40

1.   In which forms is the verb εἶμι preferred to ἔρχομαι?

2.   Translate the following using the verbs ἔρχομαι and εἶμι.

(1) You are coming.	(9) Should I come?
(2) You were coming.	(10) I might come.
(3) She was coming.	(11) She came.
(4) She has come.	(12) We have come.
(5) I wish to come.	(13) You (*pl.*) were coming.
(6) They chose to come.	(14) If I had come, you would have come.
(7) I came, you were coming.	(15) If I should come, you would come.
(8) If I come, you will come.	(16) If I am coming, they are coming.

3.   Give the six principal parts of ἔρχομαι.

4.   Give the six principal parts of εἶμι and εἰμί.

5.   Conjugate εἶμι in the following:
      (1) present subjunctive
      (2) present infinitive
      (3) present indicative
      (4) the nominative and genitive singular of the masculine, feminine, and neuter participle
      (5) present optative
      (6) present imperative
      (7) imperfect

6. How many different methods are at hand for constructing indirect discourse in Greek?

7. Explain the first method available for creating indirect discourse.

8. For purposes of indirect discourse with ὅτι or ὡς, which Greek verbs which you already know are counted as verbs of "saying"?

9. Translate the following short sentences into Greek.

    (1) He was chosen king. He reports that he was chosen king. He reported that he had been chosen king. (2) She will suffer evil [things]. I am saying she will suffer evil [things]. I had said that she would suffer evil [things]. I have said that she will suffer evil [things]. I said that she would suffer evil [things]. (3) They went to Socrates. We have written that they had gone to Socrates. We had written that they had gone to Socrates. We shall write that they went to Socrates. (4) You (*pl.*) are without friends. They declared that you were without friends. Having declared that you were without friends, they came to you. We shall declare that you are without friends.

10. Translate the answer key for number **9**. into English.

11. When in indirect discourse with ὅτι or ὡς one wishes to include a subordinate clause in that indirect discourse, what need one bear in mind?

12. Translate the following sentences from English into Greek.

    (1) Come (*use aorist*) into the house! (2) You said that they are coming into the house. (3) The man, having been chosen king, declared that his wife would no longer be treated ill by anyone. (4) Come on, let's go into the marketplace, announcing that the general has won the war! (5) My friends declared that the provisions were inside and that they would send them outside with some servants. (6) Immediately the servants came to my friends and said that soldiers had written that their general had been killed. (7) We said that although we are not fond of suffering, we would gladly suffer on behalf of our city. (8) Hey you! Go into the marketplace; and let us judge whether the people have suffered enough or not. (9) It was explained to us that whilst the king was going to his friends (*use part. phrase*), a great lion attacked him and killed him. (10) Let us choose a king kindly disposed toward those who suffer on behalf of friendship, kindness, and justice.

13. For extra practice, turn to the key for Lesson 40, **12.**, and translate those Greek sentences into English.

Lesson 41

1. Give the six principal parts of the verb φημί.

2. Translate the following using the verb φημί.

    (1) I might say something.
    (2) I deny that.
    (3) They are saying.
    (4) We were saying this.
    (5) Let's say something.
    (6) If only you would say something!
    (7) Let her say!
    (8) They were saying.
    (9) He denies that.
    (10) You (*s.*) say.
    (11) Were you (*s.*) saying that?
    (12) Should I say something?
    (13) Saying these things, he wished to say more.
    (14) Let them say this to us!

3. (a) Compare and contrast the first form of indirect discourse we learned with the second form of indirect discourse we are learning. (b) Translate the following sentences into Greek. (1) He wrote that Socrates had killed a man. (2) He thought that Socrates had killed a man. (3) I declare that we shall sell fifteen shields. (4) I declared that we would sell fifteen shields. (5) I believe that we shall sell fifteen shields. (6) I believed that we would sell fifteen shields.

4. (a) Explain the guidelines governing use of the subject in indirect discourse with the infinitive. (b) Translate the following sentences into Greek. (1) I think that I am faster than he. (2) I think that he is faster than I. (3) We judged that we were best. (4) We judged that they were best. (5) She thinks that she will be greatly loved by him. (6) She says that he will be greatly loved by herself.

5. (a) Explain the meaning of the various tenses of infinitive in a statement in indirect discourse. (b) Translate the following sentences into Greek. (1) I judged that we had won the battle. (2) I judged that we were winning the battle. (3) I judged that we would win the battle. (4) You think that we have not loved enough. (5) You think that we have not loved enough. (6) You think that we do not love enough. (7) You think that we will not love enough. (8) You will deny that you loved me. (9) You will deny that I love you. (10) You will deny that I have loved you. (11) You will deny you intend to love me again. (12) You will deny that you will love me again.

6. How does one negate an indirect statement using the infinitive?

7. Explain how to handle the particle ἄν in the form of indirect discourse which uses the infinitive.

8. Translate the following sentences from English into Greek.

(1) Although he had sold the beautiful trireme for two talents of gold (*use participial phrase*), the recently prosperous rhetor denied that he had stolen money from the city. (2) The courtesan asserted that she loved my friend and that her love was so great that she would follow him whithersoever he went. (3) Come quickly! I think that the enemy is arriving at our walls. (4) It was considered that the slowest trireme of the Athenians was even a little quicker than all those of the other city. (5) She is fond of considering her companion to be the most handsome of all men. (6) She is fond of considering herself to be the most beautiful of all women. (7) She was denying that the friendship of the enemy had turned her away from her kindness toward all other human beings. (8) What is a talent? A talent is sixty minas. What is a mina? A mina is one hundred drachmas. What is a drachma? A drachma is six obols. (9) She will assert that she has found true friendship, but that she will continue to seek true love. (10) It had been thought that the general had exchanged the trireme for one hundred minas.

9. For extra practice, turn to the key for Lesson 41, **8.**, and translate those Greek sentences into English.

Lesson 42

1. (a) Explain the formation of indirect discourse with a participle. (b) Convert the following introductory sentences and direct statements into sentences containing indirect discourse, translating your finished product.

   Example: οἶδα // ὁ ἄνθρωπος ἀποθνήσκει. =

   οἶδα τὸν ἄνθρωπον ἀποθνήσκοντα.
   I know that the man is dying.

   (1) δηλοῖ ὁ φιλόσοφος // οἱ μαθηταὶ οὐδὲν ἴσασιν. (2) ᾐσθόμεθα // αἱ θεράπαιναι τῇ δεσποίνῃ εὖ δουλεύουσιν. (3) ἀκηκόασι // οἱ πολέμιοι ἐπὶ τὰ τῆς πόλεως τείχη ἀφίκοντο. (4) ἐδήλου ὁ φιλόσοφος // ὁ φιλόσοφος οὐδὲν οἶδεν. (5) εὑρίσκομεν // ἡμεῖς οὐκ ἐθέλομεν τὴν μοῖραν ἰδεῖν.

2. (a) If an adjective modifies a noun or a pronoun functioning as the subject of indirect discourse using a participle, which case will it be in? (b) Translate the following sentences into Greek, using indirect discourse with a participle. (1) I know that I am a wise philosopher. (2) The wise philosopher has learned (by inquiry) that he was born free. (3) The wise philosopher has learned (by inquiry) that his wife was born free. (4) He has learned (by study) that I am wise philosopher. (5) Did you sense that your beautiful trireme was being detroyed?

3. Which types of verbs typically introduce indirect discourse using the participle? Give as many examples of such verbs in Greek as possible.

4. Explain what the various tenses of the participle in indirect discourse with the participle indicate.

5. Translate the following sentences using the most appropriate form of indirect discourse available for each one. (1) We know that our soldiers have not won. (2) We are saying that our soldiers have not won. (3) We think that our soldiers have not won. (4) The herald reported that the speaker had been killed. (5) The herald heard that speaker had been killed. (6) The herald heard the speaker being killed. (7) The herald denied that the speaker had been killed. (8) Is he explaining that he has not found his book? (9) Has she written that she had not found her book? (10) Is she considering herself not to have found her book? (11) Is she explaining that she has not found her book?

6. Give the six principal parts of the following verbs:

   (1) μανθάνω,
   (2) αἰσθάνομαι,
   (3) πυνθάνομαι.

7. Explain what we mean when we speak of **crasis**. Give an example.

8. Translate the following sentences from English into Greek.

   (1) The prudent man discovered that even the best [people] are not always ruled by self-control. (2) Have you heard about the old man and the old woman? It is said that they have truly found joy. (3) You will truly sense that you have acquired wisdom when you are able no longer to love money. (4) I have learned how to write books in order to teach students. (5) In turn, the students have learned (by inquiry) that their teacher is not prudent. (6) This affair seems to be out of the hands of the

prytanises. (7) Although considering himself to be the most handsome of all, this man denies that he takes joy in looking at himself. (8) You will come to perceive that Socrates has harmed many youths. (9) I found out from the prytanises that the generals had punished the evil soldiers, though they themselves had made the same mistake. (10) Do you sense a lion? I sense that a lion is coming upon us!

9. For extra practice, turn to the key for Lesson 42, **8.**, and translate those Greek sentences into English.

Lesson 43

1. For each use of the infinitive below (a) give a thorough explanation of the use; (b) create two examples in Greek of your own in illustration of the use.

   (1) complementary infinitive
   (2) object infinitive
   (3) infinitive + adjective
   (4) subject infinitive
   (5) infinitive in indirect discourse
   (6) infinitive in natural result clause

2. How may the articular infinitive be translated?

3. What case is the articular infinitive's subject found in?

4. How is the articular infinitive negated?

5. The articular infinitive is called a "verbal noun." What are the implications of this?

6. Translate the following sentences. For each, indicate how the articular infinitive is functioning within the syntax of each sentence. (1) τὸ παιδεύεσθαι καλόν ἐστιν. (2) δηλῶ σοὶ τὸ τοὺς σοφοὺς ἀεὶ σώφρονας εἶναι. (3) τὸ τοὺς πολεμίους τὴν πόλιν λελυκέναι δῆλον ἦν. (4) οὐκ αἴτιός εἰμι τοῦ τὰς ἀσπίδας κλαπῆναι.

7. In what context does πρίν mean "until"? What syntax follows it?

8. In what context does πρίν mean "before"? What syntax follows it?

9. Translate the following sentences from Greek. (1) πρὶν τὴν γυναῖκα εἰς τὴν οἰκίαν ἐλθεῖν, φιλεῖ ὁ ἀνὴρ τὴν θεράπαιναν. (2) οὐκ ἐφίλησεν ὁ ἀνὴρ τὴν γυναῖκα πρὶν ἐκείνη εἰς τὴν οἰκίαν ἦλθεν. (3) πρὶν ἂν λέγῃ ὁ ῥήτωρ, αὐτὸν οὐ νομιῶ ἀγαθὸν εἶναι. (4) πάντα τὸν θησαυρὸν συλλαμβάνω πρὶν τὸν γέροντα λῦσαι αὐτόν.

10. Translate the following sentences into Greek. (1) You cannot know how to write until you are taught by a teacher. (2) I sensed the lion coming before it saw us. (3) I did not sense the lion coming until it was necessary to flee. (4) The old lady will sell all her clothing before her husband arrives.

11. Translate the following sentences from English into Greek.

   (1) It will not be possible for you to go into the trireme until the soldiers and the horses betake themselves into it. (2) The philosopher considered

that it was necessary to pursue excellence. (3) On the one hand, it seems good for us to fight against the enemy before they attack us; on the other, we do not desire many citizens to be destroyed. (4) For the sake of us having leisure (*use articular infinitive*), our mothers make many cloaks which they sell in the marketplace. (5) I say that that man is guilty, for it is necessary to declare who is guilty of sinning this sin (*use articular infinitive*). (6) Child, I am telling you to come down this ladder now, for if you do not come, you will never stop crying because you are scared (*use participle*). (7) One must always seek excellence, truth, and justice in order to become a true philosopher. (8) "I am ready," said the old man, "to lead life in a leisurely way." (9) It was necessary for all citizens to remain in their houses before the herald reported that the army had won the war. (10) To have sought and not found the truth (*use articular infinitive*) is not a sin; not to have sought (*use articular infinitive*) is a great sin.

12. For extra practice, turn to the key for Lesson 43, **11.**, and translate those Greek sentences into English.

Lesson 44

1. As a rule of thumb, how does one form the verbal adjective in –τέος?

2. What does the verbal adjective in –τέος express?

3. Give the verbal adjective in –τέος, along with a translation, for each of the following:

    (1) θύω   (6) οἶδα
    (2) φιλέω   (7) φεύγω
    (3) σῴζω   (8) γράφω
    (4) μανθάνω   (9) πέμπω
    (5) φημί   (10) λέγω

4. When a verbal adjective in –τέος occupies the attributive position, how does it function? Give two original examples in Greek, with their translations.

5. There are two predicate uses of the verbal adjective in –τέος: the personal and the impersonal. Outline each, and give original examples.

6. Translate the following two sentences in as many ways as possible.

    (1) οὗτοι οἱ λόγοι ῥητέοι τῷ ῥήτορί εἰσιν.
    (2) τὰς ἁμαρτίας παυστέον σοι ἦν.

7. The following sentences can be translated using the verbal adjective in –τέος. Translate each twice, once using the verbal adjective personally, once impersonally.

    (1) The king needs to be chosen by the people, not the nobles (*use* ἄριστοι). (2) This road had to be traveled by the soldiers. (3) The philosophical woman ought to write down wise things. (4) We will have to fight this battle. (5) The things that need to be said are to be written [down] by the prytanis.

8. What is the sense of the verbal adjective in –τός?

9. How is the verbal adjective in –τός formed?

10. How does one form the comparative and superlative of a verbal adjective in –τός?

11. The following sentences contain verbal adjectives in –τός. Translate each of them, giving both senses of the verbal adjective in–τός when it is possible.

   (1) σὺ εἶ ὁ υἱός μου ὁ ἀγαπητός. (Mark 1.13)
   (2) ἡρπάσαμεν τὸν κλῶπα τὸν παυστόν.
   (3) παιδευτὰ τὰ τέκνα;
   (4) σπεύσωμεν ἰδεῖν τὴν θαυμαστὴν μάχην.
   (5) παυστὸς μὲν ὁ στρατός· παυστοτέρα δ᾽ ἡ τριήρης·
       παυστότατος δ᾽ ὁ στρατιώτης.

12. Give the six principal parts of the verb ἐλαύνω

13. Translate the following sentences from English into Greek.

   (1) While the triremes travel one hundred stades (*use genitive absolute*), the army must march one thousand. (2) I would be amazed at the general if he should win the war by fighting all the battles that must be fought. (3) The chorus is devoid of those who have learned what was written; it will, however, have to feel ashamed that it knows very little. (4) The prytanises will, therefore, judge this chorus to be the worst possible. (5) If the speaker is rebuked by his beloved son, he will be ashamed. (6) Until all the archons die, the citizens must not choose a king in order for him to rule them. (7) While many things are quite discoverable by inquiry (*use* πυνθάνομαι) (*use gen. abs.*), surely we sense that the gods are most knowable (*use* πυνθάνομαι) and that we must seek to discover them. (8) The generals would have felt ashamed if the soldiers had marched into battle without them. (9) While the orator said that he had seen something to be marvelled at, I do not believe that he saw it and I sense that the thing to be marvelled at never happened. (10) One must deny that life is the best when the nobles rule all others.

14. For extra practice, turn to the key for Lesson 44, **13.**, and translate those Greek sentences into English.

Lesson 45

1. List the various sub-categories of classical Greek (a) substantival subordinate clauses; (b) adjectival subordinate clauses; and (c) adverbial subordinate clauses.

2. What questions correspond to (a) a substantival subordinate clause; (b) an adjectival subordinate clause; and (c) an adverbial subordinate clause?

3. What type of subordinate clause are the clauses of fear and effort?

4. What does a clause of effort express?

5. List verbs which indicate effort.

6. Give the formula for a clause of effort.

7. Translate the following short sentences into Greek.

   (1) They were taking care not to scare the children. (2) We shall contrive

to attack the walls. (3) He took action that the woman should love him. (4) You (*s.*) were planning to get the man chosen as archon. (5) It is necessary to look [into it] that we not be killed.

8. How does the purpose clause differ from the clause of effort?

9. What specific modifications may one make to an effort clause to make it more like a purpose clause?

10. Give the six principal parts of the verb δέδοικα.

11. Translate the following using δέδοικα.

(1)	We were fearing.	(5)	She was fearing.
(2)	We fear.	(6)	She fears.
(3)	We feared.	(7)	to fear
(4)	She feared.		

12. Give the perfect active participle for δέδοικα.

13. List the expressions in Greek which may introduce a clause of fear.

14. What is the Greek formula for a clause of fear?

15. Translate the following short sentences into Greek.

    (1) We were fearing (*use* δέδοικα) lest the whole army be killed. (2) There will be a danger for us that the archon might not rule justly. (3) Let us be on our guard lest the chorus be ashamed. (4) They feared lest the children be stolen by thieves. (5) There is fear for the people that the city might be destroyed.

16. What is curious about the verbs ὁράω, σκοπέω, and φυλάττομαι in regard to the main point of this lesson?

17. Translate the following sentences into Greek.

    (1) Being ashamed that there is not enough food, I fear that my guests will go back to their houses before they eat. (2) Therefore I shall find a contrivance that the servants might steal food in the marketplace. (3) Indeed, you see, it is necessary to look into [it] that you have enough sleep and food before riding your horse all day. (4) I desire to plan for us to attack the walls of this city, while the other army sleeps in its camp (*use gen. abs.*). (5) Take care of the old man and the old woman, dear son, and take care to eat enough food. (6) The children, seeing the soldiers and their shields, were afraid lest they be stolen from their mothers and fathers. (7) There was a great fear among (*use* ἐν) the citizens that the general would not contrive cleverly to win the battle. (8) You (*pl.*) fear, being very prudent, lest your children not be well educated. (9) Although he had much leisure, the prytanis continued making plans to make his city better. (10) Having seen the great tumult, the archons took care that their houses would not be destroyed by the army which had just won a great victory.

18. For extra practice, turn to the key for Lesson 45, **17.**, and translate those Greek sentences into English.

Lesson 46

1. What makes –μι verbs distinct from standard –ω verbs?

2. Study the paradigm of the verb δίδωμι on pages 320–321 of Groton, and answer the following questions. (a) In the present system, when is the stem vowel ω used, and when is the stem vowel ο used? (b) In what forms of the indicative is the stem of the verb reduplicated? (c) In what forms of the imperative, the subjunctive and the optative is the stem reduplicated?

3. Study the paradigm of the verb ἵστημι on pages 322 and 323 of Groton, and answer the following questions. (a) In the present system, when is the stem vowel η used, and when is the stem vowel α used? (b) In what forms of the indicative is the stem of the verb reduplicated, and what constitutes reduplication for the verb ἵστημι? (c) In what forms of the imperative, the subjunctive, and the optative is the stem reduplicated?

4. In which forms is the verb ἵστημι transitive? In which forms is it intransitive?

5. Translate the following.

    (1) I was standing. We were standing. You (*pl.*) were standing. She was standing.
    (2) I gave. They gave. We gave. It gave.
    (3) If you should give, he would stand.
    (4) I am giving. I am being given. He is giving for himself. They are giving.
    (5) He is being given. They are being given. He is giving. They were giving.
    (6) You (*s.*) are giving. You (*s.*) are giving for yourself. You (*s.*) gave.
    (7) You (*pl.*) are giving for yourself. You (*pl.*) are giving. You (*pl.*) were giving.
    (8) I wish to give. I wish to stand.
    (9) I wish to make the shield stand. I command the shield to be given.
    (10) We hasten to stand.
    (11) Having stood up, the young girl began crying.
    (12) Having been stood up, the shield was snatched by a soldier.
    (13) If they stand up shouting, we shall give gifts.
    (14) If you were standing up the shield, she would be giving gifts.
    (15) If they had stood up the shield, we would have given gifts.
    (16) We are contriving to give gifts. We are contriving to stand up. We are contriving to be given. We are contriving to stand up the shield.
    (17) Give us gifts, despot, in order that we might stand in the marketplace.
    (18) She gave him a book in order that he might stand it up.
    (19) Stand (*s.*) up! Stand (*pl.*) the book up! Let them give gifts!
    (20) Give gifts! Let them give gifts! Let us stand up, giving gifts!

6. Give the six principal parts of the verb ὠνέομαι.

7. What is unique about the third principal part of the verb ὠνέομαι? What is unique about the fifth and sixth?

8. Give the six principal parts of the verb ἐπίσταμαι.

9. Give the following forms of the verb ἐπίσταμαι: (a) present indicative; (b) imperfect indicative; (c) aorist optative.

10. Give the relative, indefinite, direct interrogative, and indirect interrogative, in that order, for the following: τοσοῦτος and τοῖος.

11. Give the six principal parts of the verb δίδωμι.

12. Give the six principal parts of the verb ἵστημι.

13. Translate the following sentences from English into Greek.

(1) It is necessary for you to know how to write books before you [come to] understand (*use aor.*) philosophy. (2) He is able to teach us both his skill and his understanding. (3) Having been punished on account of standing in the marketplace (*use articular infinitive*), the old philosopher sought to punish those who had harmed him. (4) Standing under this tree we shall surely be able to see to it that we not be struck by the gods from heaven. (5) For how much was this shield bought? I bought my shield for ten drachmas. Let us never buy such poor shields for so great a price. (6) I understand that, while the orator had given his treasure to his children, he gave his books to all the citizens that they might be stood up in the marketplace and bought and sold. (7) We do not even know what sort of human being would eat his own children. (8) Having stood the couch up, I stood next to the door shouting to my husband to come down the ladder. (9) These animals were given to the king in order to stand around him. (10) Having bought so much food, I do not understand how we shall eat it.

14. For extra practice, turn to the key for Lesson 46, **13.**, and translate those Greek sentences into English.

Lesson 47

1. Conjugate the verb τίθημι in the following:
    (1) the present active indicative;
    (2) the aorist middle indicative;
    (3) the present middle/passive imperative;
    (4) the imperfect middle passive;
    (5) the aorist active indicative;
    (6) the present middle/passive indicative;
    (7) the present infinitive;
    (8) the aorist active participle.

2. Conjugate the verb ἵημι in the following:

    (1) the present active indicative;
    (2) the aorist middle indicative;
    (3) the present middle/passive imperative;
    (4) the imperfect middle passive;
    (5) the aorist active indicative;
    (6) the present middle/passive indicative;
    (7) the present infinitive;
    (8) the aorist active participle.

3. Translate the following into Greek.

    (1) He is placing; I placed; they have placed; should we place?

(2) He is throwing; I threw; they have thrown; should we throw?
(3) Place (*s.*)! place (*pl.*)! she might place; she will place; they were placed.
(4) Throw (*s.*)! throw (*pl.*)! she might throw; she will throw; they were thrown.
(5) Having placed the shield against the wall, the soldier was throwing a book.
(6) The woman told me to place the book on the ladder.
(7) Let them not throw books! Let them place the books on the couch.
(8) We would have been thrown out of the city if we had not placed the wagons in the marketplace.
(9) If only they would not throw the children through the door!
(10) We threw rocks in order to place the enemy in danger.

4. Conjugate the verb κεῖμαι in:

   (1) the present imperative;
   (2) the imperfect;
   (3) the present indicative; and
   (4) the present subjunctive.

5. Give the six principal parts of:

   (1) ἵημι;
   (2) κεῖμαι;
   (3) ἠμί;
   (4) δύναμαι;
   (5) τίθημι.

6. In what forms is the verb ἠμί found?

7. What are three common compounds of ἵημι?

8. Conjugate δύναμαι in the present indicative.

9. Translate the following sentences into Greek.

(1) "We were able," said I, "to lie upon the beautiful beds." (2) If indeed your parents placed you under a tree in order for you to die, blind man, why can you not forgive yourself? (3) "Where," said he, "do the shields lie?" I therefore said to him that I had placed them in the trireme. (4) Although the king is powerful, is his power able to contrive for him to be loved and honoured by all people? (5) What then can you do, mistress? If indeed your maidservants place the plants on the house, and not under a tree, the plants will surely die. (6) Let them therefore throw the plants down from the house in order that we might place them under a tree. (7) Will wise and prudent people lie among animals? If they wish to live their life leisurely, let them lie upon couches in houses. (8) There is a wave of fear that the general is placing the army into great danger. (9) "Put your fear out of your soul," said I, lying down, "and throw away your griefs, o servant, for you have been released from your master." (10) Standing with the prytanises, we gave to the archons, who had established many good laws, many gifts.

10. For extra practice, turn to the key for Lesson 47, **9.**, and translate those Greek sentences into English.

Lesson 48

1. How does the verb δείκνυμι differ from other –μι verbs we have so far learned?

2. (a) Give the six principal parts of the verb δείκνυμι. (b) Give the following forms of δείκνυμι:
    (1) present indicative active;
    (2) imperfect indicative middle/passive;
    (3) present imperative;
    (4) aorist passive optative;
    (5) present middle/passive subjunctive;
    (6) all infinitives;
    (7) nominative and genitive singular of all present tense participles.

3. Translate the following short sentences into Greek.

    (1) He was showing the book. (2) Let them show the book. (3) Should I show the book? (4) She might show the book. (5) If only they would be shown! (6) Showing the books, the prytanis ordered them to be destroyed. (7) Show the books (for yourself)!

4. How does the formation of the present optative and subjunctive of verbs in the –νυμι class differ from the formation of –μι verbs in the root class?

5. What other verbs fall into the –νυμι class of –μι verbs?

6. Explain in your own words how one expresses an unattainable wish in Greek. Account for both methods of doing this and discuss negation.

7. Translate the following short sentences into Greek.

    (1) If only these books had been shown in the marketplace! (*use both methods*) (2) If only these books were being shown in the marketplace! (*use both methods*) (3) If only these books would be shown in the marketplace! (4) Would that we had eaten better food! (*use both methods*) (5) Would that we were eating better food! (*use both methods*) (6) Would that we might eat better food!

8. Explain in your own words the phenomenon of prolepsis.

9. Translate the following sentences into English.

    (1) ἐθέλομεν εἰδέναι τὸν ἄνθρωπον ὁποῖον ζῷόν ἐστιν. (2) ἀποδείκνυ τὸν λόγον πότερον ἀληθής ἐστιν. (3) τοῦτον τὸν ῥήτορα ὁπόθεν ἦλθεν, εἰπέ. (4) τὸν στρατηγὸν τὸν πόλεμον οὗτινος ἕνεκα ἦρξεν ἐρωτήσατε. (5) μὴ θαυμάσῃς τὰς τριήρεις πόσον σῖτον οἷαί τ᾽ εἰσιν ἐνεγκεῖν.

10. Translate the following sentences into Greek using prolepsis.

    (1) I have discovered from what kind of race the gods were born. (2) The herald reported how many soldiers had died. (3) She came to understand whither the orators were leading the city. (4) Do you know how much clothing was bought for ten obols? (5) They had learned whom Socrates had corrupted.

11. Translate the following sentences from English into Greek.

    (1) If only he had discovered where the treasure lay! (2) Prove, if you are

able, o wise philosopher, how it is possible to confess that the gods are similar to humans! (3) For the sake of learning many things (*use articular infinitive*) we ought to have sought for truth in all things. (4) Let the dog be an example to us all! Let us never care for food in such a way that we seek it from our enemies! (5) "I agree entirely with you, o Socrates," said I, "but do we really suppose that the world was made with some model?" (6) "We are of the race of the sun," said the king, "and we shall conquer all who do not agree with us!" (7) The words having been shown to the orator, the people began to think that some great evil had been done. (8) At that time, they thought that he was an evil man, but now they are amazed at what kind of man he is. (9) Let us show our houses to our guests in order that they will wish to be invited to dinner. (10) We contrived that the servant would stop stealing our treasure from us.

12. For extra practice, turn to the key for Lesson 48, **11.**, and translate those Greek sentences into English.

Lesson 49

1. Give the six principal parts of βαίνω and γιγνώσκω.

2. Give the form of the following:

(1)	ἔβησαν	(13)	βῇς
(2)	βήσεσθαι	(14)	βήσοι
(3)	βαίης	(15)	ἐβέβασθε
(4)	βήτω	(16)	ἐβαίνομεν
(5)	βάντι	(17)	ἔβημεν
(6)	βαθήσονται	(18)	βάντων
(7)	βαῖμεν	(19)	βάσαις
(8)	βῶ	(20)	βᾶσι
(9)	βῆτε	(21)	βαίνωσιν
(10)	βέβαται	(22)	βαῖεν
(11)	βεβήκαμεν	(23)	βῆναι
(12)	ἐβεβήκην	(24)	βηθῆναι

3. Give the form of the following:

(1)	γνωσθῆναι	(13)	ἐγνώκην
(2)	γνῶναι	(14)	ἐγνώκαμεν
(3)	γνοῖεν	(15)	ἔγνωται
(4)	γιγνώσκωσιν	(16)	γνῶτε
(5)	γνόσιν	(17)	γνῶ
(6)	γνούσαις	(18)	γνοῖμεν
(7)	γνόντων	(19)	γνωσθήσονται
(8)	ἔγνωμεν	(20)	γνόντι
(9)	ἐγιγνώσκομεν	(21)	γνώτω
(10)	ἔγνωσθε	(22)	γνοίης
(11)	γνώσοιτο	(23)	γνώσεσθαι
(12)	γνῶς	(24)	ἔγνωσαν

4. Translate the following short sentences into Greek.

(1) If only she had known this. (2) If only we knew this. (3) If only they might know this. (4) We went into the marketplace. (5) You (*pl.*) might go into the marketplace. (6) Let me go into the marketplace!

5. Give the Greek suffixes indicating the following: (1) place whence; (2) place whither; (3) place where.

6. Translate the following:

(1)	ἐκεῖσε	(7)	δεῦρο
(2)	οἴκοι	(8)	Ἀθήναζε
(3)	ἐνθάδε	(9)	οἴκοθεν
(4)	Ἀθήνηθεν	(10)	ἄλλοθι
(5)	ὁμοῦ	(11)	ἐκεῖθεν
(6)	ἄλλοσε	(12)	ὁμόσε

7. Translate the following sentences into Greek.

(1) We bought beautiful clothes in Athens. (2) Whither are you going? I am going home. (3) We have arrived here from another place. (4) How can you say that you walked from the same place? (5) My parents are standing there, under that tree. (6) When will you go hence?

8. Explain the accusative and dative of respect.

9. Translate the following sentences from English into Greek.

(1) Do you remember our family? I remember that we were treated poorly by our parents. (2) Where is Athens? How is it possible to walk to Athens? (3) The walls having already fallen, the city will surely fall. (4) Mother and father, do you really love one another, or do you only pretend to be fond of each other? (5) Having come to know that the general would be unable to remind the soldiers of their homeland, the archons sent letters to them. (6) Each one at Athens has received many obols from the allies of the Athenians. (7) One maid walked into the house; the other did not know whither she should go. (8) Is your family large? Ours is [the] same, although [our] parents have died (*use gen. abs.*). (9) They have received many gifts from one another, having invited one another often to dinner. (10) Don't you see the sun? Are you therefore blind in the eyes? Don't you however remember me? Truly you have become extremely old in age.

10. For extra practice, turn to the key for Lesson 49, **9.**, and translate those Greek sentences into English.

Lesson 50

1. Explain the use of redundant μή.

2. What moods are contained in cautious assertions and cautious denials using μή and μή οὐ respectively?

3. What might οὐ μή indicate?

4. Translate the following short sentences into English.

(1) φυλάττεται ὁ φύλαξ τὰς ἀσπίδας μὴ κλαφθῆναι. (2) ὅπως μὴ πίῃ τὸ ὕδωρ. (3) μὴ κωλύηται ὁ στρατηγός. (4) οὐ μὴ λήσουσιν αὐτὴν τρέχοντες. (5) μὴ οὐ λήσουσιν αὐτὴν τρέχοντες. (6) τί με κωλύεις τὸ μὴ βλάπτειν τοὺς ἵππους. (7) οὐκ ἐκώλυσαν τοὺς πολεμίους τοῦ μὴ οὐ τὴν πόλιν λῦσαι. (8) μὴ τρέχει ἡ θεράπαινα διὰ τοῦ πεδίου. (9) οὐ μὴ τρέχῃ ἡ θεράπαινα διὰ τοῦ πεδίου. (10) οὐ μὴ τρέχῃς διὰ τοῦ πεδίου. (11) μὴ οὐ τρέχῃ διὰ τοῦ πεδίου.

5. Explain the phenomenon of attraction in Greek.

6. Translate the following sentences and for each one, give the sentence without attraction.

(1) δῶρα πολλὰ ἐδόθη τοῖς πολίταις οἷς εἷλεν ὁ βασιλεύς. (2) ἕστηκα οὗ ἔφυγον ἀπὸ τῶν Ἀθηνῶν. (3) τί νομίζεις περὶ ὧν ἔλεγεν ὁ φιλόσοφος; (4) ἆρα μέμνηνται τῶν εἰρημένων ὧν ἔλαθε καὶ τοὺς σοφούς; (5) ἐθέλω βῆναι ὅθεν ἔφυγον. (6) ἆρα γιγνώσκετε οὓς ἐτύχετε ἐν τῇ ἀγορᾷ;

7. Explain the syntax of μέχρι and the special syntax of ἕως.

8. Explain the accusative absolute.

9. Translate the following sentences from English into Greek.

(1) I have been hindered often by the general from attacking our enemy. (2) Until the dinner, let us drink in order that our sorrows escape our notice. (3) When will this evil befall the city? If the city happens to be prosperous, fortune will take away its great treasure. (4) Fortune is a false thing. As long as fortune rules, human beings will experience a harsh life. (5) Let the chorus drink; let the plain be struck by its free foot; let the hills hear the sound of its joy. (6) This wisdom has escaped the notice of the minds of even the best philosophers. (7) We did not escape the notice of the prytanises in becoming enemies of the city. (8) I sensed that my horse had drunk too much water; but the other horse escaped the notice of the general in drinking too much. (9) O wise philosopher, is the world really ruled by a huge mind, by fate, or merely by chance? (10) "Do not tell me false things," said I, "but tell me a true account of what happened to you."

10. For extra practice, turn to the key for Lesson 50, **9.**, and translate those Greek sentences into English.

Answer Key to Ancillary Exercises

Lesson 1

1.
(1)	Β, β	(12)	Υ, υ
(2)	Φ, φ	(13)	Ξ, ξ
(3)	Α, α	(14)	Ω, ω
(4)	Μ, μ	(15)	Λ, λ
(5)	Ζ, ζ	(16)	Θ, θ
(6)	Γ, γ	(17)	Π, π
(7)	Σ, σ, ς	(18)	Δ, δ
(8)	Ε, ε	(19)	Τ, τ
(9)	Ψ, ψ	(20)	Χ, χ
(10)	Ρ, ρ	(21)	Ι, ι
(11)	Κ, κ	(22)	Η, η
		(23)	Ο, ο

2. Check yourself against Groton §3.

3. Check yourself against Groton §3. You need not have thought of the same examples, but make sure your example is a true representation of the sound you're aiming for.

4. A diphthong is two vowels pronounced together, with the sound of the first vowel gliding into the sound of the second vowel, ultimately forming one long syllable.

5. (a) The Greek language has two types of diphthong: the proper diphthong and the improper diphthong. What distinguishes the two types from one another is that in the proper diphthong both vowels are pronounced, whereas in the improper dipthong only the first vowel is pronounced. It is interesting to note that all improper dipthongs are made of naturally long vowels followed by ι. (b) There are three ways to categorize long and short vowels in Greek: (i) always long, (ii) always short, (iii) sometimes short, sometimes long.

Always Long	Always Short	Sometimes Short, Sometimes Long
Η, η	Ε, ε	Α, α
Ω, ω	Ο, ο	Ι, ι
		Υ, υ

6. Check your answers and examples against Groton §5.

7. The iota subscript and the iota adscript are both iotas written as part of a diphthong. Conventionally, one uses the iota subscript for a word containing an improper diphthong (example: διαφορᾷ, where –ᾳ is the improper diphthong ΑΙ), while the adscripted iota is used for proper diphthongs or for improper diphthongs when the first letter of the improper diphthong is capitalized as the first letter of a proper name (examples: γυναῖκες, where –αι– is the proper diphthong ΑΙ; Ἅιδου, where the –αι– is the capitalized improper dipthong ΑΙ).

8. (a) One uses a breathing mark in classical Greek on any word that begins with a vowel or the letter ρ. (b) The breathing mark has two symbols. The symbol ʼ indicates rough breathing; that is, it indicates that the letter or diphthong above which it is placed is pronounced with an

"h" in front of it. The symbol ' indicates smooth breathing; that is, it indicates that the vowel or diphthong above which it is placed is not pronounced with an "h" in front of it. (c) A breathing mark accompanying any single lower case letter is placed directly above that letter; over proper dipthongs, whether or not the first letter is capitalized, it is placed over the second letter of the diphthong; over improper diphthongs, it is placed over the first vowel, if that vowel is lower-case; when an improper diphthong or single letter is capitalized and takes a breathing mark, the breathing mark will be placed before the vowel or the first letter of the improper diphthong.

9. The consonantal stops in classical Greek are: β, γ, δ, θ, κ, π, τ, φ, χ.

10. (a) β, π, φ; (b) δ, τ, θ; (c) κ, γ, χ.

11. When γ is followed by another palatal, it is pronounced like our English consonant cluster -ng-.

12. (a) μ, ν; (b) ζ, ξ, ψ; (c) σ/ς.

13. (a) A consonant cluster is pronounced together when a consonantal stop is followed by another consonantal stop, liquid, or nasal. It is pronounced separately if it is the same consonant twice (e.g., ττ), or if a liquid or nasal is followed by any other consonant. (b) together, separately, together, together, together, separately, together, separately, together.

14. One determines how many syllables a Greek word has by counting up the total individual vowels or diphthongs. The total number of vowels or diphthongs is the total number of syllables in the word.

15. One breaks such words into syllables by observing the following conventions: (a) a single consonant will always go with the vowel or diphthong that follows it; (b) a consonant cluster beginning with a stop will go with the vowel or diphthong that follows it; (c) a consonant cluster beginning with a liquid or nasal (λ, μ, ν, ρ) will be split such that the liquid or nasal will be part of the preceding syllable, and the remainder of the cluster will be part of the following syllable.

16. The following key is for sections (c) and (d) of this exercise.

(1)	3; κά · μη · λος	(11)	5; ἐγ · χει · ρί · δι · ον
(2)	3; ἄγ · γελ · λος	(12)	5; δι · ε · φθαρ · μέ · νη
(3)	2; ἀ · εί	(13)	4; ἀ · πο · στρο · φή
(4)	3; ἔ · πλη · ξεν	(14)	7; ἀ · πο · κο · λο · κύν · τω · σις
(5)	2; ῥά · ων	(15)	3; οὐ · ρα · νός
(6)	4; ἐ · πί · λο · γος	(16)	4; τρα · γῳ · δί · α
(7)	4; ῥη · το · ρι · κός	(17)	2; τάτ · τω
(8)	4; συμ · βου · λεύ · ειν	(18)	4; ὑ · πεί · ρο · χον
(9)	3; τρά · πε · ζα	(19)	2; χα · μαί
(10)	4; ἀ · θα · νά · των	(20)	5; ἀ · πο · βδέ · λυ · γμα

Lesson 2

1. There are three different kinds of accent in ancient Greek. They are the acute (`), the grave (´), and circumflex (ˆ).

2. Scholars think that originally the acute indicated a gliding up of pitch in the syllable over which an acute was placed; the grave indicated a gliding down of pitch in the syllable over which the grave was placed; the circumflex indicated either a rise and fall in pitch, or that the pitch remained steady. Today, we conventionally simply use the accents to place stress on the syllable that is accented.

3. If a lower-case vowel with a breathing mark, whether it's rough or smooth, also receives an acute or a grave accent, the accent is placed to the right of the breathing mark over the vowel (examples: ἤ, ἥ, ἢ, ἣ). If a lower-case vowel with a breathing mark, whether rough or smooth, receives also a circumflex, the breathing mark is placed underneath the circumflex and directly above the vowel (examples: ὦ, ὧ).

4. If an upper-case individual vowel or upper-case vowel in an improper diphthong with a breathing mark, whether it's rough or smooth, also receives an acute or a grave accent, the accent is placed to the right of the breathing mark, just to the left of the letter (examples: Ἄ, Ἅ, Ὤ, Ὥ). If an upper-case individual vowel or an upper-case vowel in an improper diphthong with a breathing mark, whether rough or smooth, receives also a circumflex, the breathing mark is placed underneath the circumflex and just to the left of the vowel (examples: Ὦ, Ὧ).

5. An accent placed over a proper diphthong is always placed over the second vowel of the diphthong (αὐθεντεῖν, λείψει, οἳ, Αἴρω).

6. Most Greek words will receive only one accent.

7. Only the last three syllables of any Greek word may receive an accent. These syllables are conventionally called the ultima (last syllable), the penult (the second-to-last syllable), and the antepenult (the third-to-last syllable).

8.
(1)	σα	(6)	there is no penult in this word; it has only 1 syllable
(2)	σας	(7)	there is no antepenult in this word; it has only 2 syllables
(3)	θυ	(8)	ται
(4)	κέ	(9)	με
(5)	νοι	(10)	there is no antepenult in this word; it has only 1 syllable

9. (a) An acute accent may appear on any of the last three syllables of the Greek word, the antepenult, the penult, or the ultima (correct examples: κάμηλος, θεασαμένη). (b) A grave accent may appear only on the last syllable of the Greek word, the ultima (examples: καὶ, αὐτὴ). (c) A circumflex may appear on either of the two last syllables of the Greek word, the penult or the ultima (examples: ταῦρον, τῶν).

10. When we say a syllable is (a) short, we mean that it has both a short vowel and it is followed by no consonant, a single consonant (excluding ζ,ξ,ψ), or a consonant cluster pronounced together (i.e., all those that are not double consonants or clusters whose first member is λ,μ,ν or ρ). When we say a syllable is (b) long by nature, we mean that it has a long vowel or a diphthong (with the exception of the diphthongs οι and αι when they are the last two letters of a word). When we say a syllable is (c) long by position, we mean that no matter the length of its vowel and no matter whether it has a diphthong, it is followed by a consonant cluster whose first letter is λ,μ,ν or ρ, a consonant cluster composed of the same letters (e.g., ττ, σσ, λλ), or a so-called double consonant (ζ,ξ,ψ).

11.
(1)	short	(6)	short
(2)	long by nature	(7)	short
(3)	long by nature	(8)	short
(4)	short	(9)	long by position
(5)	long by nature	(10)	short

12.
(1)	short	(6)	short
(2)	long by nature	(7)	short
(3)	short	(8)	long by position
(4)	long by nature	(9)	short
(5)	short	(10)	short

13. Check your answers against Groton §15.1,2.

14.
(1) B; ἄγ · γε · λος
(2) C; δι · ε · φθαρ · μέ · νη
(3) A; σταῦ · ρον
(4) B; ἐ · τύ · μων
(5) C; πα · ραγ · γέλ · μα · σιν
(6) A; ἀ · νάρ · σι · ος
(7) B; γυ · ναι · κὸς
(8) A; θε · οὺς
(9) C; δε · κά · του
(10) C; κε · κομ · μέ · νος

Lesson 3

1. The parts of speech in Greek are: noun, pronoun, adjective, verb, adverb, conjunction, preposition, and particle.

2. A verb indicates either action (the action of the sentence) or a state of being.

3. A Greek verb has person, number, voice, mood, and tense.

4. We mean that the verb itself contains an indicator as to whether the subject of the verb is also the speaker of the sentence (first person), whether the subject of the verb is also the person to whom the sentence is directed (second person), or the subject of the verb is someone or thing other than the speaker of the sentence or its addressee.

5. We mean that the verb itself contains an indicator as to whether the subject of the verb is single, dual or plural (that is, whether one, two, or more than one person is the subject). For our purposes in learning classical Attic Greek, we omit to learn the dual as it is rarely used in this dialect in this period.

6. We mean that a Greek verb will be either active, middle, or passive. That is, we mean that the form of the verb will show us whether the subject is doing the action of the sentence, is doing the action of the sentence for itself, or is getting the action of the sentence done upon it. For the time being, we are only concerned with the active voice.

7. A Greek verb that is transitive shows that the action of the verb is carried out upon an object (example: "I am kicking the ball." Here "the ball" is the object, the recipient, of the action of the verb done by the subject.). A Greek verb that is intransitive shows that the action of the verb does not have an object (example: "She is sleeping." Here "is sleeping" is an active verb, but there is no recipient of the action of "sleep".).

8. A Greek verb will be found in one of four moods: indicative, imperative, subjunctive, or optative. A verb in the indicative mood shows that the action or state of being expressed by the verb is viewed by the speaker as actual. A verb in the imperative mood indicates that the speaker is commanding the action of the verb to be done. A verb in the subjunctive mood or the optative mood shows that the speaker views the action as

possible or imagined. For the time being, we are concerned only with the indicative and imperative moods.

9. (a) The Greek verb may be found in seven tenses: present, imperfect, future, aorist, perfect, pluperfect, and future perfect. (b) When we speak of primary tenses, we have in mind only those tenses which refer to present or future time (present, future, perfect, future perfect). When we speak of secondary tenses, we have in mind only those tenses which refer to past time (imperfect, aorist, pluperfect).

10. Every verbal tense implies an "aspect." Aspect refers to whether the action or state of being of the verb is viewed as unfinished (imperfective), as a simple occurrence (aoristic), or as finished (perfective).

11. (a) Present active indicative means that the action of the verb takes place in present time and has imperfective or aoristic aspect; that the subject of the sentence is the doer of the action expressed by the verb; and that the action is viewed as an actual occurrence. (b) Present active imperative means that the action of the verb takes place in present time and has imperfective aspect; that the subject of the sentence is the doer of the action expressed by the verb; and that the action is commanded.

12. To determine the present stem of the Greek –ω verb, one simply removes the ω from the present active indicative, first person singular. What remains is the stem. Example: We start with the first person singular, present active indicative, ἐθέλω. From this, we remove the ω and are left with ἐθελ, which is the stem.

13. (a) The Present Active Indicative of the –ω verb is formed by adding to the stem the following personal endings: –ω, –εις, –ει, –ομεν, –ετε, –ουσι(ν). (b) The Present Active Imperative of the –ω verb is formed by adding to the stem the following personal endings: –ε, –έτω, –ετε, –όντων. (c) The Present Active Infinitive of the –ω verb is formed by adding to the stem the following ending: –ειν.

14. The Greek verb has what is called a recessive accent. This means that the accent on any form of the verb wants to stay on the antepenult as an acute, if possible. However, when the ultima of a Greek verb form is long, the acute accent will be drawn off of the antepenult onto the penult. When a Greek verb form is only two syllables long and the penult is long and the ultima is short, the accent on the penult will be a circumflex.

15.
 (1) indicative, singular, first person
 (2) indicative, plural, third person
 (3) indicative, singular, third person
 (4) imperative, singular, third person
 (5) indicative, singular, second person
 (6) infinitive, no number, no person
 (7) indicative or imperative, plural, second person
 (8) indicative, plural, first person
 (9) imperative, plural, third person
 (10) imperative, singular, second person

16.
(1) ἐθέλειν		to wish	
(2) γράφω	γράφομεν	I am writing.	We are writing.
γράφεις	γράφετε	You are writing.	You are writing.
γράφει	γράφουσι(ν)	He is writing.	They are writing.
(3) σπεῦδε	σπεύδετε	Hasten!	Hasten!
σπευδέτω	σπευδόντων	Let him hasten!	Let them hasten!

(4)	κλέπτω	κλέπτομεν	I do steal.	We do steal
	κλέπτεις	κλέπτετε	You do steal.	You do steal.
	κλέπτει	κλέπτουσι(ν)	He does steal.	They do steal.
	κλέπτειν		to steal	
(5)	φύλαττε	φυλάττετε	Guard!	Guard!
	φυλαττέτω	φυλαττόντων	Let her guard!	Let them guard!
(6)	θῦε	θύετε	Sacrifice!	Sacrifice!
	θυέτω	θυόντων	Let it sacrifice!	Let them sacrifice!
	θύειν		to sacrifice	

17. See Groton §20, p. 16.

18. (1) γράφε καὶ μὴ κλέπτε. or γράφετε καὶ μὴ κλέπτετε. (2) καὶ θύομεν καὶ φυλάττομεν. (3) μὴ κλεπτέτω. παιδεύουσιν. (4) ἐθέλεις γράφειν; or ἐθέλετε γράφειν; (5) σπευδόντων φυλάττειν. (6) κλέπτειν οὐ σπεύδομεν. (7) μὴ ἔθελε κλέπτειν. or μὴ ἐθέλετε κλέπτειν. (8) καὶ γράφε καὶ θῦε. or καὶ γράφετε καὶ θύετε. (9) σπεύδειν οὐκ ἐθέλομεν. (10) σπεῦδε (or σπεύδετε) φυλάττειν· ἐθέλουσι κλέπτειν.

19. Correct your work against **18**. in the exercises for Lesson 3.

Lesson 4

1. A noun is a word which signifies a person, place, or thing. An example of a person-noun in English is "Jamie;" an example of a place-noun in English is "New York;" an example of a thing-noun in English is "dog" or "cup."

2. Yes and no. A Greek noun does inflect, that is, it does change in form. This is called "declension." However, a Greek noun does not change to show the same things a verb's changes show. A Greek noun changes to show difference in number and case.

3. (a) The various genders found among Greek nouns are: masculine, feminine and neuter. (b) When we speak of the gender of a Greek noun, we speak of **grammatical** gender, not **physical** gender, though the two may overlap. That is to say, every noun in the Greek language has a gender, either masculine, feminine, or neuter. A noun is "born" with this gender, whether or not the person, place, or thing it connotes is naturally masculine, feminine, or neuter. Take, for example, the Greek word for table, ἡ τράπεζα. This is a feminine noun. Neither we nor the Greeks think that there is anything physically "feminine" about a table; but for the Greek language, ἡ τράπεζα is grammatically feminine.

4. No. Grammatical gender is inherent in a given noun, and always sticks with that noun.

5. A Greek noun may be found in the singular, dual, or plural. For our purposes, we are interested only in the singular and the plural.

6. In an English sentence, one determines the function of a particular noun by its place in the sentence and sometimes by its form. Thus, a subject will often come before the verb in English (example: **Sven** is eating Ole's food.). The direct object will often come after the verb in English (example: Sven is eating Ole's **food**.). The indirect object will either be sandwiched between the verb and the object (example: Sven gave **Ole** a horse.) or be preceded by the word "to" (example: Sven gave a horse to **Ole**.). Possession is shown in one of two manners. Either the noun will receive an apostrophe-s or s-apostrophe (examples: Sven is eating **Ole**'s food, or Sven is eating **the Swedes**' food.) or the noun showing possession is preceded by the preposition "of" (example: Sven is riding the horse of **Ole**.).

7. One determines the function of a noun in a Greek sentence by determining its case.

8. A noun in (a) the genitive usually indicates that that noun possesses another noun in the sentence (usually one directly before or directly after the genitive noun) and sometimes is the object of a preposition that takes a genitive object; (b) the vocative indicates the addressee of the sentence; (c) the dative usually indicates that the noun is the indirect object of the sentence and sometimes is the object of a preposition that takes a dative object; (d) the accusative usually indicates that the noun is the direct object of the sentence and sometimes is the object of a preposition that takes an accusative object; (e) the nominative usually indicates that the noun is the subject of the sentence or a predicate nominative. The nominative may not be the object of a preposition.

9. (a) Generally speaking, the noun has what is called a **persistent** accent, in distinction to the verb's **recessive** accent. (b) A persistent accent is one which wants to stay on the group of letters where it is "born;" that is, when we learn the nominative singular of a noun, we should assume that the accent wants to stay over the same group of letters in all other forms of that noun.

10. See Groton §29.1–2.

11. Some feminine first declension nouns receive an α set of endings in the singular **because their stems end in ε, ι, or ρ**. If a feminine first declension noun does not end in ε, ι, or ρ, in the singular it will receive the η set of endings.

12. The feminine article in Greek is ἡ. Its full declension is as follows:

	S.	Pl.
Nom.	ἡ	αἱ
Gen.	τῆς	τῶν
Dat.	τῇ	ταῖς
Acc.	τήν	τάς

13.

(1)
ἡ ἀγορά	αἱ ἀγοραί
τῆς ἀγορᾶς	τῶν ἀγορῶν
τῇ ἀγορᾷ	ταῖς ἀγοραῖς
τὴν ἀγοράν	τὰς ἀγοράς
ἀγορά	ἀγοραί

(2)
ἡ ἐπιστολή	αἱ ἐπιστολαί
τῆς ἐπιστολῆς	τῶν ἐπιστολῶν
τῇ ἐπιστολῇ	ταῖς ἐπιστολαῖς
τὴν ἐπιστολήν	τὰς ἐπιστολάς
ἐπιστολή	ἐπιστολαί

(3)
ἡ ἡσυχία	αἱ ἡσυχίαι
τῆς ἡσυχίας	τῶν ἡσυχιῶν
τῇ ἡσυχίᾳ	ταῖς ἡσυχίαις
τὴν ἡσυχίαν	τὰς ἡσυχίας
ἡσυχία	ἡσυχίαι

(4)
ἡ χώρα	αἱ χῶραι
τῆς χώρας	τῶν χωρῶν
τῇ χώρᾳ	ταῖς χώραις
τὴν χώραν	τὰς χώρας
χώρα	χῶραι

14. See Groton §31.

15. (1) τὴν ἐπιστολὴν πέμπω. (2) τὴν ἐπιστολήν, ὦ θεά, πέμπω. (3) τὴν ἐπιστολήν, ὦ θεά, εἰς τὴν ἀγορὰν πέμπω. (4) πεμπέτω ἡ θεὰ τὴν ἡσυχίαν ἐκ τῆς σκηνῆς. (5) ἐπιστολὰς ἐν τῇ ἀγορᾷ γράφετε (or γράφε). (6) αἱ θεαὶ τῆς ἡσυχίας σπεύδουσι θύειν. (7) τῇ θεᾷ θύομεν. (8) τῇ θεᾷ ἐπιστολὰς θύομεν. (9) ἐθέλετε (or ἐθέλεις) τὰς θεὰς ἐν τῇ σκηνῇ καὶ ἐν τῇ ἀγορᾷ παιδεύειν; (10) τὰς ἐπιστολὰς ἐκ τῶν σκηνῶν κλέπτειν σπευδόντων.

16. Check your answers against **15.** in the exercises for Lesson 4.

Lesson 5

1. (a) In general, the short α feminine first declension nouns differ from the first declension feminines we already know specifically in respect to the length of the α ending in the following forms: nominative, accusative, and vocative singular; they differ also from the feminine first declension we are already familiar with in that, while the standard long α feminine first declension has an η ending in all cases in the singular on nouns whose stems do **not** end in ε, ι or ρ, in the feminine first declension, short α, the η shows up on nouns whose stems do not end in ε, ι or ρ only in the genitive and dative singular. Furthermore, while the accent on a feminine first declension long α noun may not be found on the antepenult due to the length of the ultima, many feminine first declension short α nouns do receive the accent on the antepenult in forms where the length of the ultima allows it. (b) The two feminine first declension types differ from one another in the following fashion: when the stem of the noun does not end in ε, ι or ρ, the genitive and dative singular use an η ending rather than a long α ending.

2. They are similar to one another in all cases in the plural, including the accenting oddity of the ultima of the genitive plural being accented with circumflex.

3. The reflexive use of the definite article is common not only in Greek, but in many other Indo-European languages. Quite simply, where English has a preoccupation with the possessive adjective "my, his, your, their, our", etc., ancient Greek may simply use the definite article. An example of this follows: ἡ δέσποινα κελεύει τῇ θεραπαίνῃ. Translated literally, it says, "The mistress is commanding the maidservant." But by a legitimate use of the article τῇ as reflexive, we may be perfectly comfortable translating this sentence, "The mistress is commanding her maidservant." Context will be of great help in determining whether to translate an article reflexively or not.

4.
   (1) βλάπτω   βλάπτομεν
       βλάπτεις   βλάπτετε
       βλάπτει   βλάπτουσι(ν)
   (2) ἄκουε   ἀκούετε
       ἀκουέτω   ἀκουόντων
   (3) κελεύειν

5.
   (1) accusative
   (2) accusative
   (3) genitive (for a person); accusative (for a thing)
   (4) accusative
   (5) accusative
   (6) dative or accusative
   (7) accusative
   (8) accusative

6.
(1)	ἡ θεά	αἱ θεαί
	τῆς θεᾶς	τῶν θεῶν
	τῇ θεᾷ	ταῖς θεαῖς
	τὴν θεάν	τὰς θεάς
	ὦ θεά	ὦ θεαί
(2)	ἡ μοῖρα	αἱ μοῖραι
	τῆς μοίρας	τῶν μοιρῶν
	τῇ μοίρᾳ	ταῖς μοίραις
	τὴν μοῖραν	τὰς μοίρας
	ὦ μοῖρα	ὦ μοῖραι
(3)	ἡ κλίνη	αἱ κλῖναι
	τῆς κλίνης	τῶν κλινῶν
	τῇ κλίνῃ	ταῖς κλίναις
	τὴν κλίνην	τὰς κλίνας
	ὦ κλίνη	ὦ κλῖναι
(4)	ἡ δέσποινα	αἱ δέσποιναι
	τῆς δεσποίνης	τῶν δεσποινῶν
	τῇ δεσποίνῃ	ταῖς δεσποίναις
	τὴν δέσποιναν	τὰς δεσποίνας
	ὦ δέσποινα	ὦ δέσποιναι
(5)	ἡ θεράπαινα	αἱ θεράπαιναι
	τῆς θεραπαίνης	τῶν θεραπαινῶν
	τῇ θεραπαίνῃ	ταῖς θεραπαίναις
	τὴν θεράπαιναν	τὰς θεραπαίνας
	ὦ θεράπαινα	ὦ θεράπαιναι
(6)	ἡ θάλαττα	αἱ θάλατται
	τῆς θαλάττης	τῶν θαλαττῶν
	τῇ θαλάττῃ	ταῖς θαλάτταις
	τὴν θάλατταν	τὰς θαλάττας
	ὦ θάλαττα	ὦ θάλατται

7. (1) κελευέτω ἡ δέσποινα ταῖς θεραπαίναις γράφειν ἐπιστολάς. (2) τῆς θεᾶς ἀκούετε; (3) ἐπειδὴ τὴν θάλατταν ἀκούουσιν, τῇ δεσποίνῃ ἐπιστολὰς γράφουσιν. (4) ὥρα παιδεύειν. (5) ὥρα ταῖς θεραπαίναις παιδεύειν ἐν τῇ ἀγορᾷ. (6) ἐπεὶ ὥρα ἐπιστολὰς γράφειν, μὴ βλαπτόντων αἱ δέσποιναι τὰς θεραπαίνας. (7) ἄκουε· παιδεύομεν καὶ ἐπιστολὰς γράφομεν. (8) κελεύει ἡ θεὰ τῇ δεσποίνῃ καὶ ταῖς θεραπαίναις ἐκ τῶν κλινῶν σπεύδειν καὶ εἰς τὴν ἀγοράν. (9) ἐπειδὴ τὴν θάλατταν ἀκούομεν, θύομεν τῇ Μοίρᾳ. (10) ταῖς θεραπαίναις μὴ κέλευε τὴν δέσποιναν βλάπτειν.

8. Check your answers against **7.** in the exercises for Lesson 5.

Lesson 6

1. The future active indicative may have either aoristic or imperfective aspect.

2. The future active indicative is formed from the second principal part of the Greek verb.

3. Both the first and second principal part of the Greek verb need to be memorized because while the second principal part often is formed according to predictable rules, it is with a certain amount of frequency also formed in unpredictable ways. By learning the second principal part by memory, one assures oneself of being correct in forming the future active indicative of a given verb.

4. The standard stem change that takes place in the formation of the future active indicative is the addition of the consonant σ to the **present stem** of the verb. For example, the present stem of the verb θύω is derived by

removing the ω from the form. This yields θυ-. To this stem, the suffixing of a σ will yield the future active stem. The second principal part is simply the first person singular of the future active indicative: θύσω.

5.

(1)	ψ	(6)	ξ
(2)	ψ	(7)	σ
(3)	ξ	(8)	σ
(4)	σ	(9)	ξ
(5)	ξ	(10)	ψ
		(11)	ψ

6.
(1) indicates either: β, π, φ, or ππ
(2) indicates either: stem ending in vowel, δ, τ, or θ
(3) indicates either: γ, κ, χ, or ττ

7. Possibilities   Actual Dictionary Entry

	Possibilities	Actual Dictionary Entry
(1)	λύδω, λύτω, λύθω, λύω	λύω
(2)	πλήγω, πλήκω, πλήχω, πλήττω	πλήττω
(3)	μεταπέμπω, μεταπέμφω, μεταπέμβω	μεταπέμπω
(4)	πείω, πείδω, πείθω, πείτω	πείθω
(5)	τάγω, τάκω, τάχω, τάττω	τάττω
(6)	διώγω, διώκω, διώχω, διώττω	διώκω
(7)	βουλεύω, βουλεύδω, βουλεύθω, βουλεύτω	βουλεύω
(8)	λείβω, λείπω, λείφω, λείπτω	λείπω
(9)	σείω, σείδω, σείθω, σείτω	σείω
(10)	σπεύω, σπεύδω, σπεύθω, σπεύτω	σπεύδω

8.

(1)	φυλάττω, φυλάξω	(8)	γράφω, γράψω
(2)	διώκω, διώξω	(9)	κλέπτω, κλέψω
(3)	ἀκούω, ἀκούσομαι	(10)	ἔχω, ἕξω / σχήσω
(4)	θύω, θύσω	(11)	κελεύω, κελεύσω
(5)	μέλλω, μελλήσω	(12)	παιδεύω, παιδεύσω
(6)	βλάπτω, βλάψω	(13)	ἀλλάττω, ἀλλάξω
(7)	ἐθέλω, ἐθελήσω	(14)	σπεύδω, σπεύσω
		(15)	πέμπω, πέμψω

9.

(1)	μελλήσω	μελλήσομεν
	μελλήσεις	μελλήσετε
	μελλήσει	μελλήσουσι(ν)
	μελλήσειν	
(2)	διώξω	διώξομεν
	διώξεις	διώξετε
	διώξει	διώξουσι(ν)
	διώξειν	
(3)	θύσω	θύσομεν
	θύσεις	θύσετε
	θύσει	θύσουσι(ν)
	θύσειν	

10. When μέλλω is followed by a future infinitive, its meaning is "intend to, be about to"; when it is followed by a present infinitive or by no infinitive, it means "delay [to], hesitate [to]."

11. See Groton, p. 36, NOTE under ἀλλά.

12. (1) τὴν κόρην ἐν τῇ οἰκίᾳ μηκέτι μέλλε παιδεύειν. (2) μέλλεις, ὦ θεά, τὴν κόρην εἰς δέσποιναν ἀλλάξειν. (3) ἡ θεράπαινα τὴν μοῖραν οὐ διώκει, ἀλλ᾽ ἡ Μοῖρα δέσποινα τὰς κόρας διώκει. (4) οἰκίαν ἔχεις; ἔχεις τὴν οἰκίαν φυλάττειν. (5) ἐπειδὴ τὰς ἐπιστολὰς τῇ δεσποίνῃ πέμψομεν, μελλήσει τὰς θεραπαίνας διώκειν. (6) οὐκέτι θύσετε ταῖς θεαῖς, ἀλλὰ ταῖς θεραπαίναις κελεύσετε θύειν. (7) κλέπτει ἡ θεράπαινα τὴν ἐπιστολήν. τὴν ἐπιστολὴν πάλιν κλέψω ἐκ τῆς οἰκίας. (8) ἐπεὶ

τὰς κόρας παιδεύειν μέλλεις, ἐπιστολὰς ἐν τῇ οἰκίᾳ μέλλω γράψειν. (9) τὰς δεσποίνας πάλιν εἰς κόρας, ὦ θεαί, ἀλλάξομεν; (10) καὶ τῆς κόρης καὶ τὴν θάλατταν πάλιν ἀκούειν ἐθελήσει.

13. Check your answers against **12**. in the exercises for Lesson 6.

Lesson 7

1. The case endings for the second declension masculine are as follows:

	Singular	Plural
Nom.	ος	οι
Gen.	ου	ων
Dat.	ῳ	οις
Acc.	ον	ους
Voc.	ε	οι

2. They differ in the following ways. (1) The feminine first declensions typically have α or η in their endings; the masculine second declensions typically have ο or ω in their endings. (2) The feminine first declension vocative singular is the same as the feminine first declension nominative singular, whereas the masculine second declension nominative and vocative singular differ from one another (ος vs. ε). (3) The masculine second declension has only one set of endings for all stems, the feminine first declension has different singular endings for stems ending in ε, ι or ρ. (4) The masculine second declension genitive plural is not always accented on the ultima, unlike the feminine first declension genitive plural which always is.

3. They are similar in the following ways. (1) They both have a persistent accent. (2) The nominative and vocative plurals in both declensions are the same. (3) In both declensions, the nominative and vocative plurals end in ι. (4) In both declensions, the dative plurals end in ις. (5) In both declensions, the dative singular ending has a ι-subscript. (6) In both declensions, the accusative singular ends in ν. (7) In both declensions, the accusative plural ends in ς. (8) In both declensions, genitive and dative singulars and plurals of nouns whose accent is persistent on the ultima receive a circumflex on the ultima.

4.
ὁ	οἱ
τοῦ	τῶν
τῷ	τοῖς
τόν	τούς

5.
(1)
ὁ ἵππος	οἱ ἵπποι
τοῦ ἵππου	τῶν ἵππων
τῷ ἵππῳ	τοῖς ἵπποις
τὸν ἵππον	τοὺς ἵππους
ὦ ἵππε	ὦ ἵπποι

(2)
ὁ ἀδελφός	οἱ ἀδελφοί
τοῦ ἀδελφοῦ	τῶν ἀδελφῶν
τῷ ἀδελφῷ	τοῖς ἀδελφοῖς
τὸν ἀδελφόν	τοὺς ἀδελφούς
ὦ ἄδελφε	ὦ ἀδελφοί

(3)
ἡ ἀδελφή	αἱ ἀδελφαί
τῆς ἀδελφῆς	τῶν ἀδελφῶν
τῇ ἀδελφῇ	ταῖς ἀδελφαῖς
τὴν ἀδελφήν	τὰς ἀδελφάς
ὦ ἀδελφή	ὦ ἀδελφαί

(4) See Groton §43.

6.
- (1) feminine, feminine first declension
- (2) epicene (i.e., masculine or feminine), masculine second declension
- (3) epicene (i.e., masculine or feminine), masculine second declension
- (4) feminine, masculine second declension
- (5) masculine, masculine second declension
- (6) feminine, feminine first declension

7. Check your own answer for accuracy against Groton §46.

8.
(1)	χαιρήσειν	χαίρειν
(2)	χαιρήσω	χαιρήσομεν
	χαιρήσεις	χαιρήσετε
	χαιρήσει	χαιρήσουσι(ν)
(3)	χαῖρε	χαίρετε
	χαιρέτω	χαιρόντων
(4)	χαίρω	χαίρομεν
	χαίρεις	χαίρετε
	χαίρει	χαίρουσι(ν)

9. (1) τὸν ἵππον μὴ βλάπτε. (2) τὸν ἵππον λίθοις μὴ βλάπτε. (3) μέλλει ὁ ἄνθρωπος σπεύσειν; (4) μελλήσει ὁ ἄνθρωπος σπεύδειν ἀπὸ τοῦ ποταμοῦ; (5) χαῖρε, ὦ ἄδελφε, χαῖρε τῇ λύπῃ, ἐπεὶ οἱ θεοὶ χαρὰς πέμψουσιν. (6) καὶ ὁ ἀδελφὸς καὶ ἡ ἀδελφὴ τῇ ὁδῷ χαιρήσουσιν. (7) τὰς ἀνθρώπους ἐκ τοῦ ποταμοῦ καὶ εἰς τὴν ὁδὸν διωκόντων οἱ ἵπποι. (8) οὐ πέμψει ἡ Μοῖρα χαρὰς, ἀλλ᾽ ἡ ἄνθρωπος ταῖς λύπαις χαιρέτω. (9) ἵππον εἰς ἄνθρωπον ἀλλάττειν ἔχουσιν οἱ θεοί; ἔχουσι καὶ ἄνθρωπον εἰς λίθον ἀλλάττειν; μὴ ἐθελόντων βλάπτειν τὸν ἄνθρωπον. (10) ὦ θεέ, ὦ μοῖρα, ὦ ἄνθρωπε, τῇ χαρᾷ χαιρήσω καὶ τοῖς θεοῖς θύσειν μελλήσω.

10. Check your answers against **9.** in the exercises for Lesson 7.

Lesson 8

1. (a) The two categories of nouns are similar in the following ways. (1) Their genitive and dative singulars and plurals are exactly alike. (2) Their accusative singular is exactly alike. (3) They are both so-called o-stem nouns. (4) Within each declension, the nominative and vocative plurals are the same form (masculine -οι; neuter -α). (5) Like all nouns, they both have persistent accent. (b) They are dissimilar in the following ways. (1) The masculine nominative and vocative singular, and nominative, accusative, and vocative plural are not like those of the neuter. (2) While the neuter nominative, accusative, and vocative singular have the same form, the masculine nominative, accusative, and vocative all differ from one another. (3) While the neuter nominative, accusative, and vocative plural have the same form, only the masculine nominative and vocative plurals are alike, while the accusative differs from them both. (4) Their gender is different.

2.
-ον	-α
-ου	-ων
-ῳ	-οις
-ον	-α
-ον	-α

3. (a)
τό	τά
τοῦ	τῶν
τῷ	τοῖς
τό	τά

   (b)
ἡ	αἱ
τῆς	τῶν

τῇ	ταῖς
τήν	τάς

(c)

ὁ	οἱ
τοῦ	τῶν
τῷ	τοῖς
τόν	τούς

4.
   - (1) neuter nominative or accusative plural
   - (2) masculine accusative singular
   - (3) masculine nominative singular
   - (4) masculine or neuter genitive singular
   - (5) feminine dative singular
   - (6) feminine nominative singular
   - (7) masculine accusative plural
   - (8) feminine genitive singular
   - (9) masculine or neuter dative plural
   - (10) neuter nominative or accusative singular
   - (11) masculine, feminine, or neuter genitive plural
   - (12) masculine or neuter dative singular
   - (13) feminine dative plural
   - (14) masculine nominative plural
   - (15) feminine accusative plural

5. When a neuter nominative plural is the subject of a sentence, the verb it governs is in the third person **singular** form, unlike what we'd normally expect. Normally, when a plural noun is the subject of a sentence, the verb reflects that plurality in being third person plural. In the following sentence, the subject is plural, as is the verb: αἱ δέσποιναι τοὺς ἵππους διώξουσιν (The mistresses will pursue the horses.). However, when the subject in a given sentence is neuter plural, the change noted above occurs in the verb: τὰ τέκνα τοὺς ἵππους διώξει (The children will pursue the horses.).

6. Adjectives are not "gendered" in the same way nouns are. In fact, an adjective's gender will change from use to use, depending on the gender of the noun it modifies.

7. (a) An adjective must agree with the noun it modifies in number, case, and gender. (b) While often this agreement in number, case, and gender will be reflected in the parity of the form of the adjective with the form of the noun it modifies (for example, τὸ καλὸν τέκνον); equally often we will encounter situations where the form of the appropriate number, case, and gender of the adjective does not match the form of the same number, case, and gender of the noun (for example, τῇ ἀξίᾳ ὁδῷ, where the noun is singular, dative, plural, as is the adjective).

8. When an adjective is listed in vocabulary of *From Alpha to Omega*, it will be given as follows: the masculine nominative singular form, followed by the feminine nominative singular ending, followed by the neuter nominative singular ending (example: ἀγαθός, -ή, -όν). From these three forms in the lexical entry of the word, we can determine several things. First of all, we see in the characteristic -o- of the masculine and neuter forms that the adjective, when formed up in those genders, will be second declension of the appropriate gender. Secondly, from the -η of the feminine nominative singular, we recognize that the feminine forms will be of the first declension, long α. In the particular instance of ἀγαθή, we recognize that in the singulars we will be using the -η forms, and not the -α forms. Thus, the adjective follows noun declensions with which we are already familiar.

9.
    (1) τῆς ἀγαθῆς δεσποίνης
    (2) ὦ καλὴ ἄνθρωπε or ὦ καλὲ ἄνθρωπε
    (3) τὰ ἄξια τέκνα
    (4) ταῖς ἀγαθαῖς ὁδοῖς
    (5) τὴν καλὴν θεάν
    (6) τὴν ἀγαθὴν θεόν
    (7) τὸν ἄξιον θεόν
    (8) τῶν καλῶν ἡσυχιῶν
    (9) τῇ ἀγαθῇ χώρᾳ
    (10) τὴν ἀξίαν σκηνήν

10. See Groton §54.(a) For an adjective to be in the attributive position, it must simply always be preceded directly by the article that goes with the noun the adjective is modifying: **τὴν καλὴν** θεάν, τὴν θεὰν **τὴν καλήν**, θεὰν **τὴν καλήν**. (2) The predicate position is occupied by an adjective when it agrees in number, case and gender with a noun but is **not** preceded by the article that agrees with the noun: ἡ θεὰ **καλή**, **καλὴ** ἡ θεά.

11.
    (1) the beautiful goddess
    (2) the goddess is beautiful
    (3) the beautiful goddess
    (4) the goddess is beautiful
    (5) the beautiful goddess

12. The attributive position is occupied by an adjective with a noun with no definite article simply by placing the adjective before or after the noun: **καλή** θεά, θεά **καλή** = a beautiful goddess.

13.
ἀγαθός	ἀγαθή	ἀγαθόν
ἀγαθοῦ	ἀγαθῆς	ἀγαθοῦ
ἀγαθῷ	ἀγαθῇ	ἀγαθῷ
ἀγαθόν	ἀγαθήν	ἀγαθόν
ἀγαθέ	ἀγαθή	ἀγαθόν
ἀγαθοί	ἀγαθαί	ἀγαθά
ἀγαθῶν	ἀγαθῶν	ἀγαθῶν
ἀγαθοῖς	ἀγαθαῖς	ἀγαθοῖς
ἀγαθούς	ἀγαθάς	ἀγαθά
ἀγαθοί	ἀγαθαί	ἀγαθά

14.
    (1)
λείψω	λείψομεν
λείψεις	λείψετε
λείψει	λείψουσι(ν)
	λείψειν

    (2)
εὕρισκε	εὑρίσκετε
εὑρισκέτω	εὑρισκόντων
	εὑρίσκειν

    (3)
ἀπολείπω	ἀπολείπομεν
ἀπολείπεις	ἀπολείπετε
ἀπολείπει	ἀπολείπουσι(ν)

15.
    (1) ἀπολείπω, ἀπολείψω
    (2) εὑρίσκω, εὑρήσω
    (3) λείπω, λείψω

16. (1) τὸν ἀγαθὸν βίον, ὦ δέσποινα Μοῖρα, ἀπολείψω; (2) ἀξία τοῦ καλοῦ δώρου ἡ δέσποινα. (3) τὸ ἀγαθὸν ἔργον εὑρήσομεν. (4) τὴν ἀξίαν χώραν εὑρίσκουσιν οἱ καλοὶ ἵπποι. (5) ἀπολείπει τὰ τέκνα τὰ φυτὰ τὰ καλά. (6) λίθοις βλάψει τὰ τέκνα οἰκίαν τὴν καλήν. (7) ἵπποις ἀξίοις τὰς κόρας τὰς ἀγαθὰς διώξουσιν. (8) ἐπειδὴ τὸν ἀγαθὸν βίον ἀπολείψω, τὰ ἔργα τὰ ἄξια μὴ λεῖπε. (9) μηκέτι κλεπτόντων δῶρα καλὰ ἐκ θησαυροῦ τοῦ ἀξίου. (10) μηκέτι κλεπτέτω τὰ τέκνα δῶρα καλὰ ἐκ θησαυροῦ τοῦ ἀξίου. (11) μηκέτι κλεπτόντων οἱ ἄνθρωποι δῶρα καλὰ ἐκ θησαυροῦ τοῦ ἀξίου.

(12) σπεύδετε φυτὰ καλὰ εὑρήσειν; ὥρα τὰς θεραπαίνας εἰς τὴν χώραν ἵπποις πέμπειν. ἔτι καλὴ ἡ χώρα. μὴ μελλόντων αἱ θεράπαιναι φυτὰ εὑρίσκειν, ἀλλὰ τὰ ἔργα μελλόντων λείψειν.

17. Check your answers against **16.** in the exercises for Lesson 8.

Lesson 9

1. In the first declension, one finds also α and η stem masculine nouns.

2. Just as in the first declension feminines in α/η, the variation between α and η takes place in the singular. In the first declension masculines, furthermore, as in the first declension feminines, if the stem of the noun ends in ε, ι or ρ, the α form of the singular will be used, while for nouns with stems ending in all other letters, the η form of the singular will be used.

3. It is a combination of factors, each of which should be present, each of which is supplied in the lexical entry form of a noun, used in determining the declension of a particular noun. In order to be certain that you've encountered a masculine first declension noun, the nominative form should have the ending -ας or -ης. The genitive singular form should end in -ου, and the article should be ὁ.

4.   (1) first declension masculine   (4) first declension feminine
     (2) second declension masculine (5) second declension neuter
     (3) first declension masculine   (6) second declension
                                           masculine, feminine

5.   (1)

ὁ δεσπότης	οἱ δεσπόται
τοῦ δεσπότου	τῶν δεσποτῶν
τῷ δεσπότῃ	τοῖς δεσπόταις
τὸν δεσπότην	τοὺς δεσπότας
ὦ δέσποτα	ὦ δεσπόται

     (2)

ὁ νεανίας	οἱ νεανίαι
τοῦ νεανίου	τῶν νεανιῶν
τῷ νεανίᾳ	τοῖς νεανίαις
τὸν νεανίαν	τοὺς νεανίας
ὦ νεανία	ὦ νεανίαι

6.   (1)

ὁ ἐλεύθερος μαθητής	οἱ ἐλεύθεροι μαθηταί
τοῦ ἐλευθέρου μαθητοῦ	τῶν ἐλευθέρων μαθητῶν
τῷ ἐλευθέρῳ μαθητῇ	τοῖς ἐλευθέροις μαθηταῖς
τὸν ἐλεύθερον μαθητήν	τοὺς ἐλευθέρους μαθητάς
ὦ ἐλεύθερε μαθητά	ὦ ἐλεύθεροι μαθηταί

     (2)

ὁ καλὸς οἰκέτης	οἱ καλοὶ οἰκέται
τοῦ καλοῦ οἰκέτου	τῶν καλῶν οἰκετῶν
τῷ καλῷ οἰκέτῃ	τοῖς καλοῖς οἰκέταις
τὸν καλὸν οἰκέτην	τοὺς καλοὺς οἰκέτας
ὦ καλὲ οἰκέτα	ὦ καλοὶ οἰκέται

     (3)

ἡ ἀξία θεός	αἱ ἄξιαι θεοί
τῆς ἀξίας θεοῦ	τῶν ἀξίων θεῶν
τῇ ἀξίᾳ θεῷ	ταῖς ἀξίαις θεοῖς
τὴν ἀξίαν θεόν	τὰς ἀξίας θεούς
ὦ ἀξία θεέ	ὦ ἄξιαι θεοί

     (4)

ὁ ἀγαθὸς νεανίας	οἱ ἀγαθοὶ νεανίαι
τοῦ ἀγαθοῦ νεανίου	τῶν ἀγαθῶν νεανιῶν
τῷ ἀγαθῷ νεανίᾳ	τοῖς ἀγαθοῖς νεανίαις
τὸν ἀγαθὸν νεανίαν	τοὺς ἀγαθοὺς νεανίας
ὦ ἀγαθὲ νεανία	ὦ ἀγαθοὶ νεανίαι

7. **Similarities**: in the singular, they modulate between α and η endings,

depending on whether the stem ends in ε, ι or ρ; they have the same endings in the dative and accusative singular and in all cases of the plural; they always accent the genitive plural on the ultima with a circumflex; accent on these nouns, as all nouns, is persistent; if accent is persistent on the ultima, the genitive and dative singular and plurals will always receive circumflex. **Differences**: the masculine nominative singular ends in -ας or -ης, while the feminine ends in -α or -η; the masculine genitive singular ends in -ου while the feminine ends in -ας or -ης; the masculine vocative singular will always end in -α, while the feminine modulates between -η and -α; the article of the masculine first declension is the masculine article, while for the feminine it is the feminine article.

8. Compare your answer against Groton §61.

9. (1) οἱ **ἐν τῇ ἀγορᾷ** ἄνθρωποι; not substantive; "the human beings in the marketplace" or "the in-the-marketplace human beings"

   (2) αἱ **καλαί**; substantive; "the beautiful [women, girls]"

   (3) τῷ **ἐν τῇ οἰκίᾳ** δεσπότῃ; not substantive; "for the master in the house" or "for the in-the-house master"

   (4) τῶν **ἀθανάτων**; substantative; "of the immortal [things, gods, people, or women]"

   (5) τὰ **ἀγαθὰ** ἔργα; not substantive; "the good works"

   (6) τοῦ **ἐν τῇ καλῇ οἰκίᾳ** δώρου; not substantive; "of the master in the beautiful house" or "of the in-the-beautiful-house master"

   (7) τὰ **ἐν τῇ ἀγορᾷ**; substantive; "the things in the marketplace" or "the in-the-marketplace things"

   (8) αἱ **ἀθάνατοι** θεαί; not substantive; "the immortal goddesses"

   (9) τῇ **ἐν τῇ οἰκίᾳ**; substantive; "for the [woman] in the house" or "for the in-the-house woman]"

   (10) τῶν θεῶν τῶν **ἀθανάτων**; not substantive; "of the immortal gods or goddesses"

   (11) τὰ **ἀγαθά**; substantive; "the good things"

   (12) τοῦ **καλοῦ**; substantive; "of the good thing, man, or person of unspecified gender"

10. See Groton §61, last ¶.

11. There are two basic ways, each with its own variations. (1) The noun showing possession, the genitive noun, may either directly precede the article and noun it possesses, or may directly follow the two: ἡ σκηνὴ τοῦ ἀνθρώπου (the human's tent), or τοῦ ἀνθρώπου ἡ σκηνή (the human's tent). (2) The noun showing possession, the genitive noun, may also be placed in the attributive position: ἡ τοῦ ἀνθρώπου σκηνή (the person's tent; lit., the of-the-person tent), or ἡ σκηνὴ ἡ τοῦ ἀνθρώπου (the person's tent; lit., the tent, the [one] of the person).

12. (1) οἱ ἐν τῇ οἰκίᾳ δοῦλοι τῷ δεσπότῃ δουλεύσουσιν. (2) οἱ ἐν τῇ οἰκίᾳ τῷ δεσπότῃ δουλεύσουσιν. (3) αἱ ἐν τῇ οἰκίᾳ τῷ δεσπότῃ δουλεύσουσιν. (4) πεμπέτω ὁ οἰκέτης ἐπιστολὴν τῷ μαθητῇ τῷ ἀναξίῳ. (5) πεμπέτω ὁ δοῦλος οἰκέτης ἐπιστολὴν τοῖς ἀναξίοις οἰκέταις. (6) μηκέτι δουλευόντων τοῖς νεανίαις οἱ ἐλεύθεροι. (7) μηκέτι δουλευόντων ταῖς θεαῖς ταῖς ἀθανάτοις αἱ δοῦλαι. (8) ἐπεὶ δεσπότην τὸν πρότερον ἀπολείπεις, μέλλεις εὑρήσειν καὶ δουλεύσειν δεσποίνῃ ἀναξίῳ; (9) τὰ κακὰ ἐν τῇ ἀγορᾷ λείπετε καὶ τοὺς νεανίας τοὺς καλοὺς εἰς τὰς σκηνὰς διώκετε. (10) τῇ κακῇ καὶ ἀναξίῳ ἐθέλομεν δουλεύειν; (11) ἐθέλομεν τοῖς κακοῖς καὶ ἀναξίοις δουλεύειν; (12) ἐθέλετε τοὺς ἵππους λίθοις διώκειν ἀπὸ τοῦ ποταμοῦ; (13) ἐθέλεις τοὺς μαθητὰς τοὺς καλοὺς ἀπὸ τοῦ ἐν τῇ οἰκίᾳ δεσπότου διώκειν; (14) τὰ τέκνα ἐλεύθερα λυπῶν; ταῖς λύπαις μηκέτι δουλευέτω, ἀλλὰ τῇ χαρᾷ δουλευέτω. (15) ἐν τῇ ἀγορᾷ τὴν τοῦ ἀναξίου δεσπότου οἰκίαν τὴν κακὴν εὑρήσομεν.

13. Check your answers against **12**. in the exercises for Lesson 9.

Lesson 10

1. The imperfect active indicative is formed from the first principal part of the verb, the first person singular present active indicative.

2. Imperfect active indicative means the following: As to mood, it means that it expresses what the speaker portrays as an actual occurrence. As to tense, it indicates that the action takes place in past time. As to aspect, it indicates that the action is viewed by the speaker as on-going or continuous. As to voice, it indicates that the subject is the doer of the action expressed in the verb.

3. The imperfect active indicative is formed from the first principal part of the verb by first dropping the personal ending from the verb. Begin with λείπω, for example. Drop the ω, and one is left with λειπ-. To this, one adds the ε augment to the front, as a prefix, yielding ἐλειπ-. One then adds to the stem as suffixes the personal endings appropriate to the imperfect active: -ον, -ες, -ε(ν), -ομεν, -ετε, -ον.

4.
(1)	η	(6)	η
(2)	η	(7)	ῳ
(3)	ῃυ	(8)	ῃυ
(4)	ω	(9)	long ι
(5)	long υ	(10)	η

5. When one wishes to add the ε augment to a verb that begins with a prepositional prefix, one inserts the ε between the prefix and the stem of the verb. Generally, if the last letter of the prefix is a vowel, that letter will drop out in order to give way to the ε.

6. The ε augment in Greek always indicates that the verb is in an indicative historical tense, i.e., either in imperfect, aorist, or pluperfect, the last two of which need not concern us now.

7. The imperfect active indicative in Greek always has a recessive accent, as nearly all Greek verbs have.

8.
(1) ἐδίωκον   ἐδιώκομεν
     ἐδίωκες   ἐδιώκετε
     ἐδίωκε(ν)   ἐδίωκον

you were chasing, you [always] chased, you would chase, you kept on chasing, you continued to chase, you used to chase

(2) ἤθελον   ἠθέλομεν
     ἤθελες   ἠθέλετε
     ἤθελε(ν)   ἤθελον

you were willing, you [always] wanted, you would want, you kept on willing, you continued to will, you used to want

(3) ἔθυον   ἐθύομεν
     ἔθυες   ἐθύετε
     ἔθυε(ν)   ἔθυον

you were sacrificing, you [always] sacrificed, you would sacrifice, you kept on sacrificing, you continued to sacrifice, you used to sacrifice

(4) ἐδούλευον   ἐδουλεύομεν
     ἐδούλευες   ἐδουλεύετε
     ἐδούλευε(ν)   ἐδούλευον

you were serving, you [always] served, you used to serve, you would serve, you kept on serving, you continued to serve

(5) ἔλεγον   ἐλέγομεν
     ἔλεγες   ἐλέγετε
     ἔλεγε(ν)   ἔλεγον

you were saying, you [always] said, you used to say, you would say, you kept on saying, you continued to say

(6)	ἔφευγον	ἐφεύγομεν
	ἔφευγες	ἐφεύγετε
	ἔφευγε(ν)	ἔφευγον

you were fleeing, you [always] fled, you used to flee, you would flee, you kept on fleeing, you continued to flee

(7)	ἔπραττον	ἐπράττομεν
	ἔπραττες	ἐπράττετε
	ἔπραττε(ν)	ἔπραττον

you were doing, you [always] did, you used to do, you would do, you kept on doing, you continued to do

(8)	ἀπέλειπον	ἀπελείπομεν
	ἀπέλειπες	ἀπελείπετε
	ἀπέλειπε(ν)	ἀπέλειπον

you were abandoning, you [always] abandoned, you used to abandon, you would abandon, you kept on abandoning, you continued to abandon

9. The augment does not lengthen the ε as we might expect, to η, but to ει.

εἶχον	εἴχομεν
εἶχες	εἴχετε
εἶχε(ν)	εἶχον

10. (a) "indeed"; (b) "but" or "and"; (c) they function as correlatives, "on the one hand…, on the other hand…."

11. We mean that they occupy not the first position in the clause in which they are found. Typically, they will be found in the second position of their respective clauses. But see Groton §68, ¶ 4. Example: τῇ μὲν θεᾷ θύω, τῷ δὲ θεῷ οὔ. (I am sacrificing to the goddess, but not to the god.)

12. In the singular, one should translate it as "this one [on the one hand]…, that one [on the other hand]…" Example: ἡ μὲν τὰ τέκνα διώκει, ἡ δὲ τοὺς ἵππους = this one [on the one hand] is chasing the children, that one [on the other], the horses. In the plural, one should translate it as "some [on the one hand]…, others [on the other hand]…." Example: αἱ μὲν τὰ τέκνα διώκουσιν, αἱ δὲ τοὺς ἵππους = some [women] are chasing the children, others [women, of course], the horses.

13. (1) ἡ μὲν τοῖς μαθηταῖς φίλη, ἡ δ' οὔ. (2) αἱ μὲν ἀναξίοις μαθηταῖς φίλαι, αἱ δ' οὔ. (3) τὸν ἵππον τῇ ἀληθείᾳ ἐδίωκον, ἐπεὶ τοὺς οἰκέτας ἔφευγεν. (4) οἱ μὲν δεσπόται λεγόντων, οἱ δ' οἰκέται μὴ λεγόντων. (5) τὸν οὖν βίον ἀπελείπετε; (6) ἔργα ἀγαθὰ ἔπραττες; οὐκ ἔπραττον ἀγαθὰ ἔργα. οἱ οὖν δοῦλοι ἔργα ἀγαθὰ πραττόντων. (7) ἐφεύγομεν μὲν καὶ τὸν θάνατον καὶ τὸν κίνδυνον, ἐδίωκον δὲ τὴν μοῖραν τὴν φίλην. (8) ὁ μὲν ἵππος τῷ νεανίᾳ τῷ καλῷ φίλος, ἡ δὲ κόρη τῇ ἀληθείᾳ οὐ φίλη τῷ νεανίᾳ. (9) αἱ μὲν ἐπιστολὰς ἔγραφον, αἱ δ' οὔ. (10) οἱ μὲν ἐπιστολὰς ἔγραφον, οἱ δὲ ταῖς τῆς μοίρας θεαῖς ἔθυον. (11) τὰ μὲν ἐλέγομεν, τὰ δ' ἔλεγον. τὴν ἀλήθειαν εὑρίσκειν ἔχομεν; (12) τοὺς φίλους οὐ φεύγω, ἀλλὰ τὴν ἀλήθειαν λέξω. (13) ὁ μὲν δεσπότης τῇ δεσποίνῃ φίλος. (14) οἱ μὲν μαθηταὶ ἐπαίδευον τὸν δεσπότην, ὁ δὲ δεσπότης οὐκ εἶχεν τοὺς μαθητὰς παιδεύειν. (15) ἐπιστολὰς ἐγράφομεν ταῖς κόραις, αἱ δ' οὐκ ἔλεγον τὴν ἀλήθειαν. (16) ἐδίωκον μὲν οἱ θεοὶ τοὺς ἀνθρώπους, οἱ δ' ἄνθρωποι τῶν θεῶν ἐλεύθεροι.

14. Check your answers against **13.** in the exercises for Lesson 10.

Lesson 11

1. In the active voice, the form of the verb's personal ending is determined by its subject, and the subject does the action expressed by the verb (example: The girl **is petting** the dog.). In the middle voice, the form of the verb's personal ending is also determined by its subject, the subject also does the action expressed by the verb, but the action of the verb is implied to be in the interest of the subject (example: The girl **is petting** the dog [**for herself**].). In the passive voice, the form of the verb's personal ending is determined by its subject, but the subject does not do the action expressed by the verb, but is rather acted upon by the verb (example: The dog **is being petted** by the girl.).

2. future: middle only
   imperfect: middle/passive
   present: middle/passive

3.
   (1) present middle/passive indicative: first principal part
   (2) imperfect middle/passive indicative: first principal part
   (3) present middle/passive imperative: first principal part
   (4) future middle indicative: second principal part
   (5) present middle/passive infinitive: first principal part

4. (a) (1) Take the first principal part and remove from it the personal ending (example: θύ/ω). (2) This leaves remaining the present stem (θυ-). (3) To the present stem, add the appropriate primary personal ending for the indicative (-ομαι, -η/ει, -εται, -όμεθα, -εσθε, -ονται), or for the imperative (-ου, -έσθω, -εσθε, έσθων), or impersonal ending for the infinitive (-εσθαι). (b) (1) Take the second principal part and remove from it the personal ending (example: ἐθελήσ/ω). (2) This leaves remaining the future stem (ἐθελησ-). (3) To the future stem, add the appropriate primary personal ending for the indicative (-ομαι, -η/ει, -εται, -όμεθα, -εσθε, -ονται), or the impersonal ending for the infinitive (-εσθαι). (c) (1) Take the first principal part and remove from it the personal ending (example: θύ/ω). (2) This leaves remaining the present stem (θυ-). (3) To this stem, prefix the ἐ- augment (ἔθυ-). (4) To the present stem plus ἐ- augment, add the appropriate secondary personal ending (-όμην, -ου, -ετο, -όμεθα, -εσθε, -οντο).

5.
   (1) διώξομαι   διωξόμεθα
       διώξῃ   διώξεσθε
       διώξεται   διώξονται
       It will chase [for itself].
   (2) θύσεσθαι
       to [be about to] sacrifice [for oneself]
   (3) ἐλεγόμην   ἐλεγόμεθα
       ἐλέγου   ἐλέγεσθε
       ἐλέγετο   ἐλέγοντο
       It was being said. She was saying [for herself].
   (4) ἠθελόμην   ἠθελόμεθα
       ἠθέλου   ἠθέλεσθε
       ἠθέλετο   ἠθέλοντο
       It was being wished. He was wishing [for himself].
   (5) φεύγου   φεύγεσθε
       φευγέσθω   φευγέσθων
       Let it be fled. Let it flee [for itself].
   (6) πράττομαι   πραττόμεθα
       πράττῃ   πράττεσθε
       πράττεται   πράττονται
       It is being done. She is doing [for herself].

       (7) δουλεύεσθαι
            to be served; to serve [for oneself]
       (8) these forms do not exist
       (9) this form does not exist

6. The agent of a passive verb in Greek is expressed in one of two ways. (a) If the agent is a person or persons, use ὑπό + the genitive case. (b) If the agent is a thing or things, use the dative of means (see Groton §46 and §74).

7. Often, but not always, when a middle/passive verb is being used in the middle, it will have a direct object in the appropriate case (often accusative, though exceptions exist, like ἀκούω or δουλεύω). Example: διώκομαι **τὸν ἵππον**, "I am chasing **the horse** [for myself]." Often, but not always, when a middle/passive verb is being used in the passive, the sentence in which it is found will have a genitive of personal agent (ὑπὸ + genitive) or a dative of means. Examples: διώκομαι **ὑπὸ τοῦ κακοῦ δεσπότου**, "I am being chased **by the evil master**;" διώκομαι **λίθοις**, "I am being chased **with rocks**."

8. (1) ἀλλάττονται, "they are changing [for themselves]," or "they taking [something] in exchange for [something]"

   (2) φυλάττονται, "they are guarding [for themselves]," or "they are on guard against [something or someone]"

   (3) γράφονται, "they are writing [for themselves]," or "they are indicting [someone]"

   (4) παιδεύονται, "they are teaching [for themselves]," or "they are having [someone] taught"

   (5) πείθονται, "they are obeying"

   (6) τρέπονται, "they are betaking themselves"

9. (1) accusative and **genitive**: ἀλλάττῃ <u>τὸν κακὸν ἵππον</u> **τῆς καλῆς οἰκίας**, "You are exchanging the ugly horse **for the beautiful house**."

   (2) **dative**: πείθεσθε **τῷ ἀγαθῷ δεσπότῃ**, "Obey **the good master**!"

10.   (1) imperfective or aoristic
         (2) imperfective only
         (3) imperfective
         (4) imperfective or aoristic

11. (1) πείσω. (2) πείσομαι. (3) πείθῃ. (4) ἔπειθες. (5) τὸν ἵππον τρέπει. (6) εἰς τὴν οἰκίαν τρέπεται. (7) τὴν κόρην εἰς ἵππον ἠλάττομεν. (8) τὴν κόρην ἵππου ἠλαττόμεθα. (9) τὰ τέκνα παιδεύσεσθε. (10) τὰ τέκνα παιδεύσετε. (11) τὸ κακὸν ἐφυλαττόμην. (12) ἐν τῇ σκηνῇ ἐφύλαττον. (13) τοὺς οἰκέτας γράψει. (14) ἐπιστολὴν γράψει. (15) ἐπιστολὴν γράψεις. (16) φεύξομαι. (17) ἀκουσόμεθα. (18) ἀκουόμεθα. (19) τὸ δῶρον λειπέσθω. (20) οἱ λίθοι εὑρισκέσθων. (21) ὑπὸ τῆς δεσποίνης ἐβλάπτεσθε. (22) τὴν δέσποιναν ἐβλάπτεσθε.

12. Check your answers against **11**. in the exercises for Lesson 11.

13. Check your answer against Groton §76.

14. (1) ὑπὸ τὴν ἅμαξαν μὴ τρέπου, ὦ δοῦλε κακέ. (2) ἐπεὶ λέγει ὁ δεσπότης, τοὺς μαθητὰς πείθει· πεισόμεθα τῷ δεσπότῃ; (3) οἱ μὲν ὑπὸ τῶν μαθητῶν ἠκούοντο, οἱ δ᾽ ὑπὸ τῶν τέκνων ἐβλάπτοντο. (4) ἔχουσι τοῦ δεσπότου οἱ τρόποι ὑπὸ τῶν θεῶν ἀλλάττεσθαι; (5) ὑπὸ τῇ σκηνῇ τὴν μοῖραν φυλάττομαι. (6) ἁμάξῃ τρεπέσθων πόρρω τῆς κακῆς μικρᾶς λίμνης καὶ τῆς ἀγορᾶς. (7) ἐδιώκετε μὲν τὰ τέκνα ὑπὸ τῆς σκηνῆς εἰς τόπον κακόν, ἐφυλάττοντο δ᾽ οἱ ἵπποι ἐν τόπῳ καλῷ ὑπὸ τῶν θεραπαινῶν. (8) ὁ ἐν τῇ ἁμάξῃ θησαυρὸς πόρρω ἐν λίμνῃ λείπεται. (9) παιδευσόμεθα μὲν τὰ τέκνα, παιδεύονται δ᾽ οἱ μαθηταὶ ὑπὸ τοῦ ἀγαθοῦ δεσπότου. (10) τῇ Μοίρᾳ, ὦ ἄνθρωπε, πείθου.

15. Check your answers against **14**. in the exercises for Lesson 11.

Lesson 12

1. See Groton §79.

2. See Groton §79.

3. See Groton §79.

4. See Groton §79.

5. See Groton §79.

6.
(1)	They are.	(10)	You are.
(2)	He will be.	(11)	You will be.
(3)	Be!	(12)	Be!
(4)	They were.	(13)	You were.
(5)	to [be about to] be	(14)	You are.
(6)	We are.	(15)	They will be.
(7)	I shall be.	(16)	Let her be!
(8)	Let them be!	(17)	to be
(9)	You were.	(18)	I was. It was.

7. The enclitic forms of εἰμί are found only in the present active indicative. All forms of the present active indicative are enclitic **with the exception of the second person singular, εἶ.**

8. In all of these forms, εἰμί bears a recessive accent.

9. When we say a word has an enclitic accent, we mean that it relies on the foregoing word for its accent.

10. (1) The enclitic will receive an acute or a grave on its ultima, depending upon whether it's followed by another word. Example: οἰκέτης ἐστίν. οἰκέτης ἐστὶν ὁ μαθητής.

    (2) The proclitic will, uncharacteristically, receive an acute accent. This will happen no matter whether the following enclitic is one or two syllables. Example: ὁ μαθητὴς **οὔκ ἐστιν** ἐν τῇ ἀγορᾷ.

    (3) The preceding word will both retain its acute on the antepenult **and** receive another acute on the ultima. Examples: αἱ **δέσποιναί εἰσι** καλαί. **ἄνθρωπόν γε** φεύγει ὁ θεός.

    (4) The accent will not change; the enclitic will receive no accent, no matter the number of syllables it has. Examples: τῶν **θεραπαινῶν ἐστι** τὰ δῶρα. **καλῆς γε** οὔσης τῆς θεᾶς.

    (5) The preceding word will both retain its circumflex on the penult **and** receive another acute on the ultima. Examples: ἡ **Μοῖρά ἐστι** καλή. **φεῦγέ γε.**

    (6) The grave on the preceding word will simply convert from a grave into an acute, remaining on the same syllable on which it started. This occurs no matter the length of the enclitic word. Examples: **καλά γε** τὰ τέκνα. **καλά ἐστι** τὰ τέκνα

    (7) The acute on the penult of the preceding word remains as is. No further accents are added either to the preceding word or to the enclitic. Example: **μοίρᾳ γε** ὁ θάνατος.

    (8) In this case, since the accent is gone from the preceding word, it will fall on the last syllable of the enclitic. Example: οἱ **δ' εἰσὶ** καλοί. **οἱ δ' εἰσί.**

    (9) The preceding enclitic receives an acute on its ultima. Example: φίλοι **ἐσμέν γε.**

11. We mean that a verb described as being deponent will, at least in some tenses, be middle or passive in form but active in meaning.

12. So far, only three verbs we have encountered are deponent in the future:

φεύγω, φεύξομαι
ἀκούω, ἀκούσομαι
εἰμί, ἔσομαι

13. (1) τὸν ἵππον φεύγω. (2) τὸν ἵππον φεύξομαι. (3) ἐν τῇ ἀγορᾷ εἶ. (4) ἐν τῇ ἀγορᾷ ἔσῃ; (5) ὑπὸ τοῦ δεσπότου ἀκουόμεθα. (6) We shall hear the despot. (7) We are listening to the despot for ourselves. (8) We are listening to the despot. (9) You will flee the horse. (10) He is fleeing the horse.

14. See Groton §81, NOTE under εἰμί, ἔσομαι.

15. See Groton §81, NOTE under εἰμί, ἔσομαι.

16. (1) ἐπεὶ ἔστι τὸν πόλεμον λύειν τὴν χώραν, πεμπέτω ἡ θεὰ τὴν εἰρήνην. (2) ἐν ἀρχῇ ἦν ὁ λόγος. (3) τοὺς πολεμίους φευξόμεθα, ἐπειδὴ οἰκίας ἔλυον. (4) ἐπεὶ πόλεμον εἴχομεν, δεσπότην γε καλὸν εἴχομεν. (5) ἐχθρὸς ὁ ἄνθρωπός ἐστι τοῖς μαθηταῖς. παιδευέσθω ὁ δεσπότης τοὺς μαθητὰς πόρρω τοῦ ἀνθρώπου. (6) καλόν ἐστιν ἡ εἰρήνη. (7) καλά εἰσιν ἡ εἰρήνη καὶ ἡ ἡσυχία. (8) ἔλεγεν ἡ δέσποινα λόγον ἐχθρὸν ταῖς θεραπαίναις. (9) διὰ τῆς ἀγορᾶς εἰρήνη ἦν, ἐπεὶ πόρρω ἐδίωκεν ἡ θεὰ τὸν πόλεμον. (10) διὰ τὸν τοῦ οἰκέτου κακὸν λόγον, πόλεμος μὲν ἔστω, ἡ δ᾽ εἰρήνη μή.

17. Check your answers against **16.** in the exercises for Lesson 12.

Lesson 13

1. The standard adjective is placed after an article that goes with the noun. Examples: ἡ ἀγαθὴ κόρη, αἱ κόραι αἱ ἀγαθαί, κόραι αἱ ἀγαθαί. The demonstrative is placed in predicate position: οὗτος ὁ ἄνθρωπος. See Groton § 84.

2. See Groton § 83.

3.
   (1) ὅδε, ἥδε, τόδε
   (2) οὗτος, αὕτη, τοῦτο
   (3) ἐκεῖνος, ἐκείνη, ἐκεῖνο

4. Simply append the suffix –δε to the appropriate form of the article. For example, to modify a feminine, dative, singular noun, simply take the article τῇ and add –δε = τῇδε. Note: the unaccented articles ὁ, ἡ, οἱ, αἱ receive the accent acute on the penult when combined with -δε to make the demonstrative.

5. Similarities:
   • Masculine the same in all cases in singular and plural
   • Accent persistent
   • Feminine the same in all cases in the singular and plural as first declension –η
   • Neuter the same in all cases in singular and plural except the singular nom. and acc.

   Differences:
   • Neuter singular nom. and acc. end in –o in the demonstrative, while they end in –ov in the adjective

6. Stem is: In the following forms:
   οὑτ–   masc. nom. sing. and pl.

τοῦτ–   all cases of masculine except nom. sing. and pl.; all cases of neuter except nom. and acc. pl.; fem. gen. pl.

αὕτ–   fem. nom. sing. and fem. nom. pl.

ταῦτ–   all cases of feminine except nom. sing. and pl., gen. pl.; neut. nom. and acc. pl.

7.

 (1) this, this one; masc. nom. sing.; subject or predicate nominative

 (2) those, those ones; fem. nom. pl.; subject or predicate nominative

 (3) these, these ones; fem. acc. pl.; direct object

 (4) this, this one; masc. nom. sing.; subject or predicate nominative

 (5) that, that one; fem. nom. sing.; subject or predicate nominative

 (6) of these, of these ones; masc., fem., or neut. gen. pl.; possession

 (7) of those, of those ones; masc., fem., or neut. gen. pl.; possession

 (8) to these, to these ones; fem. dat. pl.; indirect object

 (9) of this, of this one; fem. gen. sing.; possession

 (10) this, this one; masc. acc. sing.; direct object

 (11) to/for that, to/for that one; fem. dat. sing.; indirect object

 (12) to/for this, to/for this one; masc. or neut. dat. sing.; indirect object

 (13) for this, for this one; masc. or neut. dat. sing.; indirect object

 (14) this, this one; neut. nom. or acc. sing.; subject, predicate nominative, or direct object

 (15) to/for these, to/for these ones; fem. dat. pl.; indirect object

 (16) that, that one; neut. nom. or acc. sing.; subject, predicate nominative, or direct object

 (17) this, this one; fem. nom. sing.; subject or predicate nominative

 (18) to/for this one; fem. dat. sing.; indirect object

 (19) this, this one; fem. acc. sing.; direct object

 (20) these, these ones; neut. nom. or acc. pl.; subject, predicate nominative, or direct object

 (21) these, these ones; fem. nom. pl.; subject or predicate nominative

 (22) those, those things; neut. nom. or acc. pl.; subject, predicate nominative, or direct object

 (23) these, these things; neut. nom. or acc. pl.; subject, predicate nominative, or direct object

 (24) to/for those, to/for those ones; masc. or neut. dat. pl.; indirect object

8.

 (1) οὗτος ὁ ἄνθρωπος; ὁ ἄνθρωπος οὗτος

 (2) οὗτός ἐστι ἄνθρωπος.

 (3) τάδε τὰ φυτά; τὰ φυτὰ τάδε

 (4) ἐκείναις ταῖς μοίραις; ταῖς μοίραις ἐκείναις

 (5) ἐκεῖνο φυτόν.

 (6) τοῦδε τοῦ ἀνθρώπου; τοῦ ἀνθρώπου τοῦδε

 (7) ἐκείνοις τοῖς φυτοῖς; τοῖς φυτοῖς ἐκείνοις

 (8) τοῦτον τὸν οἰκέτην; τὸν οἰκέτην τοῦτον

 (9) ἐκείνου τοῦ ποταμοῦ; τοῦ ποταμοῦ ἐκείνου

 (10) οἰκέτης οὗτος.

(11) ἐκείνου τοῦ ἀνθρώπου; τοῦ ἀνθρώπου ἐκείνου
(12) ἐκεῖνα τὰ φυτά; τὰ φυτὰ ἐκεῖνα
(13) τῷδε τῷ ἀγαθῷ οἰκέτῃ; τῷ ἀγαθῷ οἰκέτῃ τῷδε
(14) εἰς ταύτην τὴν ἀγοράν; εἰς τὴν ἀγορὰν ταύτην

9.
(1) βλέπω; I am seeing
(2) βλέψομαι; I shall see
(3) βλέπεις; you see
(4) βλέπε; see!
(5) βλέπῃ; you are seen, you are being seen
(6) βλέπου; be seen!
(7) βλεπόντων; let them see!
(8) βλεπέσθω; let him/her/it see for him-/her-/itself
(9) βλεπέσθων; let them be seen!
(10) βλέψεσθε; you (*pl.*) see
(11) βλέπεσθε; be (*pl.*) seen!

10. (1) οὐκ ἔστιν αὕτη ἡ φιλοσοφία σοφή. (2) αὕτη ἡ φιλοσοφία ἡ σοφή ἐστι τῇ ἀληθείᾳ σοφία. (3) λύσει ὅδε ὁ φιλόσοφος τοῦτον τὸν λόγον. (4) θύσεται ἐκεῖνος ὁ φιλόσοφος ὁ ἀνάξιος ταύταις ταῖς θεαῖς. (5) ἡ δέσποινα ἥδε εἰς τὴν φιλοσοφίαν τὴν ἐκείνης τῆς σοφῆς βλέπει. (6) τόδε μὲν νῦν βλέπω, τοῦτο δὲ τότε βλέψομαι. (7) ἐκεῖναι γὰρ αἱ σοφαὶ θεράπαιναι τόνδε τὸν μακρὸν λόγον λύσονται. (8) ἐπειδὴ εἰς ταύτην τὴν ἀγορὰν τρέφεται τοῦτο τὸ τέκνον, τότε βλέψεται τὴν καλὴν κόρην τήνδε. (9) ἥδε μὲν οὐ σοφή, ἀλλ᾽ οὗτος σοφός. σοφὴ εἶ; (10) ἐκεῖνος ἦν φιλόσοφος· ἥδ᾽ ἐστι φιλόσοφος· αὗται καὶ σοφαὶ καὶ φιλόσοφοι ἔσονται.

11. Check your answers against **10.** in the exercises for Lesson 13.

Lesson 14

1. In classical Greek, a third person personal pronoun in the nominative case is supplied by: οὗτος, αὕτη, τοῦτο; ὅδε, ἥδε, τόδε; or ἐκεῖνος, –η, –ο. At the same time, the oblique cases (genitive, dative, and accusative) of the third person pronoun are supplied by the appropriate form of αὐτός, –ή, -ό.

2. (a) ἐγώ and ἡμεῖς
(b) ἐγώ, ἐμοῦ/μου, ἐμοί/μοι, ἐμέ/με; ἡμεῖς, ἡμῶν, ἡμῖν, ἡμᾶς

3. (a) σύ/συ and ὑμεῖς
(b) σύ/συ, σοῦ/σου, σοί/σοι, σέ/σε; ὑμεῖς, ὑμῶν, ὑμῖν, ὑμᾶς

4. When αὐτός, –ή, –ό is used in the predicate position to modify a noun, its force is intensive, and is translated as "-self" or "very"; when it is used in the attributive position to modify a noun, it is an adjective with the meaning of "same".

5. It depends. If it is in the nominative case, it functions as an intensifier (αὐτὴ ἔλεγε τάδε = She herself was saying the following things); while if in one of the oblique cases (genitive, dative, or accusative), it functions as a third person personal pronoun.

6. The dative of possession describes a way in which the Greek language uses the dative case, a form of εἰμί (or εἰμί understood), and a noun in the nominative case to express that the item in dative possesses the item in the nominative. Example: μοί ἐστιν ὁ ἵππος = I have the horse (lit., the horse is to me).

7.
(1) ἔπληττον
(2) πλήττει
(3) αὐτὰ (or αὐτοὺς or αὐτὰς) πλήξεται.
(4) ὑφ᾽ ἡμῶν πλήττονται.
(5) τὸ βιβλίον φέρουσιν αὗται.
(6) ἐφέρετο τὸ ἱμάτιον ὑπό σου.
(7) τὸ ἱμάτιον οἴσω.
(8) τὸ ἱμάτιον ἐφέρετε.
(9) τὸ βιβλίον οἰσόμεθα.
(10) [ἡμεῖς] ἐφερόμεθα.
(11) σὲ ἔπληττον.
(12) αὐτὰ (or αὐτοὺς or αὐτὰς) ἐπλήττετο.
(13) ὑπό σου ἐπλήττετο.
(14) αὕτη τὸ βιβλίον φέρει.
(15) ὑπ᾽ αὐτῶν φέρεται τὸ βιβλίον.
(16) φέρεται τὸ ἱμάτιον ὑπό σου.
(17) τὸ ἱμάτιον οἴσεις.
(18) τὸ βιβλίον φερόμεθα.
(19) τὸ βιβλίον ἐφερόμεθα.
(20) φερόμεθα

8.
(1) ἔχει τὸ τέκνον ἱμάτιον. ἔστι τῷ τέκνῳ ἱμάτιον.
(2) ἔχει τὰ τέκνα τὰ βιβλία ταῦτα. ἔστι τὰ βιβλία ταῦτα τοῖς τέκνοις.
(3) ἔχετε καλὸν ἵππον. καλὸς ἵππος ἐστὶν ὑμῖν.
(4) ἔχεις καλὸν ἵππον. καλὸς ἵππος ἐστί σοι.
(5) ἅμαξαν ἔχει ἡ ἵππος. τῇ ἵππῳ ἐστὶ ἅμαξα.
(6) ἔχουσιν ἵππους. ἵπποι εἰσὶν αὐτοῖς.
(7) βιβλία ἔχει αὕτη. Αὐτὴ ἐστὶ βιβλία.
(8) ἔχομεν ἵππους. ἵπποι εἰσὶν ἡμῖν.
(9) ἁμάξας ἔχω. εἰσί μοι ἅμαξαι.

9.
(1) personal pronoun, second person plural, nominative; you
(2) adjective, feminine nominative plural; very, same, themselves
(3) demonstrative, neuter nominative/accusative singular; that
(4) personal pronoun, first person plural, nominative; we
(5) personal pronoun, second person singular, genitive, emphatic; of you
(6) adjective, masculine nominative plural; very, same, themselves
(7) demonstrative, feminine nominative plural; these
(8) adjective or third person singular pronoun, neuter nominative/accusative singular; very, same, itself, it
(9) personal pronoun, first person plural, genitive; of us
(10) personal pronoun, second person plural, genitive; of you
(11) demonstrative, masculine nominative plural; these
(12) demonstrative, feminine nominative singular; this
(13) personal pronoun, second person plural, dative; to/for you
(14) personal pronoun, first person singular, genitive, non-emphatic; of me
(15) adjective, masculine nominative singular; very, same, himself
(16) personal pronoun, second person singular, nominative; you
(17) adjective, feminine nominative singular; very, same, herself
(18) personal pronoun, first person plural, dative; to/for us
(19) personal pronoun, first person singular, genitive, emphatic; of me
(20) demonstrative, masculine nominative singular; this

10. (1) τὸ αὐτὸ βιβλίον πλήξω. (2) αὐτὸ τὸ βιβλίον πλήξω. (3) τοῦτο τὸ βιβλίον ἔπληττον λίθοις. (4) τὰ αὐτὰ βιβλία ὑφ᾽ ἡμῶν ἐπλήττετο. (5) ταῦτα τὰ βιβλία ἐπλήττομεν ἡμεῖς. (6) σοί ἐστι καὶ τὰ βιβλία καὶ τὰ ἱμάτια. (7) μή μοι ἐπίπληττε. (8) ἡ ἅμαξα ἐπὶ τοῦ ἱματίου τοῦδε ἐστίν. (9) ἔγωγ᾽ οὐκ οἴσομαι τὸ ἱμάτιον. (10) αὐτοὺς τοὺς ἵππους οὐκ ἐπλήττου σύ.

11. Check your answers against **10.** in the exercises for Lesson 14.

Lesson 15

1. A contract verb is a verb whose stem ends in –ε, –ο, or –α; this last vowel of the stem combines with the theme vowel of the personal ending often yielding a new sound.

2. No. Contract verbs are "born" as contract verbs, whilst the remainder of Greek verbs are "born" as non-contract verbs. Thus, παιδεύω will never be found in contract form, i.e., in a form of, say, παιδευάω; nor will δηλόω ever be found as the non-contract δήλω.

3. ο/ω is the most voracious; α dominates ε; and ε is at the bottom of the food-chain.

4.
    (1) τιμαόντων
    (2) τιμάεις
    (3) φιλέου
    (4) φιλέεσθαι
    (5) δηλοόμεθα
    (6) δηλόετε
    (7) δηλόει

5.
    (1) ὠφελῶ, γελῶ, δηλῶ.
    (2) ὠφελοῦμαι, τιμῶμαι, δηλοῦμαι.
    (3) ὠφέλουν, ἐγέλων, ἐδήλουν.
    (4) ὠφελούμην, ἐτιμώμην, ἐδηλούμην.
    (5) ὠφελεῖς, γελᾷς, δηλοῖς.
    (6) ὠφελῇ, τιμᾷ, δηλοῖ.
    (7) ὠφέλεις, ἐγέλας, ἐδήλους.
    (8) ὠφελοῦ, ἐτιμῶ, ἐδηλοῦ.
    (9) ὠφέλει, γέλα, δήλου.
    (10) ὠφελοῦ, τιμῶ, δηλοῦ.
    (11) φιλεῖ, δηλοῖ, γελᾷ.
    (12) φιλεῖται, δηλοῦται, τιμᾶται.
    (13) ἐφίλει, ἐδήλου, ἐγέλα.
    (14) ἐφιλεῖτο, ἐδηλοῦτο, ἐτιμᾶτο.
    (15) φιλείτω, δηλούτω, γελάτω.
    (16) φιλείσθω, δηλούσθω, τιμάσθω.

6.
    (1) φιλούντων, τιμώντων, δηλούντων.
    (2) φιλείσθων, τιμάσθων, δηλούσθων.
    (3) ἐφιλοῦντο, ἐτιμῶντο, ἐδηλοῦντο.
    (4) ἐφίλουν, ἐτίμων, ἐδήλουν.
    (5) φιλοῦνται, τιμῶνται, δηλοῦνται.
    (6) φιλοῦσι, τιμῶσι, δηλοῦσι.
    (7) φιλεῖτε, τιμᾶτε, δηλοῦτε.
    (8) φιλεῖσθε, τιμᾶσθε, δηλοῦσθε.
    (9) ἐφιλεῖσθε, ἐτιμᾶσθε, ἐδηλοῦσθε.
    (10) ἐφιλεῖτε, ἐτιμᾶτε, ἐδηλοῦτε.
    (11) φιλεῖσθε, τιμᾶσθε, δηλοῦσθε.
    (12) φιλεῖτε, τιμᾶτε, δηλοῦτε.
    (13) ἐτιμώμεθα, ἐφιλούμεθα, ἐδηλούμεθα.
    (14) ἐτιμῶμεν, ἐφιλοῦμεν, ἐδηλοῦμεν.
    (15) τιμώμεθα, φιλούμεθα, δηλούμεθα.
    (16) τιμῶμεν, φιλοῦμεν, δηλοῦμεν.

7.
    (1) γελᾷς, γελάσῃ. The future is deponent.
    (2) κομίζουσι, κομιοῦσι. The future is contract.
    (3) ἀκούετε, ἀκούσεσθε. The future is deponent.

(4) λέγει, ἐρεῖ. The future is contract and is built from a stem that differs from the present.

(5) βάλλομεν, βαλοῦμεν. The future is contract; stem loses one λ.

(6) εἰμί, ἔσομαι. The future is deponent.

(7) φεύγουσι, φεύξονται. The future is deponent.

(8) βλέπεις, βλέψῃ. The future is deponent.

(9) φέρομαι, οἴσομαι. The future is built from a stem that differs from the present.

8. (1) καὶ τοὺς οἰκέτας ἁρπάσω καὶ ἐπὶ τοῖς δεσπόταις γελάσομαι. (2) δῆλοί σοι οἱ τρόποι οἱ τούτων; ἐγώ σοι αὐτοὺς δηλώσω. (3) αἱ μὲν τοὺς ἵππους λίθοις ἔβαλλον, οἱ δ᾽ ἐκείνας τῇ ἀληθείᾳ τοῖς αὐτοῖς βαλοῦσιν. (4) ἀλλάξονται οἱ φιλόσοφοι τὴν ἀλήθειαν τίμης; (5) μὴ γέλα, ὦ τέκνον κακόν, ἐπεὶ γελάσονται ἐπὶ σοὶ οἱ ἄνθρωποι ἀγαθοί. (6) οὗτοι οἱ αὐτοὶ ἄνθρωποι καὶ τότε ὑπὸ τῶν θεῶν ὠφελοῦντο καὶ νῦν ὑπ᾽ αὐτῶν ὠφελοῦνται. (7) τὸν φιλόσοφον διὰ τῆς ἀγορᾶς κομιῶ, τότε γὰρ τίμην ἀπὸ τῶν ἀνθρώπων κομιεῖται. (8) ὁ μὲν νεανίας λέγει τάδε· φιλῶ φιλεῖν τὴν κόρην· ἐρεῖ δ᾽ ἡ αὐτὴ κόρη τάδε· φιλῶ ὑπ᾽ αὐτοῦ φιλεῖσθαι; (9) ἐκείνην τὴν σοφίαν τὴν τοῦδε τοῦ φιλοσόφου οὐκέτι τιμῶνται οἱ δεσπόται. οὗτοι ὑπὸ τῶν οἰκετῶν μὴ τιμάσθων.

9. Check your answers against **8.** in the exercises for Lesson 15.

Lesson 16

1. A third declension noun may be either masculine, feminine, or neuter. In order to know the gender of a specific third declension noun, it is important to memorise its gender as indicated by its lexical form, in which the last element given is the gender. For example, ἀγών, –ῶνος, ὁ, is shown by the article ὁ to be a masculine noun.

2. (a) To get the stem of a first declension noun, one simply removes the nominative singular ending from it; for example, the stem of μαθητής is μαθητ–. (b) To find the stem of a second declension noun, one simply removes the nominative singular ending from it; for example, the stem of τέκνον is τέκν–. (c) To find the stem of a third declension noun, one may not rely upon the nominative singular form of the word. One must rather go to the genitive singular form and remove the –ος ending, thereby arriving at the stem of the noun. The stem of the noun ὄνομα, for example, must be gotten from its genitive singular form, ὀνόματος. The stem is ὀνοματ–.

3. See Groton §99.7

4. (a) No. It must simply agree with the noun it modifies in number, case, and gender. (b) No. An adjective of any declension, provided that it reflects the number, case, and gender of the noun it modifies, may modify a third declension noun. For example: τὸ καλὸν ὄνομα = "the good name."

5.
	Lexical Form	Stem
(1)	ἀσπίς, –ίδος, ἡ	ἀσπίδ–
(2)	φύλαξ, –ακος, ὁ	φύλακ–
(3)	χάρις, –ιτος, ἡ	χάριτ–
(4)	κλώψ, κλωπός, ὁ	κλωπ–
(5)	ῥήτωρ, –ορος, ὁ	ῥήτορ–
(6)	λέων, –οντος, ὁ	λέοντ–
(7)	ὄνομα, –ατος, τό	ὀνόματ–
(8)	ἀγών, –ῶνος, ὁ	ἀγών–

6. (1) ταῖς ἀσπίσι   (9) τῷ ῥήτορι

(2)	ὦ ἀσπί	(10)	τοῖς ῥήτορσι
(3)	τὸν φύλακα	(11)	οἱ λέοντες
(4)	τῶν φυλάκων	(12)	ὁ λέων
(5)	αἱ χάριτες	(13)	τὸ ὄνομα
(6)	τὴν χάριν	(14)	τῶν ὀνομάτων
(7)	τῶν κλωπῶν	(15)	τοῖς ἀγῶσι
(8)	ὦ κλῶπες	(16)	τοὺς ἀγῶνας

7. (1) διώκει τὸν φύλακα. (2) διώκει τὸν φύλακα ὁ κακὸς λέων. (3) διώκει τὸν φύλακα τοῦ ἀξίου τέκνου χάριν ὁ λέων ὁ κακός. (4) ἐρεῖ ὁ ῥήτωρ τάδε· ἐγὼ μὲν ἔβλεπον καὶ τοὺς κλῶπας καὶ τὰς ἀσπίδας, οἱ δὲ φύλακες ἐκείνους οὐκ ἔσπευδον διώκειν καὶ οὐκ ἤθελον ταύτας ἁρπάζειν. (5) ἢ ἀγῶνα σχήσω ἢ τοὺς λέοντας δηλώσω. (6) ἐπεὶ οἱ κλῶπες τοὺς ἵππους ἐκ τῆς χώρας ἁρπάσουσιν, καὶ ποιούντων οἱ καλοὶ φύλακες ἀσπίδας καὶ λεγόντων οἱ ἀγαθοὶ ῥήτορες λόγους μακροὺς ἐπ' αὐτούς. (7) τοῖς μὲν σοφοῖς φιλοσόφοις εἶχεν ὁ ῥήτωρ χάριν, ἐπὶ τοῖς δ' αὐτοῖς φιλοσόφοις ἐγέλων οἱ ἄνθρωποι. (8) βαλῶ μὲν τὸν λέοντα λίθοις, φυλάξω δὲ τὰ ἀγαθὰ τέκνα καλαῖς ἀσπίσι.

8. Check your answers against 7. in the exercises for Lesson 16.

Lesson 17

1. (1) (a) Genitive plural. (b) The stem of the noun τεῖχος is τειχεσ–, and one adds to this stem the standard third-declension genitive plural ending, -ων. The word in its "pre-contracted" state is thus: τειχέσων. The sigma then drops out, yielding τειχέων, at which point ε and ω contract to ω, yielding τειχῶν.

(2) (a) Genitive singular. (b) The stem of the noun γέρας is γερασ–, and one adds to this stem the standard third-declension genitive singular ending, –ος. The word in its "pre-contracted" state is thus: γέρασος. The sigma then drops out, yielding γέραος, at which point α and ο contract to ω, yielding γέρως.

(3) (a) Dative singular. (b) The stem of the noun γέρας is γερασ–, and one adds to this stem the standard third-declension dative singular ending, -ι. The word in its "pre-contracted" state is thus: γέρασι. The sigma then drops out, yielding γέραι, at which point α and ι contract to either ᾳ or αι, yielding either γέρᾳ or γέραι.

(4) (a) Genitive singular. (b) The stem of the noun Σωκράτης is Σωκρατεσ–, and one adds to this stem the standard third-declension genitive singular ending, –ος. The word in its "pre-contracted" state is thus: Σωκράτεσος. The sigma then drops out, yielding Σωκράτεος, at which point the ε and ο contract to ου, yielding Σωκράτους.

(5) (a) Accusative singular. (b) The stem of the noun τριήρης is τριηρεσ–, and one adds to this stem the standard masculine/feminine accusative singular ending, –α. The word in its "pre-contracted" state is thus: τριήρεσα. The sigma then drops out, yielding τριήρεα, at which point the ε and α contract to η, yielding τριήρη. It should be noted with the contraction of -εσ– stem nouns in the accusative singular that based upon what we have learned about contraction from contract verbs, one would expect the resultant form to be τριήρα. However, in the sigma-stem third-declension, ε and α contract to η. See also, for example, the neuter plural nominative, accusative, and vocative of the word τεῖχος.

(6) (a) Accusative singular. (b) The stem of the noun αἰδώς is αἰδοσ–, and one adds to this stem the standard masculine/feminine accusative

singular ending, –α. The word in its "pre-contracted" state is thus: αἰδόσα. The sigma drops out, yielding αἰδόα at which point ο and α contract to ω. The resultant form is αἰδῶ.

(7) (a) Nominative, accusative, or vocative plural. (b) The stem of the noun τεῖχος is τειχεσ–, and one adds to this stem the standard third-declension neuter nominative, accusative and vocative plural ending, –α. The word in its "pre-contracted" state is thus: τείχεσα. The sigma drops out, yielding τείχεα, at which point ε and α contract to η. The resultant form is τείχη. See note on (5).

(8) (a) Nominative, accusative, or vocative plural. (b) The stem of the noun γέρας is γερασ–, and one adds to this stem the standard third-declension neuter nominative, accusative and vocative plural ending, –α. The word in its "pre-contracted" state is thus: γέρασα. The sigma drops out, yielding γέραα, at which point the α and the α contract to long α, yielding γέρα.

(9) (a) Nominative, accusative, or vocative plural. (b) The stem of the noun τριήρης is τριηρεσ–, and one adds to this stem the standard masculine/feminine nominative, accusative and vocative plural ending, –ες. The word in its "pre-contracted" state is thus: τριήρεσες. The sigma drops out, yielding τριήρεες, at which point the ε and ε contract to ει, yielding τριήρεις.

2. It has only two sets of endings, one for the common masculine/feminine gender, one for the neuter gender.

3. No. For an adjective to modify a noun, the adjective must simply agree with it in number, case, and gender. Often an adjective that does agree with a noun in that way will have the same ending as the noun, as it will be of the same declension as the noun. Nonetheless, in many situations, the adjective and noun will not belong to the same declension and will therefore not have the same endings, though they agree in number, case, and gender.

4. The third declension noun may be either masculine, feminine, or neuter. Unlike many of the declensions we have learned which are gender specific, the third declension is not.

5. πρός has three different meanings, depending upon with which case it is used. It may also be used in an idiomatic expression. When πρός is used with the genitive case it means *from*, often indicating source. When used with the dative case, it means *at* or *near*. When used with the accusative, it means *toward*, *against*, *to*, or *facing*. It is also used in the idiom πρὸς θεῶν, "by the gods!"

6.
(1)	τῷ τείχει	(7)	ὦ Σώκρατες
(2)	τῆς τριήρους	(8)	ταῖς τριήρεσι
(3)	ἡ αἰδώς	(9)	τῇ αἰδοῖ
(4)	τὸ γέρας	(10)	τὰ γέρα
(5)	ὁ δαίμων	(11)	τοῦ δαίμονος
(6)	ἀληθεῖς	(12)	εὐδαίμονα

7. προσβαλῶ, προσβαλεῖς, προσβαλεῖ, προσβαλοῦμεν, προσβαλεῖτε, προσβαλοῦσι προσεβαλλόμην, προσεβάλλου, προσεβάλλετο, προσεβαλλόμεθα, προσεβάλλεσθε, προσεβάλλοντο

8. προσποίει, προσποιείτω, προσποιεῖτε, προσποιούντων προσποιοῦ, προσποιείσθω, προσποιεῖσθε, προσποιείσθων προσεποίουν, προσεποίεις, προσεποίει, προσεποιοῦμεν, προσεποιεῖτε, προσεποίουν

9. The two basic meanings of προσποιέω are "add to" and "pretend (to)." In order for προσποιέω to mean "add to" it should be used in the active. It may also be used in the passive to mean "be added to". However, when used in the middle voice (προσποιοῦμαι) and followed by an infinitive it means "pretend (to)."

10. (1) εὖ πράττει (or ἔχει) ὁ Σωκράτης. (2) κακῶς ἔχει (or πράττει) ὁ Σωκράτης. (3) προσεποιεῖτο κακῶς πράττειν (or ἔχειν) ὁ Σωκράτης. (4) ἔστι καλὴ ἡ αἰδὼς ἡ ἀληθής. (5) τῷ τείχει προσβαλλόντων οἱ πολέμιοι. (6) πρὸς τῇ λίμνῃ ἦν ἡ μακρὰ τριήρης. (7) γέρας μὲν κομιεῖ, τιμὴν δ᾽ ἐγώ. (8) τῷ δαίμονι λέγει ὁ Σωκράτης. (9) εὖ πράττει ὁ εὐδαίμων; ἔργα ἀγαθὰ πραττέτω. (10) ἀληθῆ, πρὸς θεῶν, γέρα ἔσται μοι.

11. (1) μὴ προσβαλλόντων οἱ φύλακες τῷ ῥήτορι τῷ ἀγαθῷ ἀσπίσι. (2) ὁ μὲν Σωκράτης τὴν τριήρη σπεύδει φυλάττεσθαι, οἱ δὲ μαθηταὶ κακῶς προσποιοῦνται τὸ αὐτὸ πράττειν. (3) τοῖς εὐδαίμοσι βίος καλός, αὐτοὶ γὰρ τὸ ἀληθὲς γέρας ηὕρισκον. (4) μὴ ἁρπάζετε τὰς ἀσπίδας πρὸς τοῦ τείχους, ἐκεῖναι γάρ μοι πρὸς τοῦ ἀγαθοῦ δεσπότου ἐπέμποντο. (5) ἡμεῖς μὲν τῷ τείχει προσβάλλειν προσποιησόμεθα, ὑμεῖς δὲ τῇ ἀληθείᾳ ταῖς τριήρεσι προσβαλεῖτε. (6) ἐν τοῖς ἀγῶσιν ἢ γέρα καὶ τιμὰς ἢ αἰδὼ καὶ κακὰ κομιούμεθα. (7) πρὸς θεῶν, τὰ γέρα ἀπὸ τῆς τριήρους καὶ πρὸς τὸν εὐδαίμονα Σωκράτη κόμιζε. (8) οὗτοι οἱ ἄνθρωποι αἰδὼ οὐκ ἔχουσιν, ἐγέλων γὰρ ἐπὶ τοῖς τοῦ ῥήτορος λόγοις τοῖς ἀληθέσιν. (9) μὴ πεμπόντων οἱ θεοὶ λύπας ἡμῖν, ἀλλ᾽ εὐδαίμονα βίον. (10) ἐλέγετο τάδε ὑπὸ τοῦ Σωκράτους· οἱ σοφοὶ οὗτοι τῇ ἀληθείᾳ ἀληθεῖς.

12. Check your answers against **11.** in the exercises for Lesson 17.

Lesson 18

1. "Aspect" refers to what a Greek verb indicates about the duration of the activity it expresses, for lack of a better way of putting it. The Greek verb may indicate one of the following regarding the duration of the activity it expresses. Imperfective aspect indicates that the action is conceived of as on-going or not yet complete. Perfective aspect indicates the action is conceived of as having been completed. Aoristic aspect indicates that the action is conceived of as if a "snap-shot." The aoristic aspect of the aorist verb is present in all of its forms: indicative, imperative, and infinitive. The time of the aorist verb, however, is indicated only in its indicative (there are some exceptions to this which will be discussed later). In the indicative, the aorist verb indicates past time. Other "times" indicated by the Greek verb are present and future. Thus, an aorist indicative form has both time and aspect (that is, it refers to past action conceived of as if a "snap-shot"). The aorist imperative has only "aspect" (that is, it refers to a commanded action as if a "snap-shot" without reference to time, though by implication it is futuristic). The aorist infinitive again has only "aspect", and refers to action as if a "snap-shot" without reference to time.

2. (a) It is distinct from the future in that it receives an ε– augment and its theme vowel is α. Furthermore, while there is no such thing as a future imperative, the aorist has an imperative. Its similarities with the future consist of the following: (1) its stem is suffixed with σ before receiving its personal ending; and (2) just as the future has no passive form built from the second principal part, the first aorist has no passive form built from the third principal part.

(b) It is distinct from the present in that it receives an ε– augment and its theme vowel is α, while the theme vowels of the present are o/ε. Furthermore, unlike the present system, it uses "secondary" endings. Another difference is that while the present system can form the active, middle, and passive from the first principal part, from the third principal part

Lesson 18

one can form only the active and middle. However, like the present system, the aorist system can form imperatives.

(c) It is distinct from the imperfect in that its stem typically (with few exceptions) receives a σ suffix before receiving the personal endings. Another distinction is that while the theme vowels for the imperfect are o/ε, for the first aorist the theme vowel is α. The imperfect is formed only in the indicative mood; it has no imperative or infinitive. At the same time, the aorist has the following forms: indicative, imperative, and infinitive. The imperfect does not have its own principal part: it is formed from the first principal part. The first aorist does have its own principal part, being formed from the third principal part. The final distinction consists of this: while the imperfect formed from the first principal part may have the active, middle, and passive, the aorist formed from the third principal part may have only the active and middle. The similarities between the imperfect and aorist consist of the following: both are historic tenses (secondary tenses); both use secondary endings; both are augmented with ε.

3. (1) First principal part
    (2) Second principal part
    (3) First principal part
    (4) Third principal part

4. See Groton §111.

5.
(1) ποιέω, ποιήσω, ἐποίησα
(2) βλάπτω, βλάψω, ἔβλαψα
(3) δηλόω, δηλώσω, ἐδήλωσα
(4) λύω, λύσω, ἔλυσα
(5) τρέπω, τρέψω, ἔτρεψα
(6) τιμάω, τιμήσω, ἐτίμησα
(7) ἁρπάζω, ἁρπάσω, ἥρπασα
(8) φυλάττω, φυλάξω, ἐφύλαξα
(9) κομίζω, κομιῶ, ἐκόμισα
(10) μέλλω, μελλήσω, ἐμέλλησα
(11) ἀκούω, ἀκούσομαι, ἤκουσα
(12) πείθω, πείσω, ἔπεισα
(13) ἐθέλω, ἐθελήσω, ἠθέλησα
(14) διώκω, διώξω, ἐδίωξα
(15) δουλεύω, δουλεύσω, ἐδούλευσα
(16) γράφω, γράψω, ἔγραψα
(17) βλέπω, βλέψομαι, ἔβλεψα
(18) φιλέω, φιλήσω, ἐφίλησα
(19) πέμπω, πέμψω, ἔπεμψα
(20) γελάω, γελάσομαι, ἐγέλασα
(21) σπεύδω, σπεύσω, ἔσπευσα
(22) ὠφελέω, ὠφελήσω, ὠφέλησα
(23) ἀλλάττω, ἀλλάξω, ἤλλαξα
(24) θύω, θύσω, ἔθυσα
(25) κλέπτω, κλέψω, ἔκλεψα
(26) κελεύω, κελεύσω, ἐκέλευσα

6. (a) Only the masculine nominative and accusative singular and the neuter nominative and accusative singular. These forms have the stem πολ–. (b) Check against Groton page 455.

7.
(1) ἠρώτησα / ἠρωτήσαμεν
ἠρώτησας / ἠρωτήσατε
ἠρώτησε(ν) / ἠρώτησαν
(2) πώλησαι / πωλήσασθε
πωλησάσθω / πωλησάσθων
(3) χαιρῆσαι
(4) φύλαξον / φυλάξατε
φυλαξάτω / φυλαξάντων
(5) ἠγγειλάμην / ἠγγειλάμεθα
ἠγγείλω / ἠγγείλασθε
ἠγγείλατο / ἠγγείλαντο
(6) γράψασθαι

8. (1) The messenger reported many things, while the speaker did not. (2) Will the guard announce these things? (3) The speech of the speaker is not worth many drachmas, but few. (4) The guards asked the following,

"Are the messengers announcing the war, or do we ourselves intend to announce it?" (5) He sold his privileges for many drachmas, but his shields for few. (6) Few people obeyed the speakers, while many [obeyed] the philosophers. (7) Did I alone ask about this ugly trireme? The masses do not, therefore, have a worthy character! (8) They did not only sell these shields to the thieves, but the thieves even announced the following: "Let Socrates sell us his shield for a few obols!" (9) Don't just ask the messenger about the wall, but also tell him, "Let not the enemy destroy the walls!" (10) Let the thief announce the following: "I did not steal the children, for they are ugly!"

9. (1) τὰς δραχμὰς μὴ κλεψάτω. (2) οἱ μὲν πολλοὶ οὐ σοφοί, οἱ δὲ φιλόσοφοί εἰσιν. (3) τὰ γέρα μου μόνον ὀλίγων ὀβολῶν οὐ πωλήσω. (4) τοὺς φύλακας πολλ᾽ ἐτίμησαν οἱ ἄγγελοι. (5) τὴν κόρην μὴ μόνον τιμησάτω, ἀλλὰ καὶ φιλησάτω. (6) εἰς τὴν ἀγορὰν μὴ τρέψασθε/τρέψαι. (7) τοῖς πολλοῖς ἐπιστολὴν γράψαι οὐκ ἔσπευσα. (8) τὰ τέκνα παιδευσάσθων μόνον ἐν ταῖς οἰκίαις, μὴ ἐν τῇ ἀγορᾷ. (9) τοὺς πολλοὺς ὀβολοὺς ὀλίγων δραχμῶν ἀλλαξάσθων. (10) οὗτος, τὴν ἅμαξαν ἐκ τοῦ ποταμοῦ με τρέψαι ὠφέλησον.

10. Check your answers against **9.** in the exercises for Lesson 18.

Lesson 19

1.

Second aorist	Imperfect	First aorist
INDICATIVE ACTIVE		
-ον	-ον	-α
-ες	-ες	-ας
-ε(ν)	-ε(ν)	-ε(ν)
-ομεν	-ομεν	-αμεν
-ετε	-ετε	-ατε
-ον	-ον	-αν
INDICATIVE MIDDLE		
-όμην	-όμην	-άμην
-ου	-ου	-ω
-ετο	-ετο	-ατο
-όμεθα	-όμεθα	-άμεθα
-εσθε	-εσθε	-ασθε
-οντο	-οντο	-αντο
IMPERATIVE ACTIVE		
-ε		-ον
-έτω		-ατω
-ετε		-ατε
-όντων		-άντων
IMPERATIVE MIDDLE		
-οῦ		-αι
-έσθω		-άσθω
-εσθε		-ασθε
-έσθων		-άσθων
INFINITIVE ACTIVE		
-εῖν		-αι
INFINITIVE MIDDLE		
-έσθαι		-ασθαι

2. (a) It is a pronoun that "reflects back" to the subject of the sentence, i.e., represents the same person, place, or thing that is the subject of the sentence, but in a different place in the sentence. It is often translated in English with ___self (i.e., myself, himself, etc.). (b) There is no such thing as a nominative form of the reflexive since it is logically impossible that

the subject reflect the subject: the subject already is the subject and "reflects" nothing.

3. (a) The personal pronoun is used when referring with a pronoun to a person, place, or thing in a particular sentence which is: either the subject or predicate nominative of the sentence, if nominative; or not referring back to the subject of the sentence, if in an oblique case. (b) The intensive adjective αὐτός may modify a noun or pronoun in any case in a sentence without necessarily forcing that noun or pronoun to refer back to the subject. For example: ἔβλαπτεν ἡμᾶς αὐτούς: he was harming us ourselves. In this instance, αὐτός is modifying ἡμᾶς, but does not reflect that "we" is the subject of the sentence. It simply intensifies "us".

4. (a) See Groton, p. 119, n. 1.
   (b) One would normally expect:
   εἶπε, εἴπετε, εὗρε, εὕρετε, λάβε, λάβετε

5. See Groton §117

6.
   (1) βάλλω, βαλῶ, ἔβαλον
   (2) λαμβάνω, λήψομαι, ἔλαβον
   (3) εὑρίσκω, εὑρήσω, εὗρον/ηὗρον
   (4) μένω, μενῶ, ἔμεινα
   (5) συλλαμβάνω, συλλήψομαι, συνέλαβον
   (6) λέγω, ἐρῶ, εἶπον
   (7) ἔχω, ἕξω/σχήσω, ἔσχον
   (8) φεύγω, φεύξομαι, ἔφυγον
   (9) λείπω, λείψω, ἔλιπον
   (10) φέρω, οἴσω, ἤνεγκον/ἤνεγκα

7.
	Reflexive	Personal	Translations
(1)	ἡμῶν αὐτῶν	ἡμῶν	of ourselves (our own); of us (our)
(2)	σεαυτῷ, σεαυτῇ	σοί, σοι	to/for yourself; to/for you
(3)	ἑαυτούς, -άς, -ά	αὐτούς, -άς, ά	themselves; them
(4)	ὑμᾶς αὐτοὺς, -άς	ὑμᾶς	yourselves; you
(5)		ἡμεῖς	we
(6)	ἑαυτῷ, ἑαυτῇ	αὐτῷ, αὐτῇ	to/for himself, herself, itself; to/for him/her/it
(7)		ὑμεῖς	you
(8)	ἐμαυτῷ, -ῇ	ἐμοί, μοι	to/for myself; to/for me
(9)	σαυτοῦ, σαυτῆς	σοῦ, σου	of yourself (your own); of you (your)
(10)	ἑαυτοῖς, -αῖς	αὐτοῖς, -αῖς	to/for themselves; to/for them
(11)		οὗτος, αὕτη, τοῦτο	he/she/it
		ὅδε, ἥδε, τόδε	he/she/it
		ἐκεῖνος, -η, -ο	he/she/it
(12)	ἡμᾶς αὐτούς, -άς	ἡμᾶς	ourselves; us

8. (1) βάλε (2) βάλλε (3) ἐλέγοντο (4) εἶπον (5) εἰπόντων (6) ἐροῦσι (7) εὑρήσομαι (8) εὑρόμην or ηὑρόμην (9) βαλεῖν (10) βαλεῖν (11) βαλέσθαι (12) βαλεῖσθαι (13) λήψεται (14) ἔλιπε (15) λαμβάνεσθε (16) λάβεσθε (17) ἐφερόμεθα (18) οἰσόμεθα (19) ἠνεγκάμεθα or ἠνεγκόμεθα

9. (1) αὐτὴν ἐφίλησεν. (2) αὐτὸν ἐφίλησεν. (3) ἑαυτὸν ἐφίλησεν. (4) ἑαυτὴν ἐφίλησεν. (5) τὸ ἑαυτῆς ὄνομα ἐφίλησεν. (6) τὸ ὄνομα αὐτῆς ἐφίλησεν. (7) τὸ ἑαυτοῦ ὄνομα ἐφίλησεν. (8) ἡμᾶς ἔμειναν. (9) αὐτοὶ ἡμᾶς ἔμειναν. (10) αὐτοὶ ἐμείναμεν αὐτούς. (11) τὴν ἐπιστολὴν ἐπέμψατε. (12) τὴν ἐπιστολὴν ὑμῖν αὐτοῖς ἐπέμψατε. (13) αὐτὸν ἔβαλες. (14) σαυτὴν [or σαυτὸν] ἔβαλες. (15) ἐμὲ [or ἐμαυτὸν or ἐμαυτὴν] εὑρήσω. (16) αὐτὸς [or αὐτὴ] αὐτὸν εὑρήσω. (17) τὸ αὐτοῦ βιβλίον ἤνεγκεν; (18) τὸ βιβλίον αὐτοῦ ἤνεγκεν; (19) τὸ βιβλίον ἡμῶν ἤνεγκεν; (20) τὸ ἡμῶν αὐτῶν βιβλίον ἠνέγκαμεν;

(21) τοὺς αὑτοῦ οἰκέτας ἔφυγεν ὁ δεσπότης; (22) αὐτοὺς ἔφυγεν ὁ δεσπότης; (23) τὸν ἑαυτῶν δεσπότην ἔφυγον; (24) τὸν δεσπότην αὐτῆς ἔφυγον;

10.   Check your answers against **9.** in the exercises for Lesson 19.

Lesson 20

1.   (a) When one speaks of the perfect of the Greek verb, one is indicating that the verb shows completed action in regard to the present. (b) When one speaks of the pluperfect of the Greek verb, one is indicating that the verb shows completed action in regard to a time in the past.

2.   The time-reference in the perfect verb is the present; its aspect regards action as complete. The time-reference in the pluperfect verb is the past; its aspect regards action as complete as well.

3.   (a) This tense has no augments or reduplication, and uses a theme vowel in o/ω and ε for its personal endings. This is a primary tense. (b) This tense typically has a σ suffixed to its stem before receiving its personal endings. It shares with the present a theme vowel in o/ω and ε. This is a primary tense. (c) This tense always receives an ε-augment and uses secondary personal endings themed in o/ε. This is a secondary tense. (d) This tense has two distinct formations: the first aorist and the second aorist. Typically for both, however, the verb receives an ε-augment. Both the first and second aorist have secondary endings. However, with the first aorist, the personal endings are themed in α; with the second aorist, in o/ε. (e) This tense has two distinct formations: the first and second perfect. Typically in both, however, the verb stem is reduplicated while the personal endings are themed by the vowel α. The first perfect receives a κ on the end of its stem. (f) This tense is marked by reduplication and an ε-augment. It has secondary endings.

4.   (a) The similarities between the perfect and pluperfect are that they are both built from the fourth principal part and they both typically have a reduplicated stem. (b) The similarities between the pluperfect and aorist and imperfect consist in this, that inasmuch as they are all secondary tenses, they all receive the ε-augment in some form or another.

5.   (a) fourth; (b) first; (c) second; (d) first; (e) fourth; (f) third

6.

Tense	Act.	Mid.	Pass.	Infinitive	Indicative	Imperative
Present	X	X	X	X	X	X
Imperfect	X	X	X		X	
Future	X	X		X	X	
Aorist	X	X		X	X	X
Perfect	X			X	X	
Pluperfect	X				X	

7.   The difference between the two is that the second perfect stem does not end in κ. The similarities are that both typically have a reduplicated stem and both share the personal endings themed in α.

8.   (1)   ῥίπτω, ῥίψω, ἔρριψα, ἔρριφα
          (2)   φυλάττω, φυλάξω, ἐφύλαξα, πεφύλαχα
          (3)   προσβάλλω, προσβαλῶ, προσέβαλον, προσβέβληκα
          (4)   κλέπτω, κλέψω, ἔκλεψα, κέκλοφα
          (5)   τρέπω, τρέψω, ἔτρεψα, τέτροφα
          (6)   κελεύω, κελεύσω, ἐκέλευσα, κεκέλευκα
          (7)   πέμπω, πέμψω, ἔπεμψα, πέπομφα

(8) συλλαμβάνω, συλλήψομαι, συνέλαβον, συνείληφα
(9) τιμάω, τιμήσω, ἐτίμησα, τετίμηκα
(10) βλάπτω, βλάψω, ἔβλαψα, βέβλαφα
(11) ἀπολείπω, ἀπολείψω, ἀπέλιπον, ἀπολέλοιπα
(12) πείθω, πείσω, ἔπεισα, πέποιθα / πέπεικα
(13) πλήττω, πλήξω, ἔπληξα, πέπληγα
(14) φέρω, οἴσω, ἤνεγκα/ἤνεγκον, ἐνήνοχα
(15) ποιέω, ποιήσω, ἐποίησα, πεποίηκα
(16) γράφω, γράψω, ἔγραψα, γέγραφα
(17) πράττω, πράξω, ἔπραξα, πέπραγα/πέπραχα
(18) ἀγγέλλω, ἀγγελῶ, ἤγγειλα, ἤγγελκα
(19) βλέπω, βλέψομαι, ἔβλεψα, βέβλεφα
(20) λείπω, λείψω, ἔλιπον, λέλοιπα
(21) χαίρω, χαιρήσω, ἐχαίρησα, κεχάρηκα
(22) ακούω, ἀκούσομαι, ἤκουσα, ἀκήκοα
(23) φεύγω, φεύξομαι, ἔφυγον, πέφευγα
(24) ἀλλάττω, ἀλλάξω, ἤλλαξα, ἤλλαχα
(25) διώκω, διώξω, ἐδίωξα, δεδίωχα
(26) ἐπιπλήττω, ἐπιπλήξω, ἐπέπληξα, ἐπιπέπληγα

9.

(1) διώκω, perfect active indicative, 2nd person singular, "you have pursued"
(2) διώκω, pluperfect active indicative, 2nd person singular, "you had pursued"
(3) διώκω, aorist active indicative, 2nd person singular, "you pursued"
(4) διώκω, imperfect active indicative, 2nd person singular, "you were pursuing"
(5) ποιέω, pluperfect active indicative, 3rd person plural, "they had made"
(6) ποιέω, perfect active infinitive, "to have made"
(7) ποιέω, perfect active indicative, 2nd person singular, "you have made"
(8) ἐπιπλήττω, perfect active indicative, 3rd person singular, "he has rebuked"
(9) πλήττω, pluperfect active indicative, 3rd person singular, "she had struck"
(10) ἐπιπλήττω, pluperfect active indicative, 3rd person singular, "he had rebuked"
(11) ἐπιπλήττω, aorist active indicative, 3rd person singular, "he rebuked"
(12) πλήττω, imperfect active indicative, 3rd person singular, "he was striking"
(13) γράφω, perfect active indicative, 1st person plural, "we have written"
(14) γράφω, perfect active infinitive, "to have written"
(15) γράφω, pluperfect active indicative, 1st person plural, "we had written"
(16) γράφω, 1st aorist active indicative, 1st person plural, "we wrote"
(17) ἐρωτάω, 1st aorist active indicative, 3rd person plural, "they asked"
(18) ἐρωτάω, perfect active indicative, 3rd person plural, "they have asked"
(19) ἐρωτάω, pluperfect active indicative, 3rd person plural, "they had asked"
(20) ἐρωτάω, perfect active infinitive, "to have asked"

(21) ἀκούω, 1st aorist active indicative, 2nd person plural, "you heard"

(22) ἀκούω, 1st aorist active imperative, 2nd person plural, "hear!"

(23) ἀκούω, perfect active indicative, 2nd person plural, "you have heard"

(24) ἀκούω, pluperfect active indicative, 2nd person plural, "you had heard"

(25) ἀκούω, future middle indicative, 2nd person plural, "you will hear"

(26) ἀκούω, present active indicative or imperative, 2nd person plural, "you are hearing" or "hear!"

10. (1) τὴν Μοῖραν κατὰ τοῦ οὐρανοῦ ἐβεβλήκειν ὁ θεός. (2) λίθον ἔρριφεν ὁ Ἕλλην. (3) λίθον ἔρριψεν ὁ Ἕλλην. (4) λίθον ἐρρίφειν ὁ Ἕλλην. (5) τὴν γῆν τὴν Ἑλληνικὴν ζητοῦμεν. (6) τὴν γῆν τὴν Ἑλληνικὴν ἐζητήκεμεν. (7) ἠγγέλκειν ὁ ἄγγελος τάδε· ἐπεὶ τὰς ἀσπίδας ἐρρίφεσαν οἱ Ἕλληνες, εἰς δένδρα μεγάλα ἐζήτησαν φυγεῖν. (8) ὑπὲρ ἡμῶν εἴρηκεν ὁ Σωκράτης, ἡμεῖς γὰρ αὐτὸν ἐτετιμήκεμεν καὶ ἀγῶνας ἐσχήκεμεν καὶ ἐτεθύκεμεν τοῖς ἀθανάτοις ὑπὲρ αὐτοῦ. (9) λέγεται ὁ Σωκράτης τὴν ἀλήθειαν τὴν τῆς φιλοσοφίας κατὰ τοῦ οὐρανοῦ αὐτοῦ ἐνηνοχέναι. (10) ἐπεὶ τοὺς πολεμίους κατὰ θάλατταν διῶξαι ἐζητήκεμεν, κατὰ γῆν ἵπποις ἐτρέψαντο.

11. (1) ἐπεὶ ὁ φιλόσοφος ἐζητήκει τὴν ἀλήθειαν, ἐρρίφασιν αὐτὸν οἱ πολλοὶ κατὰ τῶν τειχῶν. (2) εἶπεν ὁ φύλαξ τάδε· τετρόφαμεν τὴν ἅμαξαν ὑπὲρ τὸν ποταμόν, οἱ γὰρ πολέμιοι ἐζητήκεσαν ῥῖψαι αὐτὴν εἰς αὐτόν. (3) ἠρώτησεν ἡμᾶς ὁ δεσπότης τόδε· κεκλόφατε τὸν θησαυρόν μου; ὦ κακοὶ οἰκέται, εἴληφα αὐτὸν πρὸς τοῦ Σωκράτους καὶ προσεπεποιήκη αὐτῷ ἀπὸ τοῦ τῶν κλωπῶν θησαυροῦ. (4) ζητοῦμεν τὴν γῆν ἡμῶν, τὴν Ἑλλάδα. (5) λέγεται ὁ ἄνθρωπος εἰρηκέναι τάδε ἐπεὶ τὴν γῆν εἰς θησαυρὸν ἠλλάχειν· εὕρηκα· ἤλλαχα τὴν γῆν εἰς ἀληθῆ θησαυρόν. (6) ὁ μὲν κακὸς τοὺς δούλους πέπεικεν ἐνεγκεῖν τὰ ἑαυτοῦ γέρα εἰς τὴν οἰκίαν, οἱ δ᾽ αὐτῷ πεποίθασιν. σοφοὶ δ᾽ οὐκ ἦσαν ἐκεῖνοι καὶ ἔλυσεν αὐτοὺς ὁ κακὸς ἐπεὶ ἐκεκομίκεσαν τὰ γέρα εἰς τὴν οἰκίαν. (7) οἱ σοφοὶ τὰ ἱμάτια πεπωλήκασι πολλῶν ὀβολῶν. (8) τήνδε τὴν ἐπιστολὴν ἔγραψεν ἡ κόρη τῷ καλῷ νεανίᾳ· ὦ καλὲ καὶ ἀγαθὲ νεανία, ἐγώ σε πολὺ πεφίληκα, καὶ πέπεικα τὰς δούλας μου ταύτην τὴν ἐπιστολὴν πρός σε ἐνεγκεῖν. φιλήσεις με; τρέψαι οὖν νῦν πρός με. σὲ μεμένηκα. (9) μὴ ὠφέλει τὴν ἄνθρωπον· ὁ ῥήτωρ αὐτὴν ἤδη πολὺ ὠφέληκεν. (10) οἱ μὲν ὀλίγοι τῷ ῥήτορι τῷ κακῷ οὐ πεποίθασιν, οἱ δὲ πολλοὶ καὶ πεποίθασιν αὐτῷ καὶ πολὺ τετιμήκασιν.

12. Check your answers against **10.** in the exercises for Lesson 20.

13. Check your answers against **11.** in the exercises for Lesson 20.

Lesson 21

1. The interrogative pronoun/adjective will always receive the acute accent on the first syllable, with the exception of the contracted forms τοῦ and τῷ, while the indefinite pronoun/adjective is enclitic. For a review of enclitic accentuation, see Groton §80.

2. τίνος and τίνι; τοῦ and τῷ

3. τινός and τινί; του and τω

4. ἅττα

5.
τίς	τί
τίνος	τίνος
τίνι	τίνι
τίνα	τί

τίνες	τίνα
τίνων	τίνων
τίσι(ν)	τίσι(ν)
τίνας	τίνα

6.

τις	τι
τινός	τινός
τινί	τινί
τινά	τι
τινές	τινά
τινῶν	τινῶν
τισί(ν)	τισί(ν)
τινάς	τινά

7. See Groton §127.

8. See Groton §§ 117, 128, 129.

9. (1) φοβοῦμαι· ἐμέ τις ἀποκτενεῖ. (2) ἀπέθανεν ὁ Σωκράτης ἐπεὶ οἱ Ἕλληνες αὐτὸν διὰ τὴν φιλοσοφίαν αὐτοῦ ἀπέκτειναν. (3) πολὺς φόβος μοί ἐστι, πολλοὶ γὰρ περὶ ἐμοῦ ἀποθνήσκουσιν. (4) ἐμή ἐστιν ἡ ἀσπὶς αὕτη, οὐ σή. (5) ἡμετέρα ἐστὶν ἡ ἀσπὶς αὕτη, οὐχ ὑμετέρα. (6) αὕτη ἡ ἀσπὶς αὐτῇ ἐστίν, οὐκ αὐταῖς. (7) τί τὴν τῶν Ἑλλήνων τριήρη κεκλόφατε; (8) τίνας βέβλαφεν ὁ Σωκράτης; (9) τίσι ταύτην τὴν ἐπιστολὴν πέμψειν μέλλεις; (10) τίνων τὰ τέκνα κέκλοφας; ἐν τῇ σῇ οἰκίᾳ τῇ ἀληθείᾳ ἀποθανοῦνται. (11) μή με φόβει· πολλὰ φοβοῦμαι. (12) ἠλλάξατο ὁ Σωκράτης τι ἐκείνων τῶν ὀβολῶν. (13) ἐμοὶ εἶπεν φύλαξ τις τάδε· τινὲς μὲν φύλακες ἀπὸ τῶν τειχῶν ἐπεφεύγεσαν, τινὲς δ᾽ ὑπὲρ αὐτὰ ἐτρέψαντο.

10. Check your answers against **9.** in the exercises for Lesson 21.

Lesson 22

1. (1) first (2) second (3) fifth (4) first (5) first (6) first (7) third (8) fourth (9) fifth (10) fourth

2. See Groton §133.

3. Basically, the first consonant of the personal ending of such a verb combines with the final consonant of the stem, often forming a new consonantal sound.

4.

Stem Consonant	+ Personal Ending Consonant	= ?	Other Stem Endings
π	σ	ψ	φ, β
κ	σθ	χθ	γ, χ
λ	τ	λτ	
χ	μ	γμ	κ, γ
ρ	σ	ρσ	
δ	σθ	σθ	τ, θ, ζ
ν	any ending	Such forms do not exist (Groton §135.5)	
ζ	τ	στ	τ, δ, θ
ν	μ	σμ	τ, δ, θ, ζ
β	σ	ψ	π, φ
θ	τ	στ	τ, δ, ζ

5. (1) ἄγω, ἄξω, ἤγαγον, ἦχα, ἦγμαι
(2) βάλλω, βαλῶ, ἔβαλον, βέβληκα, βέβλημαι
(3) πείθω, πείσω, ἔπεισα, πέπεικα/πέποιθα, πέπεισμαι
(4) γράφω, γράψω, ἔγραψα, γέγραφα, γέγραμμαι
(5) φυλάττω, φυλάξω, ἐφύλαξα, πεφύλαχα, πεφύλαγμαι
(6) ἀπολείπω, ἀπολείψω, ἀπέλιπον, ἀπολέλοιπα, ἀπολέλειμμαι

(7) κλέπτω, κλέψω, ἔκλεψα, κέκλοφα, κέκλεμμαι

(8) παιδεύω, παιδεύσω, ἐπαίδευσα, πεπαίδευκα, πεπαίδευμαι

(9) προσβάλλω, προσβαλῶ, προσέβαλον, προσβέβληκα, προσβέβλημαι

(10) πλήττω, πλήξω, ἔπληξα, πέπληγα, πέπληγμαι

(11) ἀλλάττω, ἀλλάξω, ἤλλαξα, ἤλλαχα, ἤλλαγμαι

(12) λαμβάνω, λήψομαι, ἔλαβον, εἴληφα, εἴλημμαι

(13) πράττω, πράξω, ἔπραξα, πέπραγα, πέπραγμαι

(14) φέρω, οἴσω, ἤνεγκα / ἤνεγκον, ἐνήνοχα, ἐνήνεγμαι

(15) ἀγγέλλω, ἀγγελῶ, ἤγγειλα, ἤγγελκα, ἤγγελμαι

(16) λέγω, ἐρῶ, εἶπον, εἴρηκα, εἴρημαι

(17) τρέπω, τρέψω, ἔτρεψα, τέτροφα, τέτραμμαι

(18) χαίρω, χαιρήσω, ἐχαίρησα, κεχάρηκα, κεχάρημαι

(19) εὑρίσκω, εὑρήσω, εὗρον, εὕρηκα, εὕρημαι

(20) ῥίπτω, ῥίψω, ἔρριψα, ἔρριφα, ἔρριμμαι

(21) διώκω, διώξω, ἐδίωξα, δεδίωχα, δεδίωγμαι

(22) ἁρπάζω, ἁρπάσω, ἥρπασα, ἥρπακα, ἥρπασμαι

(23) ἐπιπλήττω, ἐπιπλήξω, ἐπέπληξα, ἐπιπέπληγα, ἐπιπέπληγμαι

(24) συλλαμβάνω, συλλήψομαι, συνέλαβον, συνείληφα, συνείλημμαι

(25) λείπω, λείψω, ἔλιπον, λέλοιπα, λέλειμμαι

(26) πέμπω, πέμψω, ἔπεμψα, πέπομφα, πέπεμμαι

6.

	Perf. Mid./Pass.	Plup. Mid./Pass.	Inf.	Translations
(1)	ἦγμαι	ἤγμην	ἦχθαι	I have been led
	ἦξαι	ἦξο		I had been led
	ἦκται	ἦκτο		to have been led
	ἤγμεθα	ἤγμεθα		
	ἦχθε	ἦχθε		
	(ἠγμένοι εἰσί)	(ἠγμένοι ἦσαν)		
(2)	πέπεισμαι	ἐπεπείσμην	πεπεῖσθαι	I have been persuaded
	πέπεισαι	ἐπέπεισο		I had been persuaded
	πέπεισται	ἐπέπειστο		to have been
	πεπείσμεθα	ἐπεπείσμεθα		persuaded
	πέπεισθε	ἐπέπεισθε		
	(πεπεισμένοι εἰσί)	(πεπεισμένοι ἦσαν)		
(3)	πέπληγμαι	ἐπεπλήγμην	πεπλῆχθαι	I have been struck
	πέπληξαι	ἐπέπληξο		I had been struck
	πέπληκται	ἐπέπληκτο		to have been struck
	πεπλήγμεθα	ἐπεπλήγμεθα		
	πέπληχθε	ἐπέπληχθε		
	(πεπληγμένοι εἰσί)	(πεπληγμένοι ἦσαν)		
(4)	λέλυμαι	ἐλελύμην	λελῦσθαι	I have been destroyed
	λέλυσαι	ἐλέλυσο		I had been destroyed
	λέλυται	ἐλέλυτο		to have been destroyed
	λελύμεθα	ἐλελύμεθα		
	λέλυσθε	ἐλέλυσθε		
	λέλυνται	ἐλέλυντο		
(5)	λέλειμμαι	ἐλελείμμην	λελεῖφθαι	I have been left
	λέλειψαι	ἐλέλειψο		I had been left
	λέλειπται	ἐλέλειπτο		to have been left

λελείμμεθα   ἐλελείμμεθα
λέλειφθε   ἐλέλειφθε
(λελειμμένοι   (λελειμμένοι
εἰσί)   ἦσαν)

(6)

προσβέβλημαι	προσεβεβλήμην	προσβεβλῆσθαι	I have been attacked
προσβέβλησαι	προσεβέβλησο		I had been attacked
προσβέβληται	προσεβέβλητο		to have been attacked
προσβεβλήμεθα	προσεβεβλήμεθα		
προσβέβλησθε	προσεβέβλησθε		
προσβέβληνται	προσεβέβληντο		

(7)

συνείλημμαι	συνειλήμμην	συνειλῆφθαι	I have been gathered
συνείληψαι	συνείληψο		I had been gathered
συνείληπται	συνείληπτο		to have been gathered
συνειλήμμεθα	συνειλήμμεθα		
συνείληφθε	συνείληφθε		
(συνειλημμένοι	(συνειλημμένοι		
εἰσί)	ἦσαν)		

(8)

ἤγγελμαι	ἠγγέλμην	ἠγγέλθαι	I have been announced
ἤγγελσαι	ἤγγελσο		I had been announced
ἤγγελται	ἤγγελτο		to have been
ἠγγέλμεθα	ἠγγέλμεθα		announced
ἤγγελθε	ἤγγελθε		

(ἠγγελμένοι εἰσί) (ἠγγελμένοι ἦσαν)

7. See Groton §137.

8. (1) πέπληξαί μοι. (2) πέπληγμαί σοι. (3) πολὺ αὐτὴν ἐβεβλάφειν. (4) πολὺ ἐβέβλαπτο αὐτῷ. (5) εὐδαίμονα βίον ἄξομεν. (6) εὐδαίμονα βίον ἤχαμεν. (7) εὐδαίμονα βίον ἤγομεν. (8) εὐδαίμων βίος ἡμῖν ἦκται. (9) εὐδαίμων βίος ἡμῖν ἦκτο. (10) τοῦτον τὸν νόμον ἡμῖν πέπομφεν ὁ δεσπότης. (11) οὗτος ὁ νόμος ἡμῖν πρὸς τοῦ δεσπότου πέπεμπται. (12) οἵ τε νόμοι καὶ οἱ τρόποι οἱ τῶν Ἑλλήνων αὐτοὺς ἐπεπείκεσαν ἀγαθὸν βίον ζητῆσαι. (13) τὸν βίον μου λαβέ, τὴν δὲ ψυχήν μου μὴ λαβέ. (14) οὐδ᾽ αὐτοὺς ἀπεκτόνη, οὐδ᾽ ἐτεθνήκεσαν. (15) ὑμεῖς μὲν τοῖς ῥήτορσιν ἐπιπέπληχθε, ἄλλοι δὲ πόρρω πεφεύγασιν. (16) τῇ τριήρει προσβαλεῖν ἐπέπεισθε τε καὶ ἐκεκέλευσθε· τί ἐμελλήσατε; (17) παρὰ τοὺς ἑαυτῶν νόμους τε καὶ τρόπους, ἔφυγον οἱ Ἕλληνες ἐπεὶ προσεβέβληντο. (18) ἔστι μὲν ἄνθρωπον θῦσαι, παρὰ δὲ τὸν νόμον ἐστίν. ἔστι τε θῦσαι ζῷον καὶ κατὰ τὸν νόμον ἐστίν. (19) μηδ᾽ εἴπετε μηδ᾽ ἐθελήσατε εἰπεῖν τάδ᾽· ἀποθανεῖται ὁ δεσπότης. (20) οὔτ᾽ ἐδεδίωκτο οὔθ᾽ ηὕρητο ἐπεὶ ἀπέθανεν.

9. Check your answers against 8. in the exercises for Lesson 22.

Lesson 23

1. A relative pronoun is a pronoun (a word that "stands in" for a noun) used to refer back (or forward) to another noun or pronoun (known as the "antecedent") in a sentence. A relative pronoun stands at the head of a relative clause.

2. A relative pronoun takes its number and gender from the word in the sentence to which it refers. For example, given a sentence like ἡ θεράπαινα τὰς κλίνας κέκλοφεν, a relative pronoun referring to ἡ θεράπαινα would have to be feminine singular, while a relative pronoun referring to τὰς

κλίνας would have to be feminine plural. The case of the relative pronoun, however, is not determined by the case of the noun it refers to, but by its use in its own clause. Thus, if it is the direct object of the verb in its own clause, it will typically be in the accusative; if showing possession, genitive, etc.

3. See Groton §141, esp. 1–4.

4. See Groton §142.

5. (1) ὅν (2) ᾗ (3) ἅς (4) ἧς (5) οὗ (6) οἷς (7) οὕς (8) ὅ (9) ὧν

6. (1) πάντα (2) πάσῃ (3) πάσας (4) πάσης (5) παντός (6) πᾶσι (7) πάντας (8) πᾶν (9) πάντων

7.
dat. singular	dat. plural	acc. singular	nom. plural	acc. plural
ἔτει	ἔτεσι(ν)	ἔτος	ἔτη	ἔτη
ἡμέρᾳ	ἡμέραις	ἡμέραν	ἡμέραι	ἡμέρας
νυκτί	νυξί(ν)	νύκτα	νύκτες	νύκτας

8. (1) τὴν κόρην εἶδον ἣ καλή ἐστιν. (2) τὴν κόρην εἶδον ἧς ὁ θησαυρὸς πολύς. (3) τὰς κόρας εἶδον αἷς ἐπιστολὰς ἔπεμψα. (4) τὰς κόρας εἶδον ἃς ἐφίλει ὁ δεσπότης. (5) τὸν ῥήτορα ὅς ἐστιν εὐδαίμων εἶδον. (6) οὗ ὁ λόγος ἀγαθὸς ἦν τὸν ῥήτορα ὄψομαι. (7) ὦπται / ἑώραται ὁ ῥήτωρ ᾧ ἐπέπληξαν οἱ πολλοί. (8) πάντα τὰ τέκνα ἃ συνειλήφειν ἀμφ᾽ ἑαυτὸν ὁ φιλόσοφος ἑώρακεν. (9) πάντα τὰ τέκνα ἑώρων ὧν τὰ ζῷα κλωψὶν ἐκέκλεπτο. (10) ἡ πᾶσα τριήρης ἐλέλυτο κλωψίν ἕως τοῖς τῶν πολεμίων τείχεσι προσεβάλλομεν. (11) ἐτρέποντο καθ᾽ ἡμέραν οἱ κλῶπες εἰς τὴν τῶν πολεμίων ἀγορὰν οἷς πολὺς θησαυρὸς ἦν. (12) τὴν πᾶσαν ἡμέραν ἑώραταί μοι ὁ δαίμων. (13) μόνον ὀλίγων ἡμερῶν πάσας τὰς ἀσπίδας ἃς παρὰ τῶν φυλάκων ἐκεκλόφεμεν ἐπωλήσαμεν. (14) μὴ λυσάντων τὸν θησαυρὸν ὃν τὰ τοῦ ῥήτορος τέκνα πολλὰ ἔτη συνείληφεν.

9. Check your answers against 8. in the exercises for Lesson 23.

Lesson 24

1. A participle is a word which "participates" in two parts of speech: the verb and the adjective.

2. One should expect that it will modify a noun, and agree with the noun it modifies in number, case, and gender. One should also expect that it will be able to occupy the various positions of an adjective (attributive and predicate). See Groton §145.

3. One should expect that like a verb a participle will have voice (active, middle, and passive) and tense (aorist, perfect, present, future). One should also expect that it will be able to receive objects and other verbal complements. See Groton §145.

4. A participle may be in either the attributive or predicate position. When it is in the predicate position, its use can be either circumstantial or supplementary. See Groton §151.

5. See Groton §150. Basically: (a) in the present, the participle expresses action contemporaneous with the action expressed in the main verb; (b) in the aorist, it may express action prior to the action of the main verb; (c) in the perfect, it expresses a state of complete action in respect to the time of the main verb; and (d) in the future, it expresses action subsequent to that of the main verb.

6. (1) ὄντι (2) ἡρπακυίαις (3) λιπόντος (4) πλήξων (5) εἰληφυίᾳ (6) φυγόν (7) πέμψαντα (8) ῥίπτοντες (9) ἀποκτενούσας (10) βεβλεφότων

7.   (1) ὠφελούντων
            ὠφελουσῶν
            ὠφελοῦσι(ν)
        (2) γελῶντα
            γελῶσα
            γελῶν
        (3) δηλοῦντας
            δηλούσαις
            δηλοῦντος

8.   (a) καλῶν   καλοῦσα   καλοῦν
            καλοῦντος   καλούσης   καλοῦντος
            καλοῦντι   καλούσῃ   καλοῦντι
            καλοῦντα   καλοῦσαν   καλοῦν
            καλοῦντες   καλοῦσαι   καλοῦντα
            καλούντων   καλουσῶν   καλούντων
            καλοῦσι(ν)   καλούσαις   καλοῦσι(ν)
            καλοῦντας   καλούσας   καλοῦντα
        (b) Same as above
        (c) καλέσας   καλέσασα   καλέσαν
            καλέσαντος   καλεσάσης   καλέσαντος
            καλέσαντι   καλεσάσῃ   καλέσαντι
            καλέσαντα   καλέσασαν   καλέσαν
            καλέσαντες   καλέσασαι   καλέσαντα
            καλεσάντων   καλεσασῶν   καλεσάντων
            καλέσασι(ν)   καλεσάσαις   καλέσασι(ν)
            καλέσαντας   καλεσάσας   καλέσαντα
        (d) κεκληκώς   κεκληκυῖα   κεκληκός
            κεκληκότος   κεκληκυίας   κεκληκότος
            κεκληκότι   κεκληκυίᾳ   κεκληκότι
            κεκληκότα   κεκληκυῖαν   κεκληκός
            κεκληκότες   κεκληκυῖαι   κεκληκότα
            κεκληκότων   κεκληκυιῶν   κεκληκότων
            κεκληκόσι(ν) κεκληκυίαις   κεκληκόσι(ν)
            κεκληκότας   κεκληκυίας   κεκληκότα

9.   (a) (1) I am sending this to the guardsman who loves his daughter. (2) I, loving the girl, am sending this to the guardsman. (3) I am sending this to the guardsman although he loves my girl. (4) We have received many gifts from the mistress who had invited us to dinner. (5) We received many gifts from the mistress since we had invited her whole household to dinner. (6) The child took joy in the good hospitality. (7) The child who had found the treasure took joy in the good hospitality. (8) The child rejoiced in the good hospitality when he had found the treasure of friendship. (9) The orators rejoiced in their fate although they had found their death. (10) The orators who had found hope rejoiced in their fate. (11) Without fear there is not hope. (12) I called the maidservant to the door on the pretext of hitting her. (13) The stranger has borne to you gifts worth much with the avowed intention of honouring you.
     (b) (1) attributive (2) circumstantial (3) circumstantial (4) attributive (5) circumstantial (6) no participle (7) attributive (8) circumstantial (9) circumstantial (10) attributive (11) no participle (12) circumstantial (13) circumstantial.

10.   Check your answers against **9.** in the exercises for Lesson 24.

Lesson 25

1. While all middle/passive participles (with the exception of the aorist passive, which we have not yet learned) are formed by appending –μενος, –η, –ον (with or without an intervening theme vowel) to the stem of the verb, there are several distinct formations. (a) The stem of the future middle typically ends with a σ. The future middle will always have a theme vowel in ο. The accent on the future middle is recessive. (b) The first aorist middle, like the future, has a stem typically ending in σ. The theme vowel, however, for the aorist middle is not ο, but α. The accent on the first aorist middle is recessive. (c) The perfect middle/passive is distinguished from the others by being built off of the fifth principal part. Its stem is therefore typically reduplicated. Furthermore, as with the perfect middle/passive indicatives and infinitive, the ending of the participle is attached directly to the stem of the word without any intervening theme vowel. This, of course, leads to certain stem changes when the stem ends in a consonant. A further difference between the perfect middle/passive and other middle/passive participial forms is the accent of the perfect middle/passive: its accent is not recessive, but is "at home" on the **first syllable of the participial ending**. (d) Unlike the first aorist middle participle, the second aorist variety has as its theme vowel ο. However, like the first aorist, it is formed from the stem of the third principal part and its accent is recessive (unlike its active form!).

2.

(a)	first principal part	λείπω	λειπόμενος, η, ον
(b)	second principal part	λείψω	λειψόμενος, η, ον
(c)	third principal part	ἔλιπον	λιπόμενος, η, ον
(d)	fifth principal	λέλειμμαι (=λέλειπ-μαι)	
			λελειμμένος, η, ον
			(=λελειπ-μένος)

3. (a) Check your explanation against Groton §159. (b) Examples: ἔχαιρον οἱ φύλακες τὸν θησαυρὸν φυλάττοντες. = The guards used to enjoy guarding the treasury. ἐπαυσάμην πλήττων τὸν ἵππον. = I stopped hitting the horse. ἔπαυσα τὸν φύλακα πλήττοντα τὴν ἵππον. = I stopped the guard from hitting the mare.

4.
   (1) λύοντος, λυούσης, λύοντος, λυομένου, λυομένης, λυομένου
   (2) λύσοντος, λυσούσης, λύσοντος, λυσομένου, λυσομένης, λυσομένου
   (3) λύσαντος, λυσάσης, λύσαντος, λυσαμένου, λυσαμένης, λυσαμένου
   (4) λελυκότος, λελυκυίας, λελυκότος
   (5) λελυμένου, λελυμένης, λελυμένου

5.

	masculine dative singular	feminine accusative plural
(1)	εἰπόντι, εἰπομένῳ	εἰπούσας, εἰπομένας
(2)	ἀγγείλαντι, ἀγγειλαμένῳ	ἀγγειλάσας, ἀγγειλαμένας
(3)	διδάξαντι, διδαξαμένῳ	διδαξάσας, διδαξαμένας
(4)	συλλαβόντι, συλλαβομένῳ	συλλαβούσας, συλλαβομένας
(5)	ἐνεγκόντι, ἐνεγκομένῳ	ἐνεγκούσας, ἐνεγκομένας
(6)	ἀποκτείναντι, ἀποκτειναμένῳ	ἀποκτεινάσας, ἀποκτειναμένας
(7)	εὑρόντι, εὑρομένῳ	εὑρούσας, εὑρομένας
(8)	πείσαντι, πεισαμένῳ	πεισάσας, πεισαμένας
(9)	ἀπολιπόντι, ἀπολιπομένῳ	ἀπολιπούσας, ἀπολιπομένας

6.

	neuter accusative plural	feminine accusative singular
(1)	εἰρηκότα, εἰρημένα	εἰρηκυῖαν, εἰρημένην
(2)	ἠγγελκότα, ἠγγελμένα	ἠγγελκυῖαν, ἠγγελμένην
(3)	δεδιδαχότα, δεδιδαγμένα	δεδιδαχυῖαν, δεδιδαγμένην

    (4) συνειληφότα, συνειλημμένα   συνειληφυῖαν, συνειλημμένην
    (5) ἐνηνοχότα, ἐνηνεγμένα   ἐνηνοχυῖαν, ἐνηνεγμένην
    (6) ἀπεκτονότα, _____   ἀπεκτονυῖαν, _____
    (7) εὑρηκότα, εὑρημένα   εὑρηκυῖαν, εὑρημένην
    (8) πεποιθότα, πεπεισμένα   πεποιθυῖαν, πεπεισμένην
        (πεπεικότα)   (πεπεικυῖαν)
    (9) ἀπολελοιπότα, ἀπολελειμμένα ἀπολελοιπυῖαν, ἀπολελειμμένην

7. (1) οὐκ ἐπαυσάμην διδάσκουσα. (2) οὐκ ἐπαυσάμην διδάσκουσα τοὺς μαθητάς. (3) οὐκ ἐπαυσάμην διδάσκουσα τοὺς μαθητὰς τοὺς νῦν εὖ πεπαιδευμένους. (4) οὐκ ἐπαυσάμην διδάσκουσα τοὺς μαθητὰς ἅτε εὖ πεπαιδευμένους. (5) οὐκ ἔπαυσα τοὺς διδασκάλους λέγοντας καίπερ δόξας κακὰς ἔχοντας. (6) τοὺς διδασκάλους τοὺς κακοὺς ἔπαυσας ἀλλάττοντας τοὺς νόμους τοὺς ἀγαθοὺς εἰς κακούς. (7) ἐχαίρησαν οἱ παῖδες τὰ σώματα τῶν διδασκάλων γράφοντες. (8) πολλάκις ὑπὸ τούτου τοῦ ἀναξίου ῥήτορος ἐπιπληττόμενοι, ἡμεῖς αὐτὸν τῆς δόξης ἡμῶν αὐτῶν χάριν γραψόμεθα. (9) οἱ τὰ μεγάλα γέρα ἐν τοῖς ἀγῶσι κομιούμενοι δεῖπνα πολλά τε μεγάλα τε ἐν τῇ ἀγορᾷ ποιήσουσιν. (10) ὡς πάντας τοὺς Ἕλληνας συλληψόμενος, ἔσπευσεν ὁ ῥήτωρ κατά τε γῆν κατά τε θάλατταν κελεύων τοὺς πολλοὺς καίπερ οὐκ ἐθέλοντας τρέψασθαι εἰς τὴν Ἑλλάδα.

8. Check your answers against **7.** in the exercises for Lesson 25.

Lesson 26

1. A direct question states the question verbatim; an indirect question is a rewording of a question connected with its integration into the very structure of a larger sentence. In practice this leads to several differences: (a) direct questions are usually set off from any larger sentence structure by a comma, a capital letter at the beginning, and quotation marks, whereas indirect questions are not; (b) direct questions end with a question mark, both in Greek and English, whereas indirect questions do not, unless they end a larger direct question.

2. See Groton §165, 1-7.

3.   (1) πόθεν   ποθέν   ὁπόθεν
         (2) ποῖ   ποι   ὅποι
         (3) πῶς   πως   ὅπως
         (4) ποῦ   που   ὅπου
         (5) πότε   ποτέ   ὁπότε

4. Translation
         (1) from somewhere
         (2) to somewhere
         (3) somehow
         (4) somewhere
         (5) sometime

5.   (1) ᾧτινι   to/for whom
         (2) ᾗτινι   to/for whom
         (3) ἅτινα   what
         (4) ὅ τι   what
         (5) ἅστινας   whom
         (6) ἧστινος   whose
         (7) οὕστινας   whom
         (8) ὧντινων   whose
         (9) αἷστισι(ν)   to/for whom
         (10) οἷστισι(ν)   to/for whom
         (11) ὅστις   who
         (12) ἥτις   who

6. In a Greek question using negation, two possibilities present themselves. One may, on the one hand, use a negation in μή (μή and its compounds, such as ἆρα μή and μῶν). The practical effect of this is to make the question expect a negative answer. (Example: μῶν ἔλυσας τὰ τείχη; = You didn't destroy the walls, did you?). One may also choose to use a negation in οὐ (οὐ and its compounds, such as οὐκοῦν and ἆρ᾽ οὐ). The practical effect of this is to make the question expect a positive answer. (Example: ἆρ᾽ οὐ τρεψόμεθα εἰς τὴν ἀγοράν; = Aren't we going to betake ourselves into the marketplace?)

7. (1) (a) The speaker asked me, "Are you a teacher?" (b) ἠρώτησέν με ὁ ῥήτωρ εἰ ἐγὼ διδάσκαλός εἰμί. (c) The speaker asked me whether I was a teacher. (2) (a) Let the servant ask her mistress, "Do you want to betake yourself into the marketplace, or remain at home?" (b) ἐρωτησάτω ἡ θεράπαινα τὴν δέσποιναν πότερον ἐθέλει τρέψασθαι εἰς τὴν ἀγορὰν ἢ μεῖναι ἐν τῇ οἰκίᾳ. (c) Let the servant ask her mistress whether she wants to betake herself into the marketplace or remain at home. (3) (a) I stopped them from asking, "Where are our children?" (b) ἔπαυσα αὐτὰς ἐρωτώσας ὅπου εἰσὶν οἱ παῖδες αὐτῶν. (c) I stopped them from asking where their children were. (4) (a) You asked the unworthy teacher, "Which bad opinions will you teach the children today?" (b) ἠρωτήσατε τὴν ἀναξίαν διδάσκαλον ἅστινας δόξας κακὰς τοὺς παῖδας τήμερον διδάξει. (c) You asked the unworthy teacher which bad opinions she would teach the children today.

8. (1)(a) οἱ μὲν ἡμᾶς ἤδη ἠρώτησαν, Μῶν κακὴ ἡ τοῦ σώματος μοῖρα μετὰ τὸν θάνατον; οἱ δὲ, Ἆρ᾽ οὐχ ἡ τῆς ψυχῆς μοῖρα κακὴ ἐν τούτῳ τῷ βίῳ; (b) οἱ μὲν ἡμᾶς ἤδη ἠρώτησαν μῶν κακὴ ἡ τοῦ σώματος μοῖρα μετὰ τὸν θάνατον· οἱ δ᾽ ἆρ᾽ οὐχ ἡ τῆς ψυχῆς μοῖρα κακὴ ἐν τούτῳ τῷ βίῳ. (c) Some have already asked us whether the fate of the body after death is not evil; others, whether the fate of the soul isn't bad in this life.

(2)(a) ἤρώτα ὁ Σωκράτης τοὺς μαθητάς, Ποῖ, πολλάκις ὑπὸ τῶν ἀναξίων διωκομένη, φεύξεται ἡ ψυχὴ φιλοσόφου; (b) ἤρώτα ὁ Σωκράτης τοὺς μαθητὰς ὅποι, πολλάκις ὑπὸ τῶν ἀναξίων διωκομένη, φεύξεται ἡ ψυχὴ φιλοσόφου. (c) Socrates would ask his students whither, when it is often pursued by unworthy [people], a philosopher's soul would flee.

(3)(a) ἐρωτήσει ἡμᾶς ὁ διδάσκαλος, Τίνα βιβλία μεγάλα εἴδετε, ἢ οὔ τινα εἴδετε; (b) ἐρωτήσει ἡμᾶς ὁ διδάσκαλος ἅττα βιβλία μεγάλα εἴδομεν, ἢ εἰ οὔ τινα εἴδομεν. (c) The teacher will ask us which great books we have seen, or whether we have not seen any.

(4)(a) ἥρπασεν ὁ δεσπότης τοὺς κλῶπας ἐρωτῶν, Οὐ καὶ τὰ παιδία μου ἠθέλετε κλέψαι; (b) ἥρπασεν ὁ δεσπότης τοὺς κλῶπας ἐρωτῶν εἰ οὐ καὶ τὰ παιδία αὐτοῦ ἤθελον κλέψαι. (c) The master seized the thieves, asking them whether they hadn't wanted to steal his children, too.

(5) (a) εἰς τὸν θησαυρὸν τοῖς ὀφθαλμοῖς βλέπων, πολλάκις ἠρώτα ἑαυτὸν ὁ εὐδαίμων, Τίνων χάριτι μεγάλῃ ταῦτα ἔλαβον; (b) εἰς τὸν θησαυρὸν τοῖς ὀφθαλμοῖς βλέπων, πολλάκις ἠρώτα ἑαυτὸν ὁ εὐδαίμων ὧντινων χάριτι μεγάλῃ ταῦτα ἔλαβεν. (c) Gazing at his treasure with his eyes, the prosperous [one] would often ask himself by whose great favour he had received these things.

Lesson 27

1. Six.

2. (a) present active, middle, passive; imperfect active, middle, passive.
   (b) future active and middle
   (c) aorist active and middle

    (d) perfect and pluperfect active

    (e) perfect and pluperfect middle and passive

    (f) aorist passive and future passive

3. As a secondary-tense verb form, it is prefixed with ἐ in the indicative (the infinitive, imperative and participle are not augmented). Furthermore, it is typical, with the exception of the second aorist passives, that the stem of the verb end with θ. The theme vowel of the aorist passive is η.

4. What we mean by second aorist passive is an aorist passive whose stem does not end in θ. Examples of this include: χαίρω...ἐχάρην, κλέπτω...ἐκλάπην, τρέπω...ἐτράπην, βλάπτω...ἐβλάβην, γράφω...ἐγράφην, ἀλλάττω...ἠλλάγην, πλήττω...ἐπλήγην, ἐπιπλήττω...ἐπεπλάγην.

5. These verbs are: ἀκούω, κελεύω, and γελάω.

6. (a) labials are: π, β, φ. When combined with θ, the resultant cluster is φθ.
    (b) dentals are: δ, θ, τ, ζ. When combined with θ, the resultant cluster is σθ.
    (c) palatals are: γ, χ, κ. When combined with θ, the resultant cluster is χθ.

7. In such a case, the contract vowel usually lengthens (one exception is γελάω). ο lengthens to ω. α lengthens to η. ε lengthens to η as well. The θ is appended directly to this lengthened vowel.

8. (a)

ἐλύθην	ἐλύθημεν
ἐλύθης	ἐλύθητε
ἐλύθη	ἐλύθησαν

    (b)

λυθείς	λυθεῖσα	λυθέν
λυθέντος	λυθείσης	λυθέντος
λυθέντι	λυθείσῃ	λυθέντι
λυθέντα	λυθεῖσαν	λυθέν
λυθέντες	λυθεῖσαι	λυθέντα
λυθέντων	λυθεισῶν	λυθέντων
λυθεῖσι(ν)	λυθείσαις	λυθεῖσι(ν)
λυθέντας	λυθείσας	λυθέντα

    (c)

λύθητι	λύθητε
λυθήτω	λυθέντων

    (d) λυθῆναι

9.

(1)	ἀνεῴχθην	(15)	ἐδιώχθην
(2)	ἀπεκρίθην	(16)	ἠλλάγην or ἠλλάχθην
(3)	ἠκούσθην	(17)	ἐπράχθην
(4)	ἐδηλώθην	(18)	ἐπλήγην
(5)	ἐκρίθην	(19)	ἐπεπλάγην
(6)	ἐχάρην	(20)	ἐφυλάχθην
(7)	ἐγελάσθην	(21)	ἠνέχθην
(8)	ἐζητήθην	(22)	ἤχθην
(9)	ἐκλάπην	(23)	ἐτράπην or ἐτρέφθην
(10)	ἐλήφθην	(24)	ἐβλέφθην
(11)	ἐγράφην	(25)	ἠγγέλθην
(12)	ἐκλήθην	(26)	ἐπείσθην
(13)	ἐβλήθην	(27)	ἐκομίσθην
(14)	ἐβλάφθην or ἐβλάβην		

10. (1) ἠρώτησα αὐτὴν εἰ ὁ υἱὸς ἡλικίαν ἔχει. (2) ὁ ὑπὸ τῶν θεῶν πληγεὶς τυφλὸς ἀπεκρίνατο αὐτοῖς λέγων· Ὑμεῖς, ὦ ἀθάνατοι, κακοί. (3) πάλαι τὸν δεσπότην ἠρώτησα εἰ ἤδη τὸν ἀγῶνα ἔκρινεν. (4) ἡ παλαιά, ὡς τὸ ἱμάτιον δραχμῆς ἀλλαξομένη, τὸν ῥήτορα ἠρώτησεν εἰ τὸ ἱμάτιον πωλήσει. (5) ἀνοιχθήτω ἡ θύρα καὶ ἀποκριθέντων οἱ κακοὶ ἀπὸ τῶν ἀγαθῶν. (6) οἱ μὲν παλαιοὶ παλαὶ αἰτίας πολλὰς ἤδη ἔκριναν· οἱ δὲ νέοι νέαν αἰτίαν ἄρτι κρινοῦσιν.

11. (1) The young speaker asked that old blind man whether he had ever seen. (2) We were asked by those who had judged the cases which guards we had seen in the marsh while we were turning our wagon into the marketplace. (3) Just now we responded the following to those who have harmed us, "Do not hurt us!" (4) The eyes of the blind man were opened by the immortal goddess. (5) The guard, rebuking the thief, struck with rocks the doors that had not been opened. (6) The man, once unable to see, enjoyed writing; but the ancient orator stopped making speeches with the avowed intention of no longer speaking to the masses.

12. Check your answers against **10.** in the exercises for Lesson 27.

13. Check your answers against **11.** in the exercises for Lesson 27.

Lesson 28

1. The future passive is formed from the stem of sixth principal part of the Greek verb. In order to arrive at the stem, one must take away the temporal augment along with the first person singular personal ending (for example, from the sixth principal part of θύω, ἐτύθην, the ἐ– and the –ην need to be removed, yielding τυθ). The same process is used also for the so-called second aorist passives (for example, the sixth principal part of χαίρω is ἐχάρην; the stem of this used for the future passive is χαρ). To the stem so derived, for every form of the future passive, whether indicative, infinitive, or participle, one then suffixes –ησ– (examples: τυθησ– and χαρησ–). The personal endings for the appropriate form of the future passive are the primary middle/passive endings, themed in ο/ε. As with so many other verb forms, the accent is recessive throughout.

2.
   (a) ἁμαρτηθήσομαι   ἁμαρτηθησόμεθα
       ἁμαρτηθήσει   ἁμαρτηθήσεσθε
       ἁμαρτηθήσεται   ἁμαρτηθήσονται
       ἁμαρτηθήσεσθαι
       ἁμαρτηθησόμενος, ἁμαρτηθησομένη, ἁμαρτηθησόμενον
   (b) γεννηθήσομαι   γεννηθησόμεθα
       γεννηθήσει   γεννηθήσεσθε
       γεννηθήσεται   γεννηθήσονται
       γεννηθήσεσθαι
       γεννηθησόμενος, γεννηθησομένη, γεννηθησόμενον

3.
(1)	οἶσθα	You know.
(2)	ᾔδησθα	You knew.
(3)	ἴσασι(ν)	They know.
(4)	ᾖστε	You knew.
(5)	ᾔδη	I knew.
(6)	ἴσμεν	We know.
(7)	εἴσομαι	I shall know.
(8)	εἴσονται	They will know.
(9)	εἴσεσθε	You will know.
(10)	ἴσθι (Know!)	ἴστε (Know!)
	ἴστω (Let him/her/it know!)	ἴστων (Let them know!)
(11)	εἰδέναι	to know
(12)	εἰδότος	knowing
(13)	εἰδυίαις	knowing
(14)	εἰδόσι(ν)	knowing

4. (a) πιστεύω, πιστεύσω, ἐπίστευσα, πεπίστευκα, πεπίστευμαι, ἐπιστεύθην; (b) ἁμαρτάνω, ἁμαρτήσομαι, ἥμαρτον, ἡμάρτηκα, ἡμάρτημαι, ἡμαρτήθην; (c) γεννάω, γεννήσω, ἐγέννησα, γεγέννηκα, γεγέννημαι, ἐγεννήθης; (d) οἶδα, εἴσομαι, _____ , _____ , _____ , _____ .

5. (1) I led the horse [for myself]. (2) I was led by the horse. (3) Will you have the children taught? (4) Will you be taught alone by books? (5) Will we miss the way? (6) Will the way be missed? (7) The speakers will be believed. (8) The speakers will believe [for themselves]. (9) The thief feared as if about to be destroyed. (10) You're not about to exchange your drachmas for a few obols, are you? (11) The drachmas aren't about to be exchanged for a few obols, are they? (12) The evil ones know how to destroy roads. (13) Know the things which have been said by wise people. (14) Let him know the things said by wise people. (15) Let them know the things which will be said by wise people. (16) The prosperous will, during their lifetime, gather together a great treasure. (17) A great treasure will be gathered together by the prosperous during their lifetime.

6. (1) εἶπέν μοι ὁ κύριος, Υἱός μου εἶ σύ, ἐγὼ τήμερον γεγέννηκά σε. (2) τούτων τῶν ἀγώνων οὔποθ᾽ ἁμαρτήσομαι. (3) οὗτοι οἱ ἀγῶνες ὑπ᾽ ἐμοῦ οὔποθ᾽ ἁμαρτηθήσονται. (4) μῶν ἡμάρτετε; (5) πάσας τὰς ἁμαρτίας εἰσόμεθα ὅτι ὑπὸ τοῦ δεσπότου ἡμῖν δηλωθήσονται. (6) ἠρώτησε πότερον πάντα τὰ ἐν τῷ κόσμῳ αὐτῇ δηλωθήσεται ἢ εἴσεται μόνον ὀλίγα. (7) τέκνα γεννῆσαι μήποτε ζητεῖτε, ζῷα γάρ ἐστιν. (8) Πότ᾽ ἐγέννησέ σε ἡ δέσποινα; (9) διὰ τοῦτ᾽ οὔποτ᾽ εἰσόμεθα εἰ τῇ ἀληθείᾳ ἐγεννήθησαν οἱ θεοί, ὅτι ἡμῖν ἐκέλευσεν ὁ Σωκράτης μὴ πιστεύειν εἰς αὐτούς. (10) διὰ τοῦτο τέκνα πολλὰ γεννήσομαι, ὅτι ἐγεννήθην ἐγώ. (11) ἐν τῇ οἰκίᾳ ταύτῃ κύριός ἐστιν ὁ δεσπότης, ὅτι πάντες οἱ δοῦλοι αὐτῷ εἰσίν. (12) μηκέτι λυσάτω ἡ δέσποινα τὰς θεραπαίνας, αὐταὶ γὰρ μέγα ἥμαρτον. (13) ἑαυτοὺς ἔθυσαν οἱ κλῶπες τήν τε ἁμαρτίαν καὶ τὴν μοῖραν εἰδότες. (14) μήποτ᾽ ἔστων κύριοι οἱ ῥήτορες· οὔπω γὰρ τοὺς τῶν παλαιῶν νόμους ἴσασι τιμῆσαι. (15) μῶν κύριαι κριθησόμεθα; οὐκ ἴσμεν εἰ πιστευθησόμεθα.

7. Check your answers against 5. in the exercises for Lesson 28.

8. Check your answers against 6. in the exercises for Lesson 28.

Lesson 29

1. ἡ πόλις

    τῆς πόλεως — Differs from the standard –ος ending due to quantitative metathesis; note accent is irregular

    τῇ πόλει — Differs slightly from standard –ι ending, though ι is still present

    τὴν πόλιν — –ν instead of –α on the example of a noun like χάρις, which is χάριν in the accusative singular

    αἱ πόλεις — Differs from standard –ες ending due to replacement of ι in the stem with –ε; the resultant contraction is -εις. Cf. Groton §180.2

    τῶν πόλεων — Standard genitive plural –ων ending; accent is odd on the strength of analogy with the genitive singular

    ταῖς πόλεσιν — Relatively standard; note, however, presence of –ε– at stem's end

    τὰς πόλεις — One would expect –εας; this particular form reflects the form of the nominative plural

2. ἡ μήτηρ — No ending; lengthened stem vowel (instead of the stem showing μήτερ, it shows μήτηρ)

    τῆς μητρός — Standard –ος ending; –ε– of stem is absent, both here and in dative singular and plural; accent irregular, as if a monosyllabic third declension noun

    τῇ μητρί — Standard –ι ending; –ε– of stem is absent,

	both here and in the genitive singular and dative plural; accent irregular, as if a monosyllabic third-declension noun
τὴν μητέρα	Standard –α ending; note presence of full stem; accent unexpectedly on penult
μῆτερ	Stem of the noun; no ending
αἱ μητέρες	Standard masc./fem. nominative plural ending; full stem present; note difference from stem of nominative singular
τῶν μητέρων	Standard accentuation; standard third declension genitive plural ending; note presence of full stem
ταῖς μητράσι(ν)	Standard third declension dative plural ending (–σι(ν)); note addition of –α– between ending and stem to ease pronunciation; note absence of –ε– from stem
τὰς μητέρας	Standard third declension masc./fem accusative plural ending; full stem returns

3.

τὸ ἄστυ	ὁ βασιλεύς	ἡ θυγάτηρ	ὁ πατήρ
τοῦ ἄστεως	τοῦ βασιλέως	τῆς θυγατρός	τοῦ πατρός
τῷ ἄστει	τῷ βασιλεῖ	τῇ θυγατρί	τῷ πατρί
τὸ ἄστυ	τὸν βασιλέα	τὴν θυγατέρα	τὸν πατέρα
ἄστυ	βασιλεῦ	θύγατερ	πάτερ
τὰ ἄστη	οἱ βασιλεῖς	αἱ θυγατέρες	οἱ πατέρες
τῶν ἄστεων	τῶν βασιλέων	τῶν θυγατέρων	τῶν πατέρων
τοῖς ἄστεσι(ν)	τοῖς βασιλεῦσι(ν)	ταῖς θυγατράσι(ν)	τοῖς πατράσι(ν)
τὰ ἄστη	τοὺς βασιλέας	τὰς θυγατέρας	τοὺς πατέρας
ἄστη	βασιλεῖς	θυγατέρες	πατέρες

4. (1) ὁ πρύτανις ἠρώτησεν εἰ οἱ στρατηγοὶ τῷ ἄστει προσέβαλον. (2) ὁ πατὴρ ὁ τούτου τοῦ πρυτάνεως, καίπερ ποτὲ βασιλεὺς ὢν τῆς πόλεως, νῦν πόρρω ἐν τῇ χώρᾳ οἰκίαν ἔχει. (3) τὸ μὲν ἄστυ τείχη τε οἰκίαι τε καὶ ἀγορά· ἡ δὲ πόλις ἄνθρωποι — βασιλεῖς, μητέρες, πατέρες, θυγατέρες, υἱοί, στρατηγοί, ῥήτορες, δέσποιναί τε καὶ δοῦλοι — καὶ νόμοι. (4) τῆς ἑσπέρας εἰς τὸν οὐρανὸν τὸν κακὸν ἐβλέψαμεν ἐρωτοῦντες εἰ ἡ μοῖρα ἐφ᾽ ἡμᾶς τρέψεται. (5) ἔσπευσαν οἱ στρατηγοὶ καὶ οἱ φύλακες μετὰ τῶν πρυτάνεων εἰς τὴν ἀγορὰν ὡς παύσοντες τοὺς πολλοὺς θόρυβον ποιοῦντας. (6) μόνοι οἱ στρατηγοὶ καὶ οἱ φύλακες ἦσαν παῦσαι τοὺς πολλοὺς θόρυβον ἐν τῇ ἀγορᾷ ποιοῦντας. (7) πότερον, ὦ στρατηγοί, πολλοῖς ἄστεσι προσβαλεῖτε ἢ τῇ ἀληθείᾳ μόνον προσποιήσεσθε πολέμιοι ἄλλαις πόλεσιν εἶναι; (8) οὐκ οἶδα πότερον προσβαλοῦσιν οἱ στρατηγοὶ πολλοῖς ἄστεσιν ἢ τῇ ἀληθείᾳ μόνον προσποιήσονται πολέμιοι ἄλλαις πόλεσιν εἶναι. (9) τὴν ἅμαξαν εἰς τὸ ἄστυ τρέψας, τοῦ μεγάλου θορύβου παρὰ τῇ θαλάττῃ ἁμαρτήσει. (10) ἐγεννήθη ἐν τούτῳ τῷ ἄστει ὁ βασιλεὺς ὃν ἐφίλει πᾶς ἄνθρωπος (11) ἐγεννήθη ἐν τούτῳ τῷ μικρῷ ἄστει τῷ οὐ πολλοῖς ὡμμένῳ ὁ βασιλεὺς ὁ πάντας φιλῶν. (12) ὁ βασιλεύς, γεννηθεὶς ἐν τούτῳ τῷ ἄστει, τὴν πόλιν μέγ᾽ ἐφίλει. (13) τῇ ἑσπέρᾳ ἐτρέψατο ὁ πατήρ μου εἰς τὴν ἡμετέραν οἰκίαν τὴν κλίνην εὑρίσκων. (14) τὴν πᾶσαν ἡμέραν ἐζητήκειν ἡ μήτηρ ἀσπίδας τε καὶ ἱμάτια τὰ ὑφ᾽ αὐτῆς ποιηθέντα ἐν τῇ ἀγορᾷ (15) μῶν τὸν νέον ἄρτι γεννηθέντα βασιλέα εἴδετε; οὐκ ἴσμεν αὐτὸν εὑρεῖν οὐδὲ ὅπου ἐστίν.

5. Check your answers against **4.** in the exercises for Lesson 29.

Lesson 30

1.
ἀκούω	ἀκούσομαι	I hear; I shall hear.
ἁμαρτάνω	ἁμαρτήσομαι	I do err; I shall err.
ἀποθνῄσκω	ἀποθανοῦμαι	I am dying; I shall die.
βλέπω	βλέψομαι	I see; I shall see.
γελάω	γελάσομαι	I do laugh; I shall laugh.
εἰμί	ἔσομαι	I am; I shall be.
λαμβάνω	λήψομαι	I am receiving; I shall receive.
οἶδα	εἴσομαι	I know; I shall know.
ὁράω	ὄψομαι	I am seeing; I shall see.
φεύγω	φεύξομαι	I flee; I shall flee.

2. We mean that a verb so described will have middle or passive *forms* but be *active* in meaning. The term "deponent" comes from the Latin word *deponens*, meaning "putting off"; deponent verbs in a sense "put off" or "shed" their active endings and use middle or passive endings in place of the active endings, while remaining active in meaning.

3. The two are distinguished simply by whether the aorist form is built off of the third or the sixth principal part. Deponents with a third principal part are called "middle deponent", since in the aorist their *form* is middle, while deponents with an aorist from the sixth principal part are called "passive deponents", their aorist being passive in *form*.

4. (1) fully deponent, middle; (2) semi-deponent; (3) fully deponent, passive; (4) fully deponent, middle; (5) semi-deponent; (6) fully deponent, middle

5. (1) τήμερον μὲν ἔφυγον πόρρω τῆς οἰκίας, ταύτῃ δὲ τῇ νυκτὶ πόρρω τοῦ ἄστεως φεύξομαι. (2) τῆς μὲν νυκτὸς ἀφίκοντο, τῆς δὲ ἑσπέρας ἀφίξει. (3) οὗτος μὲν φυγεῖν τὸν δεσπότην οὐκ ἐβουλήθη, αὕτη δ᾽ ἐπ᾽ αὐτῷ καὶ γελάσεσθαι μέλλει. (4) εἰς τὴν ἀγορὰν ἀφιγμένοι, τὰς ἀσπίδας νῦν πωλεῖν βουλησόμεθα. (5) μῶν ἀφικνεῖσθε εἰς τὴν ἐκκλησίαν; τοὺς πρυτάνεις φυγεῖν βουλόμεθα. (6) ἀφικνούμενοι εἰς τὴν βουλήν, ἠρώτησαν οἱ πρυτάνεις εἰ ἐβουλήθη ἡ ἐκκλησία τὴν βουλὴν αὐτῶν ἀκούειν.

6. The genitive absolute is a **circumstantial participial phrase**. There is no such thing as a genitive absolute phrase in which the main participle is in the attributive position, though one may have an attributive participle in the genitive when called for. A requirement of the genitive absolute phrase in classical Greek is that its subject, a noun in the genitive, may appear nowhere else in the sentence; indeed, such a noun, integrated into the syntax of the sentence, demands that any participial phrase which it governs have a participle agreeing with it in number, case, and gender. The tense of a participle in a genitive absolute phrase indicates the same temporal relationship with the main verb as would any other participle of the same tense (see Groton §150).

7. (1) τοῦ ἵππου λίθοις βληθέντος, ἐτράπη ἡ ἅμαξα εἰς τὸν ποταμόν. (2) τῆς ἐκκλησίας φυγούσης, ἐπαύσαντο οἱ ῥήτορες λέγοντες. (3) αἱ κόραι οὐδένα ἐφίλουν, οὐδενὸς ἀνδρὸς ἀξίου εὑρηθέντος. (4) ἐκάλεσαν τοὺς πολλοὺς οἱ κήρυκες μιᾷ φωνῇ, τοῦ θορύβου πολὺ μεγάλου ὄντος. (5) οἶσθα ὅποι ἔφυγον οἱ Ἕλληνες, τῆς πατρίδος λυθείσης;

8. (1) ὁ ἵππος λίθοις βληθεὶς τὴν ἅμαξαν εἰς τὸν ποταμὸν ἔτρεψεν. (2) ἐπαύσαντο λέγοντες οἱ ῥήτορες τῇ ἐκκλησίᾳ φυγούσῃ. (3) αἱ κόραι, οὐδένα ἄνδρα εὑροῦσαι φιλεῖν ἑαυτάς, οὐδέν᾽ ἐφίλουν. (4) ἐκάλεσαν οἱ κήρυκες μιᾷ φωνῇ τοὺς πολλοὺς διὰ τοῦ θορύβου πολὺ μεγάλου ὄντος. (5) οἶσθα ὅποι οἱ Ἕλληνες ἔφυγον ἀπὸ τῆς πατρίδος λυθείσης;

9. | εἷς | μία | ἕν |
    | ἑνός | μιᾶς | ἑνός |
    | ἑνί | μιᾷ | ἑνί |
    | ἕνα | μίαν | ἕν |

10. | οὐδείς | οὐδεμία | οὐδέν |
    | οὐδενός | οὐδεμιᾶς | οὐδενός |
    | οὐδενί | οὐδεμιᾷ | οὐδενί |
    | οὐδένα | οὐδεμίαν | οὐδέν |

11. | μηδείς | μηδεμία | μηδέν |
    | μηδενός | μηδεμιᾶς | μηδενός |
    | μηδενί | μηδεμιᾷ | μηδενί |
    | μηδένα | μηδεμίαν | μηδέν |

12. They cancel one another out only when the two following conditions are met in the same clause: (a) the first negation is a compound and (b) the second is a simple οὐ or μή. Otherwise they simply reinforce one another.

13. (1) No one has not come into the marketplace. = Someone has come into the marketplace. (2) No one has come into the marketplace. (3) Let no one know this! (4) Let no one not know this! = Let someone know this! (5) No one sent me anything. (6) No one sent me anything. (7) She did not send me nothing. = She sent me something.

14. (1) ἅτε πολλῶν κοινῶν τοῖς τε νόμοις καὶ τῇ σοφίᾳ, πολὺ διδαχθήσεται ἡμῖν ὑπὸ ῥητόρων τε καὶ φιλοσόφων. (2) ταύτην τὴν βουλὴν οὔτ᾽ ἤνεγκον οἱ ἄγγελοι οὔτ᾽ ἔλαβον οἱ πρυτάνεις, καίπερ τῆς ἐκκλησίας βουληθείσης κελεῦσαι τοῖς στρατηγοῖς προσβαλεῖν τοῖς πολεμίοις. (3) προσεποιήθη τῇ ἐκλλησίᾳ καθ᾽ ἕνα. (4) ἐπειδὴ οὐκ ἤκουσα οὐδεμίαν φωνήν, τοὺς ἄλλους ἐρωτήσω πότερόν τινα ἤκουσαν ἢ οὐκ οὐδεμίαν. (5) τῶν στρατηγῶν τὴν πατρίδα λυσόντων, ἀφικόμεθα ἐπὶ τὴν θάλατταν καὶ τρεψάμενοι εἰς τὰς τριήρεις τοῖς δούλοις καὶ ταῖς μητράσιν, τοῖς υἱοῖς καὶ ταῖς θυγατράσιν εἰς αὐτὰς ἀφίξεσθαι ἐκελεύσαμεν. (6) οὐδενὸς ἀληθοῦς ἀνδρὸς ἐν τῇ πατρίδι ὄντος, πόθεν φύλακας ληψόμεθα; (7) καίπερ τῆς τοῦ θορύβου φωνῆς οὔπω ὑπὸ τῶν τέκνων φοβηθείσης, οὐ βούλονται οὔθ᾽ αἱ μητέρες οὔθ᾽ οἱ πατέρες διὰ τὸν ἑαυτῶν φόβον εἰς τὰς κλίνας τρέψασθαι.

15. Check your answers against **5.**, **7.**, **8.**, **13.**, and **14.** in the excercises for Lesson 29.

Lesson 31

1. An adverb of manner is built from an adjective and is a word used to describe (a) a verb, (b) an adjective, or (c) a prepositional phrase. Examples:

    (a) The car *nearly* struck the pedestrian.
    (b) The *relatively* new house sold for *much* less than it was worth.
    (c) This action is *barely* within the realm of acceptable behaviour.

2. First of all, in English there are a number of adjectives that do not receive –*ly*, but are used in their adjectival forms also as adverbs. Such words include *much, fast,* etc. Secondly, there is a group of words whose adjectival form cannot function adverbially. To circumvent the problem with these words one can use what is known as an adverbial phrase. To use "ancient" adverbially, for example, one might say, "in an ancient way," "in ancient fashion," "in ancient manner," but not "anciently."

3. (a) One way is by removing from the genitive plural of the adjective its final -ν, and adding a -ς in its place. For instance, κακός in the genitive plural is κακῶν. Removing its final -ν and replacing it with -ς yields κακῶς = "badly" or "in an ugly or poor fashion". This manner of forming the adverb is by far and away commonest.

(b) There is, however, a number of adjectives which do not permit the manipulation above. These, rather, use either the neuter accusative singular or neuter accusative plural as their adverbial form (e.g., νέος becomes νέον when used adverbially, and πολύς becomes πολλά or πολύ when used adverbially).

4.
(1) κακῶς	(8) ἀξίως	(15) ἀληθῶς
(2) καλῶς	(9) εὖ	(16) εὐδαιμόνως
(3) δῆλον/δῆλα	(10) ἐχθρῶς	(17) μόνον
(4) μέγα/μεγάλα	(11) κοινῶς	(18) πρότερον
(5) ὧδε	(12) μικρόν/μικρά	(19) πάντως
(6) οὕτως	(13) μακρόν/μακρά	(20) φιλοσόφως
(7) ἀθανάτως	(14) ὀλίγον/ὀλίγα	(21) πολεμίως

5. (1) ἀναξίως ἔλαβε τὸ γέρας. (2) μοὶ πολεμίως προσέβαλες. (3) φιλοσόφως ἐγράφη τοῦτο τὸ βιβλίον. (4) ὧδ᾽ εἶπεν. (5) μὴ τυφλῶς ἀφικνοῦ. (6) ἆρα τῇ δεσποίνῃ δούλως πείσῃ; (7) εὖ πεπαίδευμαι. (8) Ἑλληνικῶς τὴν ἀλήθειαν ζητήσομεν. (9) αὕτη μὲν ἡ ἐπιστολὴ καλῶς ἐγράφη, ἐκεῖνο δὲ τὸ βιβλίον οὐκ αὕτως. (10) εὐδαιμόνως ἤγαγε τὸν βίον.

6. A result clause is a dependent adverbial clause which expresses either real or putative outcome.

7. The actual and natural result clauses both are introduced by the conjunction ὥστε (often correlative with such words as οὕτως, τοσοῦτος, and τοιοῦτος, etc.) and both express *outcome* or *result*.

They differ from one another in the following areas: (a) verb mood, (b) subject case, and (c) negation. The verb of an actual result clause is in the "fact mood", the indicative. This is not surprising since the indicative is used to report actions which are treated more or less as actual occurrences. The verb of a natural result clause, on the other hand, is in the infinitive.

The subject of the actual result clause, if expressed, is always in the nominative case. In the natural result clause, the subject, if expressed, is in the accusative.

The negation of the actual result clause is accomplished by οὐ and its compounds, while the negation of the natural result clause is accomplished by using μή and its compounds.

8. (1) οὕτως αἰσχρῶς ἔζην ὥστε σε μὴ πιστεῦσαι. (2) τόσοις διδασκάλοις πεπαιδεύμεθα ὥστε νῦν τὸ πᾶν ἴσμεν. (3) οὕτως ῥάδιον τοῦτο τὸ ἔργον ὥστε καὶ παιδίον αὐτὸ πράττειν. (4) τὸ ἔργον οὕτως ῥαδίως ἔπραξεν ὥστε ἕξει ταύτῃ τῇ ὥρᾳ αὐτῇ εἰς τὴν οἰκίαν ἀφίξεσθαι. (5) ἆρ᾽ οὐκ ἀεὶ οἱ ἀθάνατοι ζήσουσιν; (6) οὕτως αἰσχρῶς ἔζην ὥστε καὶ αἰσχρῶς ἀπέθανεν. (7) τοσούτοις διδασκάλοις πεπειδεύμεθα ὥστε τὸ πᾶν εἰδέναι. (8) οὕτως ῥάδιον τοῦτο τὸ ἔργον ἦν ὥστε παιδίον αὐτὸ ἔπραξεν. (9) ῥαδίως τὸ ἔργον ἔπραξεν ὥστε εἰς τὴν οἰκίαν ταυτῇ τῇ ὥρᾳ αὐτῇ ἀφικέσθαι. (10) μῶν ἀεὶ ζήσουσιν οἱ ἀνάξιοι κλῶπες ὥστε τοῖς τέκνοις ἔσεσθαι ἐχθροί; (11) τῆς βουλῆς τῶν πρυτάνεων ἀκουσάσης, ἤγγειλεν ὁ κῆρυξ τὴν βουλὴν τῇ ἐκκλησίᾳ ὥστε ἦν μέγας θόρυβος. (12) οὗτός ἐστιν ὁ ἀνήρ μου, ὃν ζῶσα φιλήσω. (13) ὡς αἰσχρῶς οὗτοι οἱ οὐ φιλοσόφοις πεπαιδευμένοι ζῶσιν. οὕτως αἰσχρῶς ζῶσιν ὥστε καὶ τοὺς θεοὺς ἀφ᾽ ἑαυτῶν τρέψαι. (14) καίπερ οὐδενὸς ῥήτορος οὐκ ἀληθῶς εἰπόντος, ἔμελλεν ἡ ἐκκλησία πιστεύειν τοῖς λόγοις. (15) τοσαύτη ἦν ἡ φωνὴ ὥστε αὐτὰς τὰς θύρας τῆς οἰκίας ἀνέῳξεν.

9. Check your answers against **8.** in the exercises for Lesson 31.

Lesson 32

1. In Greek, the typical ending for the comparative adjective is -τερος, -α, -ον.

2. In Greek, the typical ending for the superlative adjective is -τατος, -η, -ον.

3. The typical comparative adverb is formed by using the neuter accusative singular ending of the typical comparative adjective suffix -τερος, -α, -ον.

4. The typical superlative adverb is formed by using the neuter accusative plural ending of the typical superlative adjective suffix -τατος, -η, -ον.

5. The comparative and superlative adjectives of καινός are formed as follows: First of all, one must arrive at the stem of the positive degree. This is καιν-. Then one must determine whether the last syllable of the stem, in this case, καιν-, is long or short (for more on this, see Groton §15). In the case of καιν-, it is long. This being the case, the stem prefers the shorter of its two choices for a buffer vowel (ο/ω) between itself and the suffix -τερος or -τατος. The accent is recessive, staying as close to the antepenult as possible. The resultant form for the comparative is καινότερος, καινοτέρα, καινότερον. For the superlative, it is καινότατος, καινοτάτη, καινότατον. The adverbial form of the comparative is the neuter accusative singular, καινότερον. The adverbial form of the superlative is the neuter accusative plural, καινότατα.

6. The comparative and superlative adjectives of φίλος are formed as follows: First of all, its formation is a bit irregular, in that one does not use either ο or ω as the buffer vowel between the stem and the suffixes, but rather either appends the suffix directly to the stem or uses the intervening diphthong –αι- on the analogy of the formation of the comparative and superlative of παλαιός. Two variations of both the comparative and the superlative are thus available: φίλτερος, φιλτέρα, φίλτερον together with φίλτατος, φιλτάτη, φίλτατον, on the one hand, and φιλαίτερος, φιλαιτέρα, φιλαίτερον together with φιλαίτατος, φιλαιτάτη, φιλαίτατον, on the other. The accent is recessive, of course. The adverbial form of the comparative is the neuter accusative singular, either φίλτερον or φιλαίτερον; and the adverbial form of the superlative is the neuter accusative plural, either φίλτατα or φιλαίτατα.

7. The comparative and superlative adjectives of Ἑλληνικός are formed as follows: First of all, one must arrive at the stem of the positive degree. This is Ἑλληνικ-. Then one must determine whether the last syllable of the stem, in this case, -νικ-, is long or short (for more on this, see Groton §15). In the case of -νικ-, it is short. This being the case, the stem prefers the longer of its two choices for a buffer vowel (ο/ω) between itself and the suffix -τερος or -τατος. The accent is recessive, staying as close to the antepenult as possible. The resultant form for the comparative is Ἑλληνικώτερος, Ἑλληνικωτέρα, Ἑλληνικώτερον. For the superlative, it is Ἑλληνικώτατος, Ἑλληνικωτάτη, Ἑλληνικώτατον. The adverbial form of the comparative is the neuter accusative singular, Ἑλληνικώτερον. The adverbial form of the superlative is the neuter accusative plural, Ἑλληνικώτατα.

8. The comparative and superlative adjective of εὐδαίμων is formed as follows: First of all, one must arrive at the stem of the positive degree. For a third declension adjective, this is the stem of the genitive singular, -ευδαιμον-. As with all regularly formed third declension comparatives and superlatives, one adds to this stem –εσ-. There is no buffer vowel

between this and the suffix -τερος or -τατος, which are appended directly to εὐδαιμονεσ-. The accent is recessive, staying as close to the antepenult as possible. The resultant form for the comparative is εὐδαιμονέστερος εὐδαιμονεστέρα, εὐδαιμονέστερον. For the superlative, it is εὐδαιμονέστατος, εὐδαιμονεστάτη, εὐδαιμονέστατον. The adverbial form of the comparative is the neuter accusative singular εὐδαιμονέστερον. The adverbial form of the superlative is the neuter accusative plural, εὐδαιμονέστερα.

9.
(1) σοφωτέρας
(2) φιλοσοφωτέρας
(3) ἀθανατωτάτων
(4) ἐλευθερώτατον
(5) νεωτέραις
(6) δουλοτάτῳ
(7) αἰτιώτεροι
(8) ἀληθεστάτοις
(9) πολεμιωτέρου

10. (1) σοφωτέρα ἐστὶν αὐτοῦ. (2) ὡς Ἑλληνικώτατα ἔζων. (3) τίς ἀθανατώτερος τῶν θεῶν ἔχει γίγνεσθαι; (4) οἱ φίλοι μου φίλτατοί μοί εἰσιν. (5) ταύτης τῆς ἁμαρτίας αἰτιώταταί ἐστε. (6) ἀναξιώτατα ἀπεκρίναντο. (7) εἶπε μὲν ὁ πρύτανις δῆλον· ὁ δὲ ῥήτωρ δηλότερον· ὁ δὲ κῆρυξ δηλότατα. (8) αὕτη ἡ ὁδὸς μακροτέρα ἐκείνης. (9) σοφώτερός ἐστιν ὁ Σωκράτης πάντων τῶν παλαιτάτων φιλοσόφων. (10) ζῇ, ὦ φίλε, εὐδαιμονέστερον καὶ ἀληθέστατα.

11.
(1) γίγνει/ῃ — You are becoming.
(2) γενομένῳ — [to it] having become
(3) ἐγεγενήμεθα — We had become
(4) γενήσεσθαι — to be about to happen
(5) γεγονυίας — [of her/it] having become
(6) γεγενημένον — [him/it] having been born
(7) γενέσθων — Let them be born
(8) γιγνέσθω — Let him/her/it become

12.
(1) σῴζετε — You are bringing safely
(2) σωσάσης — [of her/it] having saved
(3) σέσωσται — He/she/it has saved/been brought safely
(4) σωθῆναι — to be saved
(5) ἐσεσώκεσαν — They had brought safely
(6) σεσωκόσι(ν) — [to them] having brought safely
(7) σώθητι — Be saved!
(8) σῶσον — Save!

13. (1) ἠρώτησέ με ἡ κακὴ δέσποινα ὡς ἀναξιώτατα εἰ ἐζήτησα μᾶλλον τὰ τέκνα ἢ τὰ ζῷα σῶσαι. (2) καὶ μὴν αὐτὴ τοῦ θανάτου αὐτῶν αἰτιωτάτη. (3) τοῦ λοιποῦ οὗτος ὁ νέος ἀνὴρ ὁ δεινότατος τῶν νεωτέρων πρυτάνεων δεσπότης γενήσεται τῆς πόλεως ἡμῶν. (4) τοῖς πολλοῖς αἰσχρὰ εἶπεν ὁ κῆρυξ μεγάλῃ φωνῇ ὡς ἐρῶν ἀληθέστατα. (5) ἀλλὰ μὴν ἐσώθη ἀπὸ τῶν κλωπῶν ὁ θησαυρὸς ὁ μάλιστα ζητούμενος ὥστε γέρας τῆς ἡμετέρας πόλεως γίγνεσθαι. (6) μὴ αἴτιος τοσῆσδε ἁμαρτίας ὁ βασιλεὺς γενέσθω ὥστε εὐδαιμονέστερος τῶν θεῶν τῶν ἀθανάτων γενήσεσθαι. (7) ἐκείνη ἡ ἑσπέρα ἡ μετὰ τῆς τοῦ δεσπότου κόρης φιλτέρα μοι ἦν ἢ ἡ μήτηρ καὶ ὁ πατήρ μου. (8) τοὺς ἐχθροὺς ἡρπακὼς, εἶπεν ὁ ῥήτωρ τάδε· σύ, ὦ πόλι ἐμή, πασῶν λυπῶν ὡς ἐλευθερωτάτη γενήσῃ. (9) λοιπὸν οὐκ εἶπέ μοι τὴν ἀλήθειαν οὐδεὶς τῶν οἰκετῶν τῶν δουλοτάτων. (10) σώσατε, ὦ θεοὶ ἀθάνατοι, τὴν πόλιν ἡμῶν ἀπὸ τῶν πολεμίων, καὶ ζητήσατε ὅτι ἀληθέστατα ἡμῖν βίον εὐδαιμονέστατον πέμψαι.

14. Check your answers against **13.** in the exercises for Lesson 32.

Lesson 33

1.
    (1) much, many   πολύς, πλείων, πλεῖστος
    (2) shameful   αἰσχρός, αἰσχίων, αἴσχιστος
    (3) easy   ῥᾴδιος, ῥᾴων, ῥᾷστος
    (4) [morally] good   ἀγαθός, βελτίων, βέλτιστος
    (5) bad [in might]   κακός, ἥττων, ἥκιστος
    (6) beautiful   καλός, καλλίων, κάλλιστος
    (7) [morally] bad   κακός, κακίων, κάκιστος
    (8) sweet   ἡδύς, ἡδίων, ἥδιστος
    (9) good [in ability/worth]   ἀγαθός, ἀμείνων, ἄριστος
    (10) great, large   μέγας, μείζων, μέγιστος
    (11) good [in might]   ἀγαθός, κρείττων, κράτιστος
    (12) little, few   ὀλίγος, ἐλάττων, ὀλίγιστος
    (13) bad [in ability/worth]   κακός, χείρων, χείριστος
    (14) small   μικρός, μικρότερος, μικρότατος
           μικρός, ἐλάττων, ἐλάχιστος
    (15) hostile   ἐχθρός, ἐχθίων, ἔχθιστος

2.
    (1) much, many   πολύ, πλεῖον, πλεῖστα
    (2) shameful   αἰσχρῶς, αἴσχιον, αἴσχιστα
    (3) easy   ῥᾳδίως, ῥᾷον, ῥᾷστα
    (4) [morally] good   εὖ, βέλτιον, βέλτιστα
    (5) bad [in might]   κακῶς, ἧττον, ἥκιστα
    (6) beautiful   καλῶς, κάλλιον, κάλλιστα
    (7) [morally] bad   κακῶς, κάκιον, κάκιστα
    (8) sweet   ἡδέως, ἥδιον, ἥδιστα
    (9) good [in ability/worth]   εὖ, ἄμεινον, ἄριστα
    (10) great, large   μέγα, μεῖζον, μέγιστα
    (11) good [in might]   εὖ, κρεῖττον, κράτιστα
    (12) little, few   ὀλίγως, ἔλαττον, ὀλίγιστα
    (13) bad [in ability/worth]   κακῶς, χεῖρον, χείριστα
    (14) small   μικρόν μικρότερον, μικρότατα
           μικρόν, ἔλαττον, ἐλάχιστα
    (15) hostile   ἐχθρῶς, ἔχθιον, ἔχθιστα

3.

M&F	N	M&F	N
πλείων	πλεῖον	καλλίων	κάλλιον
πλείονος	πλείονος	καλλίονος	καλλίονος
πλείονι	πλείονι	καλλίονι	καλλίονι
πλείονα (πλείω)	πλεῖον	καλλίονα (καλλίω)	κάλλιον
πλεῖον	πλεῖον	κάλλιον	κάλλιον
πλείονες	πλείονα	καλλίονες	καλλίονα
(πλείους)	(πλείω)	(καλλίυυς)	(καλλίω)
πλειόνων	πλειόνων	καλλιόνων	καλλιόνων
πλείοσι(ν)	πλείοσι(ν)	καλλίοσι(ν)	καλλίοσι(ν)
πλείονας	πλείονα	καλλίονας	καλλίονα
(πλείους)	(πλείω)	(καλλίους)	(καλλίω)
πλείονες	πλείονα	καλλίονες	καλλίονα
(πλείους)	(πλείω)	(καλλίους)	(καλλίω)

4.
    (1) μεγάλου, μείζονος, μεγίστου
    (2) μικρῷ, ἐλάττονι, ἐλαχίστῳ
    (3) ἀγαθά, βελτίονα (βελτίω), βέλτιστα
    (4) κακή, χείρων, χειρίστη
    (5) ἀγαθέ, κρεῖττον, κράτιστε

(6) κακαί, κακίονες (κακίους), κάκισται

(7) ἀγαθάς, ἀμείνονας (ἀμείνους), ἀρίστας

(8) κακοῖς, ἥττοσι(ν), ἡκίστοις

(9) ἡδέων, ἡδιόνων, ἡδίστων

5. See Groton §205.

6. One may indicate the degree of difference in one of two ways. (a) One may use an adverb, or (b) one may use the dative of degree of difference. These may be illustrated by translating the following English sentence into Greek using the two different methods:

The girl speaks a **little** more clearly than the youth.

(a) ἡ κόρη ὀλίγον δηλότερον λέγει τοῦ νεανίου.

(b) ἡ κόρη ὀλίγῳ δηλότερον λέγει τοῦ νεανίου.

In example (a), the adverb ὀλίγον modifies δηλότερον and shows the girl's speech to be "a little clearer" than the boy's. In example (b), essentially the same notion is expressed as in (a), except that instead of the adverbial form of ὀλίγος, it uses the neuter dative singular—the dative of degree of comparison—and shows by how much the girl's speech is clearer than the boy's: she speaks "clearer by a little".

The dative of degree of difference can also be used with nouns, in whatever number and gender they require. An example follows:

ἐκεῖνο τὸ ἄστυ ὀλίγοις ἀνθρώποις μεῖζον ἢ τὸ ἡμέτερον ἄστυ.

That city is larger than our city by a few human beings.

7. (1) κακίων βασιλεὺς γενήσεται οὗτος ὁ στρατηγός. (2) πολλῷ κακίων ἔσται ἢ οἱ πρότεροι βασιλεῖς. (3) ἡδέως λέγει ἡ κόρη ἡ καλλίων. (4) καὶ μὴν κρείττων ἐστὶ πολλῶν ἄλλων κορῶν. (5) ὡς αἴσχιστα εἶπεν ὁ δεινὸς κῆρυξ ὥστε μὴ ἀκοῦσαι αὐτοῦ τοὺς πολλούς. (6) τίνος ἡ φωνὴ ἡδίων ἢ ἡ τῆς φιλοσοφίας; (7) πολλῷ ἐχθίονές μοι ἐγένοντο. (8) ὁ μὲν λόγος τοῦ ῥήτορος αὐτῇ ῥᾷον ἐδιδάχθη, ἡ δὲ φιλοσοφία τῆς φιλοσόφου οὐ ῥᾳδίως μοι ἐδιδάχθη. (9) καὶ μὴν πάντων τῶν μαθητῶν ἐγὼ ῥᾷστα ἐδιδάχθην. (10) πλείω μὲν θησαυρὸν ἔχει ὁ ῥήτωρ ἢ ἐγώ, τὸν δὲ πλεῖστον συνέλαβεν ὁ κράτιστος στρατηγός.

8. Check your answers against **7.** in the exercises for Lesson 33.

Lesson 34

1. The cardinal numeral is used for counting (one, two, three, etc.; εἷς, δύο, τρεῖς, κτλ); the ordinal numeral is used for ordering items by number (first, tenth, twentieth, etc.; πρῶτος, δέκατος, εἰκοστός, κτλ); and the numerical adverb expresses how many times in terms of numbers (once, five times, a thousand times, etc.; ἅπαξ, πεντάκις, χιλιάκις, κτλ).

2. They are as follow:

(1) εἷς, μία, ἕν, declined in "one" and in all numbers with a "one" in the ones column beginning with twenty-one (21, 31, 101, 1001, etc.)

(2) δύο, declined in "two" and all numbers with a "two" in the ones column beginning with twenty-two (22, 32, 102, 1002, etc.)

(3) τρεῖς, τρία, declined in "three" and all numbers with a "three" in the ones column beginning with thirteen (13, 23, 33, 103, 1003, etc.)

(4) τέτταρες, τέτταρα, declined in "four" and all numbers with a "four" in the ones column beginning with fourteen (14, 24, 34, 104, 1004, etc.)

(5) the hundreds, beginning with 200 (διακόσιοι, -αι, -α, κτλ)

(6) the thousands, beginning with 1,000 (χίλιοι, -αι, -α, κτλ)

(7) the ten-thousands, beginning with 10,000 (μύριοι, -αι, -α, κτλ)

3. (1) | Masc. & Fem. | Neuter |
   |---|---|
   | τέτταρες | τέτταρα |
   | τεττάρων | τεττάρων |
   | τέτταρσι(ν) | τέτταρσι(ν) |
   | τέτταρας | τέτταρα |

   (2) Masc., Fem., Neut.
   δύο
   δυοῖν
   δυοῖν
   δύο

   (3) | Masc. & Fem. | Neuter |
   |---|---|
   | τρεῖς | τρία |
   | τριῶν | τριῶν |
   | τρισί(ν) | τρισί(ν) |
   | τρεῖς | τρία |

   (4) | Masc. | Fem. | Neuter |
   |---|---|---|
   | εἷς | μία | ἕν |
   | ἑνός | μιᾶς | ἑνός |
   | ἑνί | μιᾷ | ἑνί |
   | ἕνα | μίαν | ἕν |

4. (a) εἷς, πρῶτος, ἅπαξ
       πεντεκαίδεκα, πεντεκαιδέκατος, πεντεκαιδεκάκις
       εἴκοσι, εἰκοστός, εἰκοσάκις
       ὀκτώ, ὄγδοος, ὀκτάκις
       τρεῖς καὶ δέκα, τρίτος καὶ δέκατος, τρεισκαιδεκάκις

   (b) τετταράκοντα, τετταρακοστός, τετταρακοντάκις
       ἐνενήκοντα, ἐνενηκοστός, ἐνενηκοντάκις
       τριάκοντα, τριακοστός, τριακοντάκις
       ἑβδομήκοντα, ἑβδομηκοστός, ἑβδομηκοντάκις
       ἑξήκοντα, ἑξηκοστός, ἑξηκοντάκις

   (c) δισχίλιοι, δισχιλιοστός, δισχιλιάκις
       μύριοι, μυριοστός, μυριάκις
       δισμύριοι, δισμυριοστός, δισμυριάκις

5. The partitive genitive is a use of the genitive which does not show possession, but that something[s] or someone[s] is part of a larger group of things or people. That larger group is expressed in the genitive, while the item which is part of the larger group is in whatever case is demanded by the syntax of the sentence. The partitive genitive also has a parallel construction using ἐκ or ἀπό + genitive to express the same as the partitive genitive.

   Seven of the men were harmed by rocks.
   ἑπτὰ τῶν ἀνδρῶν λίθοις ἐβλάβησαν.
   ἑπτὰ ἐκ τῶν ἀνδρῶν λίθοις ἐβλάβησαν.

6. (1) ἐλύθησαν πέντε καὶ εἴκοσι τῶν ἑκατὸν τριήρων. (2) ὀκτάκις προσέβαλον οἱ στρατηγοὶ τῷ ἄστει, χιλίων ἐκ τῶν τοῦ ἄστεως ἀνδρῶν ζητούντων τοὺς πολεμίους ἀποκτεῖναι. (3) ὀκτὼ ἡμέρας ἐκεῖνον τὸν καλὸν ἄνδρα ζητήσας ἰδεῖν, τῇ ὀγδόῃ αὐτὸν τῇ ἀληθείᾳ εἶδον. (4) τετράκις σοι εἶπον τόδε· τέτταρσι τέκνοις ἵπποι τέτταρες ἦσαν παρὰ τῶν τεττάρων πατέρων. (5) μία ἐκ τῶν ἕξ καλῶν κορῶν πολλῷ καλλίων τε καὶ ἀξιοτέρα καὶ ἀμείνων ἦν τῶν πέντε ἄλλων ὥστε ἐννέα τῶν δέκα νεανιῶν αὐτὴν ῥᾳδίως φιλῆσαι. (6) τὰς μὲν πεντακοσίας τριήρεις ταῖς διακοσίαις τῆς ἄλλης πόλεως προσποιήσαντες, εἴχομεν λύπην ὡς πλείστην ἐπὶ τοὺς πολεμίους ἐνεγκεῖν. (7) ὁ μὲν πρῶτος βασιλεὺς ἄριστος· ὁ δὲ δεύτερος ὀλίγῳ χείρων· ὁ δὲ τρίτος πολλῷ ὁ χείριστος. ἆρ᾽ ἐστὶ ἐλπίς τις ἔχειν ἀμείνονα βασιλέα; (8) μυρίας καὶ χιλίας ἐπιστολὰς τῇ θυγατρὶ γέγραφα ἢ οὐκ ἔλαβεν οὐδεμίαν αὐτῶν. (9) ἐννεακαίδεκα μὲν εἰσι ἐν τῇ οἰκίᾳ ἀσπίδες, τριάκοντα δύο δὲ ἄνδρες εἰσίν. τίνες τρεῖς καὶ δέκα ἐξ

αὐτῶν οὐ βούλονται ἀσπίδας ἔχειν. (10) τόσον προσεποίησε τῷ θησαυρῷ ὁ βασιλεὺς ὥστ᾽ ἐκεῖνος νῦν δραχμὰς δεκακισμυρίας ἔχει.

7. Check your answers against **6.** in the exercises for Lesson 34.

Lesson 35

1. Generally the subjunctive indicates that while the action of a verb in the subjunctive is viewed by the speaker as possible or potential, it is not actual. Compare the two questions below, for example:

    τί ποιοῦμεν; What are we doing? (views the action expressed as actual)

    τί ποιήσωμεν; What should we do? (views the action expressed as
    possible or potential)

2. The subjunctive can be formed in three tenses: the present, aorist, and perfect. It is commonly found in both the present and aorist, and is rarely found in the perfect.

3. The difference in meaning has nothing to do with the "time" facet of Greek tense, but only with the "aspect" facet. Thus, the simple difference between the present of the subjunctive and the aorist of the subjunctive is that while the present views the action it expresses as ongoing, the aorist views it as aoristic, or snap-shot.

4. (a) built off of the stem of the sixth principal part; primary active ending with lengthened theme vowel; accentuation on first syllable of personal ending; (b) built off of the stem of the first principal part; primary active ending with lengthened theme vowel; accentuation recessive; (c) built off of the stem of the third principal part; primary active ending with lengthened theme vowel; accentuation recessive; (d) built off of the stem of the first principal part; primary middle/passive endings with lengthened theme vowel; accentuation recessive; (e) built off of the third principal part; primary middle/passive endings with lengthened theme vowel; accentuation recessive.

5.
    (1) βουληθῶ   βουληθῶμεν
    βουληθῇς   βουληθῆτε
    βουληθῇ   βουληθῶσι(ν)

    (2) ἀφίκωμαι   ἀφικώμεθα
    ἀφίκῃ   ἀφίκησθε
    ἀφίκηται   ἀφίκωνται

    (3) εὕρω   εὕρωμεν
    εὕρῃς   εὕρητε
    εὕρῃ   εὕρωσι(ν)

    (4) σῴζω   σῴζωμεν
    σῴζῃς   σῴζητε
    σῴζῃ   σῴζωσι(ν)

    (5) φέρωμαι   φερώμεθα
    φέρῃ   φέρησθε
    φέρηται   φέρωνται

    (6) no such form exists

6.
    (1) ὠφελῶμαι   ὠφελώμεθα
    ὠφελῇ   ὠφελῆσθε
    ὠφελῆται   ὠφελῶνται

    (2) γελῶμαι   γελώμεθα
    γελᾷ   γελᾶσθε
    γελᾶται   γελῶνται

(3) δηλῶ   δηλῶμεν
     δηλοῖς   δηλῶτε
     δηλοῖ   δηλῶσι(ν)

(4) δηλῶμαι   δηλώμεθα
     δηλοῖ   δηλῶσθε
     δηλῶται   δηλῶνται

(5) ζητῶ   ζητῶμεν
     ζητῇς   ζητῆτε
     ζητῇ   ζητῶσι(ν)

(6) γελῶ   γελῶμεν
     γελᾷς   γελᾶτε
     γελᾷ   γελῶσι(ν)

7. (a) μάχομαι, μαχοῦμαι, ἐμαχεσάμην, _____ , μεμάχημαι, _____ .

(b)
(1) μάχῃ/μάχει
(2) μάχῃ
(3) μάχου
(4) ἐμάχου
(5) μαχοῦνται
(6) μαχεῖσθε
(7) μαχέσηται
(8) ἐμαχέσατο
(9) μαχεσάσθω
(10) μαχέσασθαι
(11) μεμαχήμεθα
(12) ἐμεμαχήμεθα
(13) μεμαχῆσθαι

8. φαίνω, φανῶ, ἔφηνα, πέφαγκα or πέφηνα, πέφασμαι, ἐφάνθην or ἐφάνην

9. The subjunctive has three independent uses: the hortatory, the prohibitive, and the deliberative. The hortatory subjunctive expresses a command or exhortation in the first person. In English we say, for example, "Let's fight with our enemies," or, "Hey, let me do that!" Both of these examples fit the mold for the hortatory subjunctive in Greek: they express a command or exhortation (somewhat akin to the Greek imperative) and they are in the first person. They translate into Greek as follow: μαχεσώμεθα τοῖς ἐχθροῖς ἡμῶν and οὗτος, τοῦτο ποιήσω. The prohibitive subjunctive is used to replace negative commands in the aorist in the second and third person. It is always found in the second or third person, always in the aorist, and always with μή. Thus, instead of saying μὴ σύλλαβε τὰ χρήματα ("Don't gather your possessions!"), a Greek would have preferred to say μὴ συλλάβῃς τὰ χρήματα ("Don't gather your possessions!"). The deliberative subjunctive is used to express deliberation over a course of action or state of being. The deliberative subjunctive may be found in either the present or aorist subjunctive, in any person, but always in a question. τί εἴπωμεν; "What should we say?" or "What ought we to say?"

10. (1) μία τῶν θεῶν τὰς ἄλλας ἐρωτᾷ εἰ φαίνωνται τοῖς τ᾽ ἀρίστοις καὶ τοῖς χειρίστοις τῶν ἀνθρώπων. (2) πότερον τῇ πόλει τῇ πολεμίᾳ μαχεσώμεθα ἢ παρασκευάσωμεν τὴν εἰρήνην ζητῆσαι; (3) ἡ τοῦ πολέμου παρασκευὴ μὴ παυθῇ. (4) μὴ γένηται μάχη ὑπὲρ τοῦ χρυσοῦ καὶ τοῦ ἀργύρου. (5) τοὺς συμμάχους μὴ καλέσητε νῦν, οὐκέτι γὰρ παρασκευὰς πολέμου ἐποιήσαμεν. (6) σύμμαχοι γενώμεθα τῇ πόλει ᾗ πλείους τριήρεις ἢ τῇ πόλει ᾗ μόνον εἴκοσίν εἰσιν. (7) σύμμαχοι γενώμεθα τῇ πόλει ᾗ πλείους τριήρεις ἢ τῇ πόλει ᾗ μόνον εἴκοσίν εἰσιν; (8) σύμμαχοί ἐσμεν τῇ πόλει ᾗ πλείους τριήρεις ἢ τῇ πόλει ᾗ μόνον εἴκοσίν εἰσιν. (9) ζητήσω κλέψαι τὰ χρήματα τὰ τοῦ κακίστου δεσπότου τοῦ αἴσχιστα τοσοῦτον χρυσὸν καὶ ἄργυρον συλλαβόντος ὥστε νῦν φαίνεται ὡς εὐδαιμονέστατος. (10) τῶν πολεμίων πλείονας μάχας μαχεσαμένων ἡμῶν, οἱ τῆς ἡμετέρας πόλεως στρατηγοὶ παρασκευὰς παλαίτερον ἢ οἱ σύμμαχοι ἐποίησαν. (11) τὸν μὲν φιλόσοφον λῦσον, τὴν δὲ φιλοσοφίαν αὐτοῦ μὴ λύσῃς. (12) δεινόν ἐστι τοῦτο τὸ χρῆμα· πότερα πᾶσι τοῖς πρυτάνεσιν περὶ αὐτοῦ εἴπωμεν, ἢ μόνον ἑνὶ αὐτῶν;

11. Check your answers against 10. in the exercises for Lesson 35.

Lesson 36

1. A verb in the optative mood in Greek implies that the speaker views the verb's action or state of being as a potential future action, as something that could, might, or should occur.

2. The optative in Greek is found in the present, the future, the aorist, and the perfect. As in the subjunctive, the tenses lose their "time" facet and retain only their "aspect"— after all, an optative by definition points to future action! Thus, a present optative points to future potential action with on-going aspect; an aorist optative points to future potential action with aoristic or "snap-shot" aspect; and a perfect optative points to future potential action with perfective or "completed" aspect. The future optative, being an exceptional case, need not be worried about now.

3.
   (1) μαχεσαίμην   μαχεσαίμεθα
       μαχέσαιο   μαχέσαισθε
       μαχέσαιτο   μαχέσαιντο
   (2) λύοιμι   λύοιμεν
       λύοις   λύοιτε
       λύοι   λύοιεν
   (3) κλαπείην   κλαπείημεν
       κλαπείης   κλαπείητε
       κλαπείη   κπλαπείησαν
   (4) ἐσοίμην   ἐσοίμεθα
       ἔσοιο   ἔσοισθε
       ἔσοιτο   ἔσοιντο
   (5) No such form exists
   (6) συλληψοίμην   συλληψοίμεθα
       συλλήψοιο   συλλήψοισθε
       συλλήψοιτο   συλλήψοιντο
   (7) λάβοιμι   λάβοιμεν
       λάβοις   λάβοιτε
       λάβοι   λάβοιεν
   (8) παρασκευασθησοίμην   παρασκευασθησοίμεθα
       παρασκευασθήσοιο   παρασκευασθήσοισθε
       παρασκευασθήσοιτο   παρασκευασθήσοιντο
   (9) γράψοιμι   γράψοιμεν
       γράψοις   γράψοιτε
       γράψοι   γράψοιεν
   (10) θύοιμην   θύοιμεθα
       θύοιο   θύοισθε
       θύοιτο   θύοιντο

4.
   (1) ποιοίην   ποιοῖμεν
       ποιοίης   ποιοῖτε
       ποιοίη   ποιοῖεν
   (2) γελῴμην   γελῴμεθα
       γελῷο   γελῷσθε
       γελῷτο   γελῷντο
   (3) δηλοίμην   δηλοίμεθα
       δηλοῖο   δηλοῖσθε
       δηλοῖτο   δηλοῖντο
   (4) ἐρωτῴην   ἐρωτῷμεν
       ἐρωτῴης   ἐρωτῷτε
       ἐρωτῴη   ἐρωτῷεν
   (5) ὠφελοίμην   ὠφελοίμεθα
       ὠφελοῖο   ὠφελοῖσθε
       ὠφελοῖτο   ὠφελοῖντο

(6) δηλοίην   δηλοῖμεν
δηλοίης   δηλοῖτε
δηλοίη   δηλοῖεν

(7) εἴην   εἴημεν
εἴης   εἴητε
εἴη   εἴησαν

5. The two independent uses of the optative are the wish-optative and the potential optative. Each of them is found in fundamentally different syntaxes. The wish-optative, which expresses a future wish, is often preceded by either εἴθε or εἰ γάρ, if positive, or by μή, if negative. The positive wishes can be translated in one of three ways:

Would that the subject might _____.
If only the subject might _____   .
May the subject _____.

The easiest way to translate the negative wish is to use the following model:

May the subject not _____.

The three examples below demonstrate the three main ways in which the wish-optative may be constructed in Greek, followed by English translations:

εἴθε εὐδαίμονα βίον ἄγοι.
        Would that she might live a prosperous life!
        May she live a prosperous life!
εἰ γὰρ πάλιν γελάσαιτε.
        If only you might laugh again!
μὴ αἰσχρῶς τυθείη.
        May he not be slaughtered shamefully!

The potential optative, which indicates that the action of the verb is conceived of as a potential occurrence, is always used with particle ἄν. It is negated by οὐ and when negated retains ἄν. Two examples follow, one positive, the other negative:

τοῦ ῥήτορος ἀκούσαιμεν ἄν. We might listen to the speaker.
τοῦ διδασκάλου οὐκ ἂν ἀκούσαιμεν. We might not listen to the teacher.

6. (1) τὸν ἵππον διώξαιεν ἂν οἱ νεανίαι. (2) εἴθε διώξαιεν τὸν ἵππον οἱ νεανίαι. (3) τὸν ἵππον οὐκ ἂν διώξαιεν οἱ νεανίαι. (4) εἰ γὰρ αἱ θυγατέρες μου ὑπὸ πάντων ἀνδρῶν τιμηθείησαν. (5) μηδεὶς μὴ τιμῴη τὰς θυγατέρας μου. (6) ὑπὸ πάντων ἀνδρῶν οὐκ ἂν τιμηθείησαν αἱ θυγατέρες μου. (7) εἰ γὰρ πάντες ἄνδρες τὰς θυγατέρας μου τιμήσαιεν. (8) εἰ γὰρ οἱ φιλόσοφοι πάσας ἁμαρτίας δηλοῖεν. (9) οἱ φιλόσοφοι πάσας ἁμαρτίας οὐκ ἂν δηλοῖεν. (10) μὴ δηλοῖεν οἱ φιλόσοφοι πάσας ἁμαρτίας.

7. χράομαι, χρήσομαι, ἐχρησάμην, _____, κέχρημαι, ἐχρήσθην

8. (a) Present Indicative and Subjunctive   (b) Present Optative

χρῶμαι	χρώμεθα	χρῴμην	χρῴμεθα
χρῇ	χρῆσθε	χρῷο	χρῷσθε
χρῆται	χρῶνται	χρῷτο	χρῷντο

9. (1) εἰ γὰρ ἡ στρατιὰ ἑτοίμη γένοιτο μαχέσασθαι μάχην τῇ στρατιᾷ τῇ πολεμίᾳ. (2) ἔσοιντο ἂν ὀλίγῳ χρησιμώτεροι ἡμῖν ὁ πρῶτος στρατιώτης καὶ ὁ δεύτερος ἢ ὁ τρίτος καὶ ὁ τέταρτος. (3) πᾶσι μὲν τοῖς χρήμασιν ὁ βασιλεὺς χρήσαιτο ἂν ἀγαθὰ τοῖς πολλοῖς ποιῶν· τῷ δὲ χρυσῷ καὶ ἀργύρῳ μὴ χρῷτο πλείους δούλους κομιζόμενος. (4) γένοιτ' ἂν ὁ στρατὸς ἡμῶν ἱκανὸς φανῆναι τοῖς πολεμίοις ὡς δεινότατος; (5) καίπερ τῶν χρημάτων χρησίμων ὄντων καὶ τοῦ ἀργύρου χρησιμωτέρου ὄντος, χρησιμώτατος πάντων ὁ χρυσός. (6) εἴθε τῇ ἡδείᾳ ἡσυχίᾳ χρήσαιτο ἡ ἡμετέρα πόλις, καὶ εἰ γὰρ νίκῃ ἡδίονι χρῷντο οἱ στρατηγοί. (7) τοῦ στρατοπέδου ὑπὸ τῶν κατὰ γῆν ἀφικομένων στρατιωτῶν χρησθέντος, ἐχρήσθη τὸ ἄστυ ὑπὸ τῶν ἀπὸ τῶν τριήρων τῶν κατὰ θάλασσαν ἀφικομένων. (8) εἰ γὰρ βιβλία γραφείη ὑπὸ στρατηγῶν περὶ στρατοπέδων, στρατιωτῶν καὶ στρατιῶν. (9) εἴθε εἴη ἡ νίκη τῷ ἀρίστῳ ἀνδρί.

(10) παρασκευάσωμεν, ὦ στρατηγέ, ταῖς ἀσπίσι χρήσασθαι; (11) μὴ εἴπῃς τόδε· εἴθε κριθείη ὁ κάκιστος ῥήτωρ βασιλεύς. (12) μιᾷ φωνῇ ἐρωτήσωμεν τάδε· μακροτέρῳ καὶ εὐδαιμονεστέρῳ βίῳ, ὦ νίκη, ἐν ἡμῖν χρῷο ἄν;

10. Check your answers against **9**. in the exercises for Lesson 36.

Lesson 37

1. A conditional sentence is a sentence with two clauses: a subordinate "if" clause, and a main "then" clause.

2. The two terms used to describe the clauses of a Greek conditional sentence are "protasis" (πρότασις) and "apodosis" (ἀπόδοσις). The protasis of a condition is its subordinate "if" clause; the apodosis is its main "then" clause.

3. There are four different basic types of Greek conditions. They are: simple particular, contrary-to-fact, general, and future.

4. There are nine different types of Greek conditions. They are: past simple particular, present simple particular, past contrary-to-fact, present contrary-to-fact, past general, present general, future most vivid, future more vivid, future less vivid.

5.

		Protasis	Apodosis
(1)		εἰ + optative,	optative + ἄν
		If x should_____,	y would_____.
(2)	(a)	εἰ + imperfect,	imperfect.
	(b)	aorist indicative,	aorist indicative.
	(c)	pluperfect,	pluperfect.
	(a)	If x was _____ing,	y was _____ing.
	(b)	If x _____ed,	y_____ed.
	(c)	If x had _____ed,	y had _____ed.
(3)		εἰ + optative,	imperfect.
		If x (ever)_____ed,	y_____ed.
(4)		εἰ + future indicative,	future indicative.
		If x will _____,	y will _____.
(5)		ἐάν + subjunctive,	present indicative.
		If x (ever) _____s,	y _____s.
(6)		εἰ + aorist indicative,	aorist indicative + ἄν.
		If x had _____ed,	y would have _____ed.
(7)		ἐάν + subjunctive,	future indicative.
		If x _____s,	y will _____.
(8)		εἰ + imperfect,	imperfect + ἄν.
		If x were _____ing,	y would be _____ing.

6. The conditions that meet these requirements are:
Present contrary-to-fact
　　　εἰ + imperfect,_____　　imperfect + ἄν.
　　　If x were _____ing,　y would be _____ing.
Past contrary-to-fact
　　　εἰ + aorist indicative,　　aorist indicative + ἄν.
　　　If x had _____ed,　y would have _____ed.
Present general
　　　ἐάν + subjunctive,　　　present indicative.
　　　If x (ever) _____s,　y _____s.
Future more vivid
　　　ἐάν + subjunctive,　　　future indicative.
　　　If x _____s,　　　y will _____.

Future less vivid

      εἰ + optative,   optative + ἄν

      If x should _____,   y would _____.

7. The conditions that meet these requirements are:

Past general

      εἰ + optative,   imperfect.

      If x (ever) _____ed,   y _____ed.

Future less vivid

      εἰ + optative,   optative + ἄν

      If x should _____,   y would _____.

8. The conditions that meet these requirements are:

Present simple particular

      εἰ + present indicative,   present indicative

      If x is _____ing,   y is _____ing.

                     or

      If x _____s,   y _____s.

Past simple particular

      (a) εἰ + imperfect,   imperfect.

      (b) aorist indicative,   aorist indicative.

      (c) pluperfect,   pluperfect.

      (a) If x was _____ing,   y was _____ing.

      (b) If x _____ed,   y _____ed.

      (c) If x had _____ed,   y had _____ed.

Future most vivid

      εἰ + future indicative,   future indicative.

      If x will _____,   y will _____.

9. The conditions that meet these requirements are:

Present general

      ἐὰν + subjunctive,   present indicative.

      If x (ever) _____s,   y _____s.

Future more vivid

      ἐὰν + subjunctive,   future indicative.

      If x _____s,   y will _____.

10. (1) Past simple particular (2) Past contrary-to-fact (3) Past simple particular (4) Future most vivid (5) Present general (6) Present simple particular (7) Future less vivid (8) Past general (9) Future more vivid (10) Present contrary-to-fact

11. (1) εἰ νικῴης ἀδίκως, τοὺς τῆς πόλεως νόμους ἀδικοίης ἄν. (2) ἆρα τοὺς νεανίας διαφθείροι ἄν, αὐτοὺς ἄδικα διδάσκων; (3) εἰ ἐγένετο ἡ δίκη ἡ Ἀθηναία ὡς βελτίστη, οὐκ ἂν ἀπέκτειναν οἱ Ἀθηναῖοι τὸν Σωκράτη. (4) ἐὰν σ' ἀδικῶσιν, ἐλευθέρα εἶ τῆς δίκης. (5) εἰ εἴη ἡ φύσις ἡμῶν βελτίων, ἴσως ἐφίλουν πάντες ἄνθρωποι τοὺς ἄλλους. (6) πᾶσαν δίκην διαφθερῶ εἰ παρὰ τοῦ δεσπότου τοῦ κακοῦ δίκην μὴ λήψει. (7) ἐὰν πολλοὺς ἀδικῶσιν, ἆρα τοὺς ἀδικηθέντας φυλάττειν ζητήσεις; (8) εἰ γὰρ ὁ βασιλεὺς ὁ κακὸς ἀποθάνοι. (9) εἰ θόρυβος ἐν τῷ ἄστει ἐστίν, προσβάλλουσιν οἱ πολέμιοι τοῖς τείχεσιν. (10) τοῦ διδασκάλου νῦν ἤκουες, εἰ μὴ ἐζήτεις τοὺς ἄλλους μαθητὰς διαφθερεῖν. (11) εἰ ἀπέθανεν ὁ στρατηγός, ἀπέθανεν καὶ ἡ στρατιά.

12. Check your answers against **11**. in the exercises for Lesson 37.

Lesson 38

1. Two examples in illustration of this would be as follow:

   The man **who** ate the hotdog is now talking to the street vendor.
   > (Definite)
   Whoever ate the hotdog is now talking to the street vendor.
   > (Indefinite)

   From these two examples, the difference between the definite use of the relative pronoun and the indefinite use of the relative pronoun is clear. In the first instance, the relative pronoun "who" refers back in the sentence to a specific noun (in other instances, it could refer to a specific pronoun, as well); in the second instance, the relative pronoun "whoever" refers not to any specific noun or pronoun formerly mentioned. It is therefore "indefinite."

2. A relative clause that is indefinite is treated in Greek as though it were the protasis of a conditional sentence in which "if", εἰ or the εἰ part of ἐάν, is replaced by the relative pronoun. Two examples illustrate this:

   If people harm horses, they act unjustly. (Straight condition)
   Whoever harm horses act unjustly. (Relative condition)
   ἐὰν οἱ ἄνθρωποι ἵππους βλάπτωσιν, ἀδικοῦσιν. (Straight condition)
   οἵτινες ἂν ἵππους βλάπτωσιν, ἀδικοῦσιν. (Relative condition)

3. (1) (a) εἰ λέγοιμεν, τοὺς νεανίας διαφθείροιμεν ἄν. (b) ὅτε λέγοιμεν, τοὺς νεανίας διαφθείροιμεν ἄν. (2) (a) εἰ ὁ διδάσκαλος δόξας διδάξαι, οὐκ ἀληθεῖς ἦσαν. (b) ἅστινας δόξας διδάξαι ὁ διδάσκαλος, οὐκ ἀληθεῖς ἦσαν. (3) (a) εἰ τοὺς νεανίας διέφθειρας, ἐλύθης ἄν. (b) ὃς τοὺς νεανίας διέφθειρεν, ἐλύθη ἄν. (4) (a) εἰ τοὺς νεανίας διέφθειρον, ἐλύοντο ἄν. (b) οὕστινας διέφθειρον, ἐλύοντο ἄν.

4.
   (1) ὅστις, ἥτις, οἵτινες, αἵτινες, ὅς, ἥ, οἵ, αἵ
   (2) οὗτινος, ἧστινος, ὧντινων, οὗ, ἧς, ὧν
   (3) ὅντινα, ἥντινα, οὕστινας, ἅστινας, ὅν, ἥν, οὕς, ἅς
   (4) ᾧτινι, ᾗτινι, οἷστισι(ν), αἷστισι(ν), ᾧ, ᾗ, οἷς, αἷς
   (5) οἷ, ὅποι
   (6) ὅτε, ὁπότε
   (7) ὡς, ὅπως
   (8) ὅθεν, ὁπόθεν
   (9) οὗ, ὅπου

5. (1) ὅποι/οἷ ἐτρέψατο, λύπην καὶ οὐ χαρὰν ηὗρεν ἄν. (2) ὅστις/ὃς ἄρχων κριθήσεται, τῶν Ἀθηναίων εὖ ἄρξει. (3) ὁπόθεν/ὅθεν εἰς τὴν πόλιν ἡμῶν ἀφίκοισθε, αὐτὴν εὕροιτε ἂν τόπον πολλῷ ἀμείνονα πάντων ἄλλων. (4) οὗτινος/οὗ ἂν τὸ ἱμάτιον φέρῃ, καλλίων ἐστὶ πασῶν τῶν ἄλλων κορῶν. (5) εἰς ἥντινα ἂν / ἣν ἂν πρόθυμος ᾖς, μεγάλη προθυμίᾳ καὶ εἰς σὲ χρήσεται. (6) οἷστισιν / αἷστισιν ἐβούλετο ὁ σὸς θυμὸς ἐπιστολὰς πέμψαι, προθυμότατα ἂν ἐλάμβανον αὐτάς. (7) ὅτε / ὁπότε κριθείη ἄρχων ὁ ἀνὴρ οὗτος, νόμοις ἴσοις τε καὶ δικαίοις τῶν πολλῶν ἦρχεν. (8) ὡς ἂν / ὅπως ἂν θυμῷ λέγειν ζητῇ, τοῖς λόγοις αὐτοῦ μὴ πεισθῶμεν. (9) ὅπου / οὗ τοὺς παῖδας ἀπέλιπον, αὐτοὺς ηὗρον ἄν.

6. Check your answers against **5.** in the exercises for Lesson 38.

Lesson 39

1. The difference may be articulated as follows: a natural result clause speaks of an outcome not necessarily intended, and not necessarily having occured; an actual result clause speaks of an outcome not necessarily intended, but having occured; and a purpose clause speaks of an in-

tended outcome, but does not indicate whether it occured. One may represent these various schemata in chart form as follows:

	Outcome intended?	Outcome actual?
Natural Result	Not necessarily.	Not necessarily.
Actual Result	Not necessarily.	Yes, necessarily.
Purpose	Yes.	Not necessarily.

2.

	Conjunction	Verb Mood	Negation	Subject Case
Nat. Result	ὥστε	Infinitive	μή	Acc.*
Act. Result	ὥστε	Indicative	οὐ	Nom.
Purpose	ἵνα ὅπως ὡς μή	Subjunctive or Optative	μή	Nom.

*if not the same as the subject

3. The purpose clause must always use the subjunctive when the main clause to which it is attached has a verb in a primary tense. The purpose clause may use *either* the subjunctive *or* the optative when the main clause to which it is attached has a verb in a secondary tense.

4. It is easiest to cull from all the verb forms those which are considered to be secondary tense forms. The secondary forms are the indicative of the imperfect, aorist, and pluperfect and in some instances the aorist participle, all forms whose frame of reference is past time. For this reason, the perfect is excluded from the secondary tenses because of the fact that its frame of reference is present time. Furthermore, since an aorist imperative or an aorist subjunctive or optative does not refer to past time, but to future time, it too is not listed among the secondary forms for purposes of determining the mood of the verb in a purpose clause.

5. γαμέω, γαμῶ, ἔγημα, γεγάμηκα, γεγάμημαι, _____
ἕπομαι, ἕψομαι, ἑσπόμην, _____, _____, _____
βοάω, βοήσομαι, ἐβόησα, _____ , _____, _____

6.
(1) γαμοίην / γαμοῖμεν
γαμοίης / γαμοῖτε
γαμοίη / γαμοῖεν
(2) ἐβόων / ἐβοῶμεν
ἐβόας / ἐβοᾶτε
ἐβόα / ἐβόων
(3) εἰπόμην / εἰπόμεθα
εἴπου / εἴπεσθε
εἴπετο / εἴποντο
(4) βοῶ / βοῶμεν
βοᾷς / βοᾶτε
βοᾷ / βοῶσι(ν)
(5) σποίμην / σποίμεθα
σποῖο / σποῖσθε
σποῖτο / σποῖντο
(6) γήμαιμι / γήμαιμεν
γήμαις / γήμαιτε
γήμαι / γήμαιεν

7. The verb in the indirect question under such circumstances may be in either its original mood and tense, or may be converted, retaining its original tense, into the optative mood. The impact on the sentence of following the convention of using the optative is to make the question

less vivid, while the impact of retaining the original mood and tense of the verb is to make the question more vivid.

8. (1) εἰ ταύτην τὴν γυναῖκα γῆμαι κρίναιμι, ἆρα παύσαιντο ἂν ἡ μήτηρ καὶ ὁ πατήρ μου βοῶντες ἐπ᾽ ἐμοί; (2) τῷ ἵππῳ ἕπομαι ἵνα εὕρω τὴν τοῦ δεσπότου οἰκίαν. (3) τῷ ἵππῳ ἐσπόμην ὅπως τὴν τοῦ δεσπότου οἰκίαν εὕροιμι. (4) ἆρα τῷ ἵππῳ σπῶμαι ὡς τὴν τοῦ δεσπότου οἰκίαν εὕρω; (5) μένε κάτω νυνὶ καὶ τρέψου ἀνὰ τὴν κλίμακα ὕστερον μὴ τὸ τέκνον βοήσῃ. (6) ἠρώτησαν οἱ ἄνδρες τὰς γυναῖκας εἰ ξένοις ἀνδράσιν εἰς τὴν ἀγορὰν ἕποιντο. (7) ἐρωτήσουσιν αἱ γυναῖκες τοὺς ἄνδρας ὅπως τὴν ἁμαρτίαν εὑρήσειν μέλλουσιν. (8) πάντας τοὺς πρυτάνεις ἐκάλεσεν ὁ ἄρχων εἰς τὴν οἰκίαν ὡς γάμον ποιήσαι τῇ θυγατρὶ καὶ τῷ ἐσομένῳ ἀνδρὶ αὐτῇ. (9) ἐτρέψατο ὁ στρατηγὸς ἐν τῇ τριήρει ἄνω τε καὶ κάτω, ὅπως τοῖς στρατιώταις κελεύοι ὡς κράτιστα μάχεσθαι. (10) οἱ στρατιῶται τοῦ στρατηγοῦ ἀκούσονται ἵνα νίκην νικήσωσι καὶ ὅπως βοὴ μεγάλη ᾖ ὁπόταν εἰς τὴν πόλιν πάλιν ἀφίκωνται.

9. Check your answers against **8.** in the exercises for Lesson 39.

Lesson 40

1. εἶμι is preferred to ἔρχομαι in the imperfect and future, in the present subjunctive, optative and imperative, in the future optative, present and future infinitives, present and future participles.

2.

(1)	ἔρχῃ.	(9)	ἆρ᾽ ἴω;
(2)	ἤεις.	(10)	ἴοιμι ἄν.
(3)	ᾔει.	(11)	ἦλθεν.
(4)	ἐλήλυθεν.	(12)	ἐληλύθαμεν.
(5)	ἐθέλω ἰέναι.	(13)	ᾖτε.
(6)	ἐκρίναντο ἰέναι.	(14)	εἰ ἦλθον, ἦλθες ἄν.
(7)	εἰ ᾖειν, ᾔεις ἄν.	(15)	εἰ ἴοιμι, ἴοις ἄν.
(8)	ἐὰν ἴω, εἶ.	(16)	εἰ εἶμι, ἴασιν.

3. ἔρχομαι, ἐλεύσομαι, ἦλθον, ἐλήλυθα, _____ , _____

4. εἶμι_____ , _____ , _____ , _____ , _____
   εἰμί, ἔσομαι, [ἦν], _____ , _____ , _____

5. See Groton, §238.

6. To construct indirect discourse in Greek, there are **three** methods at hand.

7. The first method available for constructing indirect discourse in Greek is used with introductory verbs of saying. The reported speech is placed into a subordinate clause preceded by ὅτι or by ὡς. With an introductory verb of saying in a primary tense, the finite verb in the indirect statement retains its original mood and tense; when the introductory verb is in a secondary tense (aorist indicative [and sometimes participle], imperfect, and pluperfect), the finite verb in the indirect statement may retain its original tense and mood, but may also be expressed in the optative form of the tense the original verb was in.

8. For purposes of indirect discourse with ὅτι or ὡς, the following verbs are counted as verbs of saying: ἀγγέλλω, ἀποκρίνομαι, γράφω, λέγω, φράζω.

9. (1) ἡρέθη βασιλεύς. ἀγγέλλει ὡς βασιλεὺς ἡρέθη. ἤγγειλεν ὡς βασιλεὺς αἱρεθείη. (2) κακὰ πείσεται. λέγω ὅτι κακὰ πείσεται. εἴρηκα ὡς κακὰ πείσοιτο. εἴρηκα ὅτι κακὰ πείσεται. εἶπον ὡς κακὰ πείσοιτο. (3) ὡς τὸν Σωκράτη ἦλθον. γεγράφαμεν ὅτι ὡς τὸν Σωκράτη ἦλθον. ἐγεγράφεμεν ὅτι ὡς τὸν Σωκράτη ἔλθοιεν. γράψομεν ὅτι ὡς τὸν Σωκράτη ἦλθον. (4) ἄνευ ἐπιτηδείων ἐστέ. ἔφρασαν ὡς ἄνευ ἐπιτηδείων εἶτε.

φράσαντες ὡς ἄνευ ἐπιτηδείων εἶτε, ὡς ὑμᾶς ἦλθον. φράσομεν ὅτι ἄνευ ἐπιτηδείων ἐστέ.

10. Check your answers against **9.** in the exercises.

11. One need bear in mind the following points when one wishes to include a subordinate clause within indirect discourse using ὅτι or ὡς.
(1) When the introductory verb of "saying" is in a secondary tense, one has the option to change the verb in the subordinate clause into the optative. For example, if in direct discourse we had the following: ἐπειδὴ ἡ τριήρης μάλα καλή **ἐστιν**, οἱ στρατιῶται **ἐθέλουσιν** εἶναι ἐν αὐτῇ (since the trireme is very beautiful, the soldiers desire to be in it), the indirect form of the same could be: εἶπον οἱ ῥήτορες ὅτι ἐπειδὴ ἡ τριήρης μάλα καλὴ **εἴη**, οἱ στρατιῶται **ἐθέλοιεν** εἶναι ἐν αὐτῇ. In this instance, the verb of the dependent clause ἐπειδὴ...ἐστιν was converted into the optative just as was the verb of what was originally an independent clause in direct spech, οἱ...αὐτῇ. If this is done in a clause that has subjunctive + ἄν, the ἄν is dropped, to avoid confusion with what might appear to have initially been a potential optative.

(2) This switching of mood from indicative or subjunctive to optative in a dependent clause is, however, not used in a situation where that verb is in a secondary tense of the indicative. This simply avoids ambiguity. For example, if we were to convert the following condition, εἰ ἦλθες εἰς τὴν τριήρη, τὰ χρήματα ηὕρες ἄν (if you had gone into the trireme, you would have found the goods) into indirect discourse preceded by a secondary tense verb, we would have to convert it into the following: εἶπον ὅτι εἰ εἰς τὴν τριήρη ἦλθες, τὰ χρήματα εὕροις ἄν (= I said that if you had gone into the trireme, you would have found the goods) and not εἶπον ὅτι εἰ εἰς τὴν τριήρη ἔλθοις, τὰ χρήματα εὕροις ἄν (= I said that if you should go into the trireme, you would find the goods).

12. (1) ἐλθὲ εἰς τὴν οἰκίαν. (2) εἶπες ὅτι εἰς τὴν οἰκίαν ἴασιν. (3) ὁ ἀνήρ, αἱρεθεὶς βασιλεύς, ἔφρασεν ὅτι ἡ γυνὴ οὐκέτι κακῶς πείσοιτο ὑπ’ οὐδενός. (4) ἴθι, ἴωμεν εἰς τὴν ἀγοράν, φράζουσαι ὡς ὁ στρατηγὸς τὸν πόλεμον νενίκηκεν. (5) ἔφρασαν οἱ ἐπιτήδειοί μου ὅτι τὰ ἐπιτήδεια ἔνδον εἴη καὶ ὡς αὐτὰ ἔξω πέμψοιεν μετὰ οἰκετῶν τινῶν. (6) ἦλθον εὐθὺς οἱ οἰκέται ὡς τοὺς ἐπιτηδείους καὶ εἶπον ὡς οἱ στρατιῶται γράψαιεν ὅτι ὁ στρατηγὸς ἀποθάνοι. (7) εἴπομεν ὅτι καίπερ οὐ φιλοῦντες πάσχειν, προθύμως πεισοίμεθα ὑπὲρ τοῦ ἄστεως. (8) οὗτος, ἐλθὲ εἰς τὴν ἀγοράν· καὶ κρίνωμεν ὁπότερον ἔπαθον οἱ πολλοὶ ἱκανὸν ἢ οὔ. (9) ἐφράσθη ἡμῖν ὅτι τῷ βασιλεῖ, ἰόντι ὡς τοὺς ἐπιτηδείους, προσβάλοι λέων μέγας καὶ ἀποκτείναι. (10) βασιλέα ἕλωμεν πρόθυμον τοῖς πάσχουσιν ὑπὲρ τῆς φιλίας, τῆς προθυμίας, καὶ τῆς δίκης.

13. Check your answers against **12.** in the exercises for Lesson 40.

Lesson 41

1. φημί, φήσω, ἔφησα, _____, _____, _____

2.
   (1) φαίην ἄν τι.
   (2) τοῦτ’ οὔ φημι.
   (3) φασίν.
   (4) τοῦτ’ ἔφαμεν.
   (5) φῶμέν τι.
   (6) εἰ γάρ τι φαίητε.
   (7) φάτω.
   (8) ἔφασαν
   (9) τοῦτ’ οὔ φησιν.
   (10) φής.
   (11) ἆρα τοῦτ’ ἔφησθα;
   (12) ἆρά τι φῶ;
   (13) ταῦτα φάσκων, πλείονα φάναι ἤθελεν.
   (14) τοῦθ’ ἡμῖν φάντων.

3. (a) For sake of ease, let's simply call indirect discourse with ὅτι or ὡς indirect discourse I and abbreviate it **i.d. I**; and indirect discourse with infinitive indirect discourse II and abbreviate it **i.d. II**. While i.d. I uses a con-

junction to introduce the discourse (ὅτι or ὡς) there is no such feature in i.d. II; indeed, i.d. II uses no conjunctions or particles to alert one of its presence. Furthermore, while in i.d. I the main verb in the indirect statement is always in a finite form, in i.d. II the main verb in the indirect statement is always in the infinitive. This particular feature raises some issues in regard to the case of the subject. We have seen already, for instance with the natural result clause, that the subject of an infinitive will be in the accusative case in most instances. This is true also for i.d. II, whereas for i.d. I, the subject is always in the nominative case. When the subject is in the accusative case, any adjectives which modify it, whether attributively or predicately, will also be in the accusative case. There is an exception to the accusative subject, however. If the subject of the indirect statement is the same as that of the introductory phrase or clause, then the subject of the indirect statement will be expressed in the nominative. Verbs in dependent clauses in the indirect discourse in i.d. II are not changed to infinitives; accordingly, their subjects are expressed in the nominative.

(b) (1) ἔγραψεν ὡς ὁ Σωκράτης ἄνθρωπον ἀπέκτεινεν. (2) ἐνόμισε τὸν Σωκράτη ἄνθρωπον ἀποκτεῖναι. (3) φράζω ὅτι ἀσπίδας πεντεκαίδεκα πωλήσομεν. (4) ἔφρασα ὡς ἀσπίδας πεντεκαίδεκα πωλήσοιμεν. (5) πιστεύω ἡμᾶς ἀσπίδας πεντεκαίδεκα πωλήσειν. (6) ἐπίστευσα ἡμᾶς ἀσπίδας πεντεκαίδεκα πωλήσειν.

4. (a) We have seen already, for instance with the natural result clause, that the subject of an infinitive will be in the accusative case in most instances. This is true also for i.d. II, whereas for i.d. I, the subject is always in the nominative case. When the subject is in the accusative case, any adjectives which modify it, whether attributively or predicately, will also be in the accusative case. There is an exception to the accusative subject, however. If the subject of the indirect statement is the same as that of the introductory phrase or clause, then the subject of the indirect statement will be expressed in the nominative. Verbs in dependent clauses in the indirect discourse in i.d. II are not changed to infinitives; accordingly, their subjects are expressed in the nominative.

(b) (1) νομίζω θάττων εἶναι αὐτοῦ. (2) νομίζω αὐτὸν θάττονα εἶναι ἐμοῦ. (3) ἐκρίναμεν ἄριστοι γενέσθαι. (4) ἐκρίναμεν αὐτοὺς ἀρίστους εἶναι. (5) ἐκείνη νομίζει μέγα φιληθήσεσθαι ὑπ᾽ αὐτοῦ. (6) ἐκείνη φησὶ αὐτὸν μέγα ὑφ᾽ ἑαυτῆς φιληθήσεσθαι.

5. (a) If an infinitive in i.d. II is in the present tense, it shows that the action expressed by that verb is happening at the same time as the action of the main verb of the sentence. If an infinitive in i.d. II is in the aorist tense, it shows that the action expressed by that verb happened prior to the action of the main verb of the sentence. Thus some aorists, when subordinated to a secondary tense introductory verb, may appear in English to be pluperfects. If an infinitive in i.d. II is in the perfect tense, it shows that the action expressed by that verb is viewed as complete as of the time when the action expressed by the introductory verb is taking place. An infinitive in i.d. II in the future tense shows action that takes place after, or subsequent to, the time of the introductory verb.

(b) (1) ἔκρινα ἡμᾶς τὴν μάχην νικῆσαι. (2) ἔκρινα ἡμᾶς τὴν μάχην νικᾶν. (3) ἔκρινα ἡμᾶς τὴν μάχην νικήσειν. (4) νομίζεις ἡμᾶς οὐχ ἱκανὸν ἠγαπηκέναι. (5) νομίζεις ἡμᾶς οὐχ ἱκανὸν ἀγαπῆσαι. (6) νομίζεις ἡμᾶς οὐχ ἱκανὸν ἀγαπᾶν. (7) νομίζεις ἡμᾶς οὐχ ἱκανὸν ἀγαπήσειν. (8) ἐμὲ ἀγαπῆσαι οὐ φήσεις. (9) ἐμὲ σὲ ἀγαπᾶν οὐ φήσεις. (10) ἐμὲ σὲ ἠγαπηκέναι οὐ φήσεις. (11) ἐμὲ πάλιν ἀγαπήσειν μέλλειν οὐ φήσεις. (12) ἐμὲ πάλιν ἀγαπήσειν οὐ φήσεις.

6. One negates an indirect statement using the infinitive as the direct form of the statement would have been negated. That is, if in the direct form of the statement one would have had οὐ or its by-forms as negation, so also

in the indirect statement in i.d. II; if in the direct form of the statement one would have had μή or its by-forms as negation, so also in the indirect statement in i.d. II.

7. The particle ἄν is retained in i.d. II.

8. (1) καίπερ τὴν καλὴν τριήρη δυοῖν ταλάντων χρυσοῦ πωλήσας, ὁ ῥήτωρ ὁ νέον εὐδαίμων οὐκ ἔφησε χρήματα κλέψαι παρὰ τῆς πόλεως. (2) ἔφησεν ἡ ἑταίρα τὸν ἑταῖρόν μου ἀγαπᾶν καὶ τὴν ἀγάπην τοσαύτην εἶναι ὥστε αὐτῷ ἕπεσθαι, οἷ ἂν ἔλθῃ. (3) ταχέως ἴθι. νομίζω τοὺς πολεμίους ἐπὶ τὰ τείχη ἡμῶν ἀφικνεῖσθαι. (4) ἐνομίσθη τὴν τριήρη τὴν βραδυτάτην τὴν τῶν Ἀθηναίων καὶ ὀλίγῳ θάττονα εἶναι πασῶν τῶν ἄλλων τῆς ἄλλης πόλεως. (5) κάλλιστον πάντων ἀνδρῶν φιλεῖ νομίζειν τὸν ἑταῖρον εἶναι. (6) καλλίστη πασῶν γυναικῶν φιλεῖ νομίζειν εἶναι. (7) οὐκ ἔφη τὴν τοῦ ἐχθροῦ φιλίαν αὐτὴν ἀπὸ τῆς πᾶσι τοῖς ἄλλοις ἀνθρώποις προθυμίας τρέψαι. (8) τί τάλαντος; ὁ τάλαντος μναῖ ἑξήκοντα. τί μνᾶ; ἡ μνᾶ ἑκατὸν δραχμαί. τί δραχμή; ἡ δραχμὴ ὀβολοὶ ἕξ. (9) τὴν μὲν ἀληθῆ φιλίαν εὑρηκέναι φήσει, τὴν δ' ἀγάπην τὴν ἀληθῆ ζητήσειν. (10) ἐνενόμιστο τὸν στρατηγὸν τὴν τριήρη ἑκατὸν μνῶν ἀλλάξασθαι.

9. Check your answers against 8. in the exercises for Lesson 41.

Lesson 42

1. (a) Indirect discourse with a participle is formed in the following fashion: After the verb which introduces the indirect discourse, one uses a participle in the predicate position to express the verb of the discourse. This participle is usually preceded by a noun or pronoun in the accusative case which functions as the participle's subject. The participle, obviously, will agree with its subject in number, case, and gender. If, however, the subject of the indirect discourse is the same as that of the verb which introduces the indirect discourse, the subject will be unexpressed and remain in the nominative case.

(b) (1) δηλοῖ ὁ φιλόσοφος τοὺς μαθητὰς οὐδὲν εἰδότας. The philosopher is explaining that his students know nothing. (2) ᾐσθόμεθα τὰς θεραπαίνας τῇ δεσποίνῃ εὖ δουλευούσας. We sensed that the maids were serving their mistress well. (3) ἀκηκόασι τοὺς πολεμίους ἐπὶ τὰ τῆς πόλεως τείχη ἀφικομένους. They have heard that the enemy have arrived at the walls of their city. (4) ἐδήλου ὁ φιλόσοφος οὐδὲν εἰδώς. The philosopher was explaining that he knew nothing. (5) εὑρίσκομεν οὐκ ἐθέλοντες τὴν μοῖραν ἰδεῖν. We find that we do not want to see our fate.

2. (a) An adjective modifying a noun or pronoun which is the subject of indirect discourse will be either in the accusative or nominative case, depending upon the case of the subject, as dictated by whether the subject of the indirect discourse is the same as that of its introductory verb or not.

(b) (1) οἶδα ὢν φιλόσοφος σοφός. (2) ἐπύθετο ὁ φιλόσοφος ὁ σοφὸς γεννηθεὶς ἐλεύθερος. (3) ἐπύθετο ὁ φιλόσοφος ὁ σοφὸς τὴν γυναῖκα ἐλευθέραν γεννηθεῖσαν. (4) ἔμαθέ με φιλόσοφον σοφὸν ὄντα. (5) ἆρα τὴν καλὴν τριήρη τὴν σὴν ᾔσθου λυομένην;

3. Verbs of knowing, showing, and perceiving typically introduce indirect discourse using a participle. Such verbs as we have learned in Greek so far include:

Knowing	Showing	Perceiving
μανθάνω	δηλόω	ἀκούω
οἶδα	φαίνω	βλέπω
		εὑρίσκω
		ὁράω
		αἰσθάνομαι
		πυνθάνομαι

4. See Groton §247.

5. (1) ἴσμεν τοὺς στρατιώτας οὐ νενικηκότας. (2) λέγομεν ὅτι οἱ στρατιῶται οὐ νενικήκασιν. (3) νομίζομεν τοὺς στρατιώτας οὐ νενικηκέναι. (4) ἤγγειλεν ὁ κῆρυξ ὅτι ἀπέθανεν ὁ ῥήτωρ. (5) ἤκουσεν ὁ κῆρυξ τὸν ῥήτορα ἀποθανόντα. (6) ἤκουσεν ὁ κῆρυξ τὸν ῥήτορα ἀποθανόντα. (7) οὐκ ἔφησεν ὁ κῆρυξ τὸν ῥήτορα ἀποθανεῖν. (8) ἆρα δηλοῖ τὸ βιβλίον οὐχ εὑρών; (9) ἆρ᾽ ἔγραψεν ὡς τὸ βιβλίον οὐχ ηὗρεν; (10) ἆρα νομίζει τὸ βιβλίον οὐχ εὑρεῖν; (11) ἆρα δηλοῖ τὸ βιβλίον οὐχ εὑροῦσα;

6. (1) μανθάνω, μαθήσομαι, ἔμαθον, μεμάθηκα, _____, _____
   (2) αἰσθάνομαι, αἰσθήσομαι, ᾐσθόμην, _____, ᾔσθημαι, _____
   (3) πυνθάνομαι, πεύσομαι, ἐπυθόμην, _____, πέπυσμαι, _____

7. Crasis is a phenomenon whereby two words, one or both of which might end with or begin with a vowel or a diphthong and which might not normally undergo elision, are brought together to make one word by "melding" or "mixing" the two words together. An example of this phenomenon is the mixture of the phrase τὸ ἱμάτιον into one word: θοἰμάτιον.

8. (1) ὁ σώφρων εὗρεν καὶ τοὺς ἀρίστους οὐκ ἀεὶ τῇ σοφρωσύνῃ ἀρχομένους. (2) ἐπύθου τοῦ γέροντος καὶ τῆς γραός; λέγεται ὅτι χαρὰν τῇ ἀληθείᾳ εὗρον. (3) τῇ ἀληθείᾳ αἰσθήσεσθε τὴν σοφίαν κομισάμενοι ὅταν ἔχητε μηκέτι τὰ χρήματα ἀγαπᾶν. (4) ἔμαθον γράφειν βιβλία ἵνα τοὺς μαθητὰς παιδεύσω. (5) αὖθις οἱ μαθηταὶ ἐπύθοντο τὸν διδάσκαλον οὐκ ὄντα σώφρονα. (6) φαίνεται τοῦτο τὸ πρᾶγμα ἐκ τῶν τῶν πρυτανέων χειρῶν εἶναι. (7) καίπερ νομίζων εἶναι ὡς κάλλιστος, οὗτος οὔ φησι χαίρειν βλέπων εἰς ἑαυτόν. (8) μέλλεις αἰσθήσεσθαι τὸν Σωκράτη πολλοὺς νεανίας βεβλαφότα. (9) εὗρον παρὰ τῶν πρυτάνεων τοὺς στρατηγοὺς παρὰ τῶν στρατιωτῶν τῶν κακῶν δίκην λαβόντας, καίπερ τὴν αὐτὴν ἁμαρτίαν ἁμαρτόντας. (10) ἆρα λέοντα αἰσθάνει; λέοντα ἐφ᾽ ἡμᾶς ἐρχόμενον αἰσθάνομαι.

9. Check your answers against 8. in the exercises for Lesson 42.

Lesson 43

1. (1) The complementary infinitive completes the thought introduced by its main verb. For example, the statement ἐθέλω ("I wish"), when coupled with an infinitive, gives a fuller sense than alone: ἐθέλω γράψαι ἐπιστολήν ("I wish to write a letter"). Another instance like this is the use of οἶδα which, when coupled with the infinitive, means "know how to...": ἴσμεν ἐπιστολὰς γράψαι ("We know how to write letters"). The subject of the complementary infinitive is not repeated since it is the same as the subject of the main verb.

   (2) The object infinitive is an infinitive at the core of an infinitive phrase (complete with an accusative subject, and any other necessary items, such as objects, adverbs, etc.). This infinitive phrase acts as the direct object of the verb that governs it. In the following example, ἐθέλω σε ἐπιστολὰς γράψαι, the phrase σε ἐπιστολὰς γράψαι, an infinitive phrase, acts as the direct object of ἐθέλω. γράψαι is thus an object infinitive. In some instances when the object infinitive is used, it would be natural to have the subject of the object infinitive also used as the indirect object of the main verb. When this is the case, the subject of the infinitive is expressed in the dative case, taking on the role of the indirect object of the main verb. It is not restated in the accusative. Thus, we would not have: φράζω αὐτῷ αὐτὸν ἐπιστολὰς γράψαι ("I declare to him that he should write letters"), but: φράζω αὐτῷ ἐπιστολὰς γράψαι ("I declare that he should write letters").

   (3) There are a certain number of ajectives which an infinitive will naturally follow. Examples include: ἄξιαι ἦσαν αἱ θεράπαιναι τὸν χρυσὸν

φυλάττειν ("The maids were worthy of guarding the gold") and πρόθυμοί ἐστε, ὦ στρατιῶται, τοῖς τείχεσιν **προσβάλλειν** ("you are ready, soldiers, to attack the walls").

(4) The subject infinitive is an infinitive that acts as the subject of another verb. Typically the subject infinitive is coupled with an impersonal verb or an impersonal expression. An exception to this is the non-impersonal use of δοκῶ. The subject of the infinitive is expressed either in the accusative or the dative, depending upon the expression it is used with. An example of an expression in which the subject infinitive is used with an accusative subject is δεῖ: example, δεῖ με ἐπιστολὰς γράψαι ("It is necessary for me to write letters"). A small handful of constructions and expression, including ἀνάγκη, ἔστι, and ἔξεστι, allow one to express the subject of the infinitive in the dative. Example: ἔξεστί μοι ἐπιστολὰς γράψαι ("It is possible for me to write letters").

(5) The infinitive in indirect discourse is often referred to as the second method of indirect discourse. This construction is typically introduced by a verb of thinking, believing, or forms of φημί. The subject of the discourse will be in accusative unless it is the same as the introductory verb. Examples:

ἐνόμισαν τοὺς Ἕλληνας σώφρονας εἶναι.
They thought that the Greeks were prudent.
ἔφην ἰέναι εἰς τὴν ἀγορὰν.
I was saying that I was going into the market.

(6) The infinitive preceded by ὥστε indicates a natural result clause. The subject of the infinitive will typically be in accusative unless it is the same as the subject of the verb of the clause introducing the result clause, in which circumstance the subject will remain unexpressed. Examples:

οὕτως ἡδὺς ἦν ὁ στρατηγὸς ὥστε ὑπὸ πάντων φιλεῖσθαι.
The general was so sweet as to be loved by all.
τοσαῦτα χρήματα εἶχεν ὁ δεσπότης ὥστε τοὺς ἄλλους μηδὲν ἔχειν.
The despot had so many possessions that the others mightn't have any.

2. The articular infinitive may be translated in one of three ways: "to _____", "_____ing", or in complex syntaxes, when the infinitive has a subject, objects and adverbs, "the fact that x is _____ing", or "x's _____ing".

3. It is always found in the accusative case.

4. It is negated with μή and its by-forms, and not οὐ.

5. The implications of the articular infinitive being a verbal noun are that it acts both as a noun and a verb. In the case of the articular infinitive, this means that as a noun it may be a subject or object in a sentence; and as a verb, it may have its own subject, objects, and adverbs.

6. (1) To be taught is a good thing. Being taught is a good thing. Subject. (2) I'm explaining to you the fact that wise people are always prudent. Direct object. (3) The fact that the enemy had destroyed the city was obvious. Subject. (4) I'm not guilty of the shields being stolen. I'm not guilty of the fact that the shields got stolen. Genitive after αἴτιος.

7. πρίν means "until" when it is in a negative sentence. When used in this sense and looking forward, it is followed by a subject in the nominative and a verb in the subjunctive + ἄν. If the negative sentence contains a verb in a secondary tense, the subjunctive may become an optative. When the verb so changes, the optative will not be accompanied by the

particle ἄν. When so used, πρίν anticipates the action of the verb contained in the clause it begins. In a negative sentence, πρίν may also precede a past indicative without ἄν if it looks back to the action of the verb contained in the clause it begins.

8. πρίν means "before" when it is in a positive sentence. When used in this sense, it is followed by an infinitive. The subject of the infinitive will be expressed in accusative unless it is the same as that of the main verb, in which case it will remain unexpressed.

9. (1) Before his wife comes into the house, the man kisses his maid. (2) The man did not kiss his wife until she came into the house. (3) Until the orator speaks I shall not consider him to be good. (4) I am collecting all the treasure before the old man destroys it.

10. (1) γράψαι οὐκ ἔχεις εἰδέναι πρὶν ἂν ὑπὸ διδασκάλου παιδεύῃ. (2) τοῦ λέοντος ἰόντος ᾐσθόμην πρὶν αὐτὸν βλέψαι ἡμᾶς. (3) τοῦ λέοντος ἰόντος οὐκ ᾐσθόμην πρὶν ἀνάγκη εἴη φυγεῖν. (4) πρὶν τὸν ἄνδρα ἀφικέσθαι, πωλήσει ἡ γραῦς πάντα τὰ ἱμάτια.

11. (1) οὐκ ἐξέσται σοι ἰέναι εἰς τὴν τριήρη πρὶν ἂν οἱ στρατιῶται καὶ οἱ ἵπποι εἰς αὐτὴν τρέπωνται. (2) ἐνόμισεν ὁ φιλόσοφος ἀνάγκην εἶναι τὴν ἀρετὴν διώκειν. (3) δοκεῖ μὲν ἡμῖν τοῖς πολεμίοις μάχεσθαι πρὶν ἡμῖν αὐτοὺς προσβαλεῖν· πολλοὺς δὲ πολίτας λυθῆναι οὐ βουλόμεθα. (4) ὑπὲρ τοῦ ἡμᾶς σχολὴν ἄγειν, ποιοῦσιν αἱ μητέρες πολλὰ ἱμάτια ἃ ἐν τῇ ἀγορᾷ πωλοῦσιν. (5) τοῦτον αἴτιον εἶναι φημί, χρὴ γὰρ φράζειν ὅστις αἴτιός ἐστι τοῦ τὴν ἁμαρτίαν ταύτην ἁμαρτεῖν. (6) λέγω σοί, ὦ τέκνον, νῦν ἰέναι κατὰ ταύτης τῆς κλίμακος. ἐὰν γὰρ μὴ ἴῃς, οὔποτε παύῃ βοῶν ἅτε φοβούμενον. (7) δεῖ ἀεὶ τὴν ἀρετὴν, τὴν ἀλήθειαν, καὶ τὴν δίκην ζητεῖν ἵνα γένηται ἀληθὴς φιλόσοφος. (8) ἕτοιμός εἰμι, ἔφη ὁ γέρων, τὸν βίον σχολῇ ἄγειν. (9) ἀναγκαῖον ἦν πᾶσι πολίταις ἐν ταῖς οἰκίαις μεῖναι πρὶν τὸν κήρυκα ἀγγεῖλαι τὸν στρατὸν τὸν πόλεμον νικῆσαι. (10) τὸ μὲν ἐζητηκέναι καὶ μὴ ηὑρηκέναι τὴν ἀλήθειαν οὐχ ἁμαρτία· τὸ δὲ μὴ ἐζητηκέναι ἁμαρτία μεγάλη.

12. Check your answers against **11**. in the exercises for Lesson 43.

Lesson 44

1. One forms the verbal adjective in –τέος by adding the appropriate suffix, –τέος, –τέα, or –τέον in the appropriate case and number to the aorist passive stem (the sixth principal part minus the termporal augment ε– and minus –θην), or the present or future stem. The verbal adjective in –τέος is always accented on the –τε– syllable of the suffix. These verbal adjectives are always easily recognisable from their –τέος, –τέα, or –τέον suffix, no matter from which stem they happen to have been formed.

2. The verbal adjective in –τέος expresses necessity or obligation.

3.
(1)	θυτέος	[needing] to be sacrificed
(2)	φιλητέος	[needing] to be loved
(3)	σωστέος	[needing] to be saved
(4)	μαθητέος	[needing] to be learned
(5)	φατέος	[needing] to be said
(6)	ἰστέος	[needing] to be known
(7)	φευκτέος	[needing] to be fled
(8)	γραπτέος	[needing] to be written
(9)	πεμπτέος	[needing] to be sent
(10)	λεκτέος or ῥητέος	[needing] to be said

4. When the verbal adjective in –τέος occupies the attributive position, it often functions as a substantive. Examples of this are:

Greek	literal translation	fluid translation
τὸ σωστέον	the needing-to-be-saved thing	the thing that needs to be saved; what needs to be saved
τὰ ἰστέα	the needing-to-be-known things	the things that need to be known; what needs to be known

5. The personal use of the verbal adjective in –τέος calls for the verbal adjective to be linked to a subject via a form of the linking verb εἰμί, and to agree with that subject in number, case, and gender. When this is done, as so often with εἰμί, the verb εἰμί need not be expressed. The agent of the action expressed by the verbal adjective is given in the dative case. The verbal adjective retains its sense of necessity or obligation. Two examples follow:

αἱ ἀσπίδες κλεπτέαι ἦσαν τοῖς κλωψίν. — The shields had to be stolen by the thieves.

τὰ ἱμάτια τοῖς οἰκέταις εἰς τὴν οἰκίαν οἰστέα. — The clothes must brought into the house by the servants.

The impersonal use of the verbal adjective in –τέος calls for the verbal adjective to be expressed **either** in the nominative neuter singular **or** in the nominative neuter plural. The verbal adjective will be in either of these two forms **regardless** of the number, case, and gender of the recipient of the action (the subjects of the sentence in the construction outlined above). Again, the agent of the action is expressed in the dative case. In this use, the verbal adjective in –τέος retains its sense of necessity or obligation. Examples follow:

τοὺς ἵππους τούτοις τοῖς ἀναξίοις ἀνδράσι κλεπτέα ἦν.
The horses had to be stolen by these unworthy men.
τὰ κακὰ φευκτέον ἐστὶ τῇ δεσποίνῃ.
The evils must be fled by the mistress.

6. (1) These speeches must / ought to / have to / need to / are to be spoken by the rhetor.
The rhetor must / ought to / has to / needs to / is to speak these speeches.
(2) Stopping your sins had to / needed to / was to be done by you.
You had to / needed to / were to / were obligated to stop your sins.

7. (1) τοῖς μὲν πολλοῖς ὁ βασιλεὺς αἱρετέος, τοῖς δ' ἀρίστοις οὔ. / τοῖς μὲν πολλοῖς τὸν βασιλέα αἱρετέα, τοῖς δ' ἀρίστοις οὔ.
(2) ἰτέα ἦν ἡ ὁδὸς αὕτη τοῖς στρατιώταις. / ἰτέα ἦν τὴν ὁδὸν ταύτην τοῖς στρατιώταις.
(3) σοφὰ τῇ φιλοσόφῳ γραπτέα. / σοφὰ τῇ φιλοσόφῳ γραπτέον.
(4) αὕτη ἡ μάχη ἡμῖν μαχετέα ἔσται. / ταύτην τὴν μάχην ἡμῖν μαχετέα ἔσται.
(5) τὰ λεκτέα ἐστὶ γραπτέα τῷ πρυτάνει. / τὰ λεκτέα γραπτέον τῷ πρυτάνει ἐστίν.

8. The verbal adjective in –τός can have one of two senses, depending upon context. One sense indicates either capability or possibility, while the other has the sense of a perfect passive participle.

9. One forms the verbal adjective in –τός by adding the appropriate suffix, -τός, -τή, or –τόν in the appropriate case and number to the aorist passive stem (the sixth principal part minus the termporal augment ε– and minus –θην), or the present or future stem. The stem for the verbal adjective in –τός will be the same for any given verb as its stem for the verbal adjective in –τέος. The verbal adjective in –τός is always accented on the ultima. These verbal adjectives are always easily recognisable from their –τός, -τή, or –τόν suffix, no matter from which stem they happen to have been formed.

10. The comparative and superlative are formed in the standard fashion; to wit, by dropping the case ending (–ος), adding ο or ω and –τερος, –α, –ον or –τατος, –η, –ον for the comparative or superlative, respectively.

11. (1) You are my beloved son. You are my lovable son. (2) We have arrested the stoppable thief. (3) Are the children educated? Are the children educable? (4) Let us hasten to see the admirable battle. Let us hasten to see the admired battle. (4) The army is stoppable; the trireme more so; and the soldier is the most stoppable.

12. ἐλαύνω, ἐλῶ, ἤλασα, ἐλήλακα, ἐλήλαμαι, ἠλάθην

13. (1) τῶν τριήρων στάδια ἑκατὸν ἰουσῶν, μύρια ἐλατέον τῷ στρατῷ. (2) τὸν στρατηγὸν θαυμάσοιμι ἄν, εἰ τὸν πόλεμον νικῆσαι μαχόμενος πάσας τὰς μάχας τὰς μαχετέας. (3) κενός ἐστιν ὁ χόρος τῶν μεμαθηκότων ἃ ἐγράφη· ἀναγκαῖον δ᾽ αὐτῷ ἔσται αἰσχύνεσθαι ὅτι ὀλίγιστα οἶδεν. (4) κρινοῦσι τοίνυν οἱ πρυτάνεις τοῦτον τὸν χόρον ὡς κάκιστον εἶναι. (5) ἐὰν ἐπιπλήττεται ὁ ῥήτωρ ὑπὸ τοῦ υἱοῦ τοῦ φιλητοῦ, αἰσχυνθήσεται. (6) τοῖς πολίταις βασιλέα οὐχ αἱρετέον ἐστὶν ἵνα αὐτῶν ἄρχῃ πρὶν ἂν ἀποθάνωσι πάντες οἱ ἄρχοντες. (7) πολλῶν πευστοτέρων ὄντων, αἰσθανόμεθα μέντοι τοὺς θεοὺς πευστοτάτους ὄντας καὶ ἡμῖν ζητέον εὑρεῖν αὐτούς. (8) ἠσχύνθησαν ἂν οἱ στρατηγοὶ εἰ οἱ στρατιῶται ἄνευ αὐτῶν εἰς τὴν μάχην ἤλασαν. (9) ὡς ὁ ῥήτωρ εἶπεν ὡς θαυμαστέον τι ἴδοι, αὐτὸν ἐκεῖνο ἰδεῖν οὐ πιστεύω καὶ αἰσθάνομαι τὸ θαυμαστέον οὔποτε γενόμενον. (10) οὐ φατέον τὸν βίον ἄριστον ὅταν οἱ ἄριστοι πάντων ἄλλων ἄρχωσιν.

14. Check your answers against **13.** in the exercises for Lesson 44.

Lesson 45

1. See Groton §261.

2. (a) What? (b) Which? (c) How? Why? or When?

3. Both of these subordinate clauses are substantival.

4. A clause of effort describes an outcome which the action of the clause on which it depends makes an effort to accomplish or avert.

5. Of those we know already, we include ὁράω, φυλάττομαι, ποιέω and πράττω. Of those introduced in this lesson, we include βουλεύω, ἐπιμελέομαι, μηχανάομαι and σκοπέω.

6. ὅπως* + future indicative**
   *the negation of the clause is ὅπως μή
   **the future indicative may be replaced by the future optative when the clause of effort is preceded by a verb in a secondary tense

7. (1) ἐπεμελοῦντο ὅπως μὴ φοβήσοιεν τὰ τέκνα. (2) μηχανησόμεθα ὅπως τοῖς τείχεσι προσβαλοῦμεν. (3) ἔπραξεν ὅπως ἡ γυνὴ αὐτὸν φιλήσοι. (4) ἐβούλευσας ὅπως αἱρεθήσοιτο ὁ ἀνὴρ ἄρχων. (5) σκεπτέον ὅπως μὴ ἀποθανοῦμεν.

8. The two clauses differ from one another in that while the purpose clause is adverbial, answering the question, "Why?" the clause of effort is substantival, answering the question, "What?" Furthermore, while the clause of effort is introduced by a clause whose action expresses general effort toward a goal, the purpose clause is introduced by a clause whose action is specific, while at the same time directed toward a goal. Lastly, their respective formulae in Greek differ.

9. One may replace the future indicative or optional future optative with a subjunctive or an optional present or aorist optative, respectively.

10. δέδοικα/δέδια (pluperfect ἐδεδοίκη/ἐδεδίη), _____, ἔδεισα, _____,
    _____, _____

11. (1) ἐδέδιμεν   (5) ἐδεδοίκει(ν)
     (2) δέδιμεν   (6) δέδοικε(ν)
     (3) ἐδείσαμεν   (7) δεδιέναι
     (4) ἔδεισε(ν)

12. δεδιώς, -υῖα, -ός

13. δέδοικα, φοβοῦμαι, φόβος ἐστί [μοι], κίνδυνός ἐστί [μοι], σκοπέω, ὁράω,
    φυλάττομαι

14. μή * + subjunctive**
    *the clause is negated by μὴ οὐ
    **an optative may replace the subjunctive when the clause is intro-
    duced by a verb in a secondary tense.

15. (1) ἐδέδιμεν μὴ πᾶς ὁ στρατὸς ἀποθάνοι. (2) κίνδυνος ἔσται ἡμῖν μὴ ὁ ἄρχων οὐ
    δικαίως ἄρχῃ. (3) φυλαξόμεθα μὴ αἰσχυνθῇ ὁ χόρος. (4) ἔδεισαν μὴ οἱ παῖδες ὑπὸ
    κλωπῶν κλαπείησαν. (5) φόβος ἐστὶ τοῖς πολλοῖς μὴ ἡ πόλις λυθῇ.

16. They may be used with either a negative clause of effort or a clause of
    fear.

17. (1) αἰσχυνόμενος ἐὰν μὴ ᾖ σῖτος ἱκανός, δέδοικα μὴ οἱ ξένοι πάλιν εἰς τὰς οἰκίας
    ἴωσι πρὶν φαγεῖν. (2) εὑρήσω τοίνυν μηχανὴν ὅπως οἱ οἰκέται σῖτον ἐν τῇ ἀγορᾷ
    κλέψουσιν. (3) σκεπτέον δὴ τοι ὅπως σοὶ ἱκανὸς ὕπνος καὶ σῖτος ἔσται πρὶν τὸν
    ἵππον τὴν πᾶσαν ἡμέραν ἐλαύνειν. (4) βούλομαι βουλεῦσαι ὅπως τοῖς ταύτης τῆς
    πόλεως τείχεσι προσβαλοῦμεν, τῆς ἄλλης στρατιᾶς ἐν τῷ στρατοπέδῳ καθευδούσης.
    (5) τοῦ τε γέροντος καὶ τῆς γραός, ὦ υἱέ, ἐπιμέλου, ἐπιμελούμενος ὅπως ἱκανὸν σῖτον
    ἔδῃ. (6) οἱ παῖδες, τοὺς στρατιώτας καὶ τὰς ἀσπίδας ὁρῶντες, ἐδέδισαν μὴ ἀπὸ τῶν
    μητέρων καὶ τῶν πατέρων κλαπείησαν. (7) φόβος πολὺς ἦν ἐν τοῖς πολίταις μὴ ὁ
    στρατηγὸς οὐ δεινῶς μηχανήσαιτο ὅπως τὴν μάχην νικήσοι. (8) δέδιτε,
    σωφρονέστεροι ὄντες, μὴ τὰ τέκνα οὐκ εὖ πεπαιδευμένα ἔσται. (9) καίπερ σχολὴν
    πολλὴν ἄγων, ὁ πρύτανις ἐβούλευεν ὅπως τὴν πόλιν ἀμείνω ποιήσοι. (10) τὸν θόρυβον
    τὸν μέγαν ἑωρακότες, ἐπεμελήσαντο οἱ ἄρχοντες ὅπως αἱ οἰκίαι μὴ λυθήσοιντο ὑπὸ
    τῆς στρατιᾶς τῆς ἄρτι νίκην μεγάλην νενικηκυίας.

18. Check your answers against **17.** in the exercises for Lesson 45.

Lesson 46

1. The –μι verb differs from the –ω verb in the following ways. First of all, it
   is athematic, which means simply that it lacks a thematic vowel (ο or ε
   for the standard –ω verb). Secondly, its stem is unstable, which is to say
   that the stem of a –μι verb will vary from form to form. Thirdly, the –μι
   verb uses a different set of personal endings in many of its forms.

2. (a) ω is used in the singular active; ο is used in the plural active and the
   middle/passive. (b) In the present and in the imperfect. (c) In the present.

3. (a) η is used in the singular active; α is used in the plural active and the
   middle/passive. (b) In the present, imperfect, perfect, and pluperfect. The
   reduplication for ἵστημι consists of the rough breathing mark. (c) In the
   present.

4. It is transitive in the following forms: present, imperfect, future, first
   aorist, perfect passive, aorist passive, future passive. It is intransitive in
   the following forms: second aorist, perfect active and pluperfect active.

5.
  (1) εἱστήκη. ἕσταμεν. ἕστατε. εἱστήκει(ν).
  (2) ἔδωκα. ἔδοσαν. ἔδομεν. ἔδωκε(ν).
  (3) εἰ δοίης, σταίη ἄν.
  (4) δίδωμι. δίδομαι. δίδοται. διδόασι(ν).
  (5) δίδοται. δίδονται. δίδωσι(ν). ἐδίδοσαν.
  (6) δίδως. δίδοσαι. ἔδωκας.
  (7) δίδοσθε. δίδοτε. ἐδίδοτε.
  (8) ἐθέλω διδόναι. ἐθέλω στῆναι.
  (9) ἐθέλω τὴν ἀσπίδα ἱστάναι. κελεύω τὴν ἀσπίδα δοθῆναι.
  (10) σπεύδομεν ἑστηκέναι.
  (11) στᾶσα ἦρξεν ἡ κόρη βοῶσα.
  (12) σταθεῖσα, ἡρπάσθη ὑπὸ στρατιώτου ἡ ἀσπίς.
  (13) ἐὰν στῶσι βοῶντες, δῶρα δώσομεν.
  (14) εἰ τὴν ἀσπίδα ἵστης, δῶρα ἐδίδου ἄν.
  (15) εἰ τὴν ἀσπίδα ἔστησαν, δῶρα ἔδομεν ἄν.
  (16) μηχανώμεθα ὅπως δῶρα δώσομεν. μηχανώμεθα ὅπως
      ἐστήξομεν. μηχανώμεθα ὅπως δοθησόμεθα. μηχανώμεθα
      ὅπως τὴν ἀσπίδα στήσομεν.
  (17) δῶρα ἡμῖν, ὦ δέσποτα, δὸς ἵνα ἐν τῇ ἀγορᾷ στῶμεν.
  (18) βιβλίον ἔδωκεν αὐτῷ ὡς αὐτὸ ἱστῇ
  (19) ἔσταθι. τὸ βιβλίον ἵστη. δῶρα διδόντων.
  (20) δῶρα δότε. δῶρα δόντων. ἑστῶμεν, δῶρα διδόντες.

6. ὠνέομαι, ὠνήσομαι, ἐπριάμην, _____, ἐώνημαι, ἐωνήθην

7. The third principal part of ὠνέομαι, ἐπριάμην, is the second aorist middle of a –μι verb whose stem is πριη/α. The fifth and sixth principal parts, unlike the rest of the verb, are not deponent.

8. ἐπίσταμαι, ἐπιστήσομαι, _____, _____, _____, ἠπιστήθην

9.
  (a) ἐπίσταμαι   ἐπιστάμεθα
      ἐπίστασαι   ἐπίστασθε
      ἐπίσταται   ἐπίστανται
  (b) ἐπιστάμην   ἐπιστάμεθα
      ἐπίστασο   ἐπίστασθε
      ἐπίστατο   ἐπίσταντο
  (c) ἐπισταθείην   ἐπισταθεῖμεν
      ἐπισταθείης   ἐπισταθεῖτε
      ἐπισταθείη   ἐπισταθεῖσαν

10. τοσοῦτος   ὅσος   ποσός   πόσος   ὁπόσος
    τοῖος   οἷος   ποιός   ποῖος   ὁποῖος

11. δίδωμι, δώσω, ἔδωκα, δέδωκα, δέδομαι, ἐδόθην

12. ἵστημι, στήσω, ἔστησα / ἔστην, ἕστηκα, ἕσταμαι, ἐστάθην

13. (1) χρή σε ἐπίστασθαι βιβλία γράψαι πρὶν ἐπιστηθῆναι τὴν φιλοσοφίαν. (2) οἷός τ᾽ ἐστιν ἡμᾶς καὶ τὴν τέχνην καὶ τὴν ἐπιστήμην διδάσκειν. (3) δίκην διὰ τὸ ἐν τῇ ἀγορᾷ ἑστηκέναι δούς, ἐζήτησεν ὁ φιλόσοφος ὁ παλαιὸς δίκην παρὰ τῶν αὐτὸν βλαψάντων λαβεῖν. (4) ἑστηκότες ὑπὸ τῷ δένδρῳ τούτῳ, οἷοί τ᾽ ἐσόμεθα δὴ σκέψασθαι ὅπως μὴ ὑπὸ τῶν θεῶν ἀπὸ τοῦ οὐρανοῦ πληχθησόμεθα. (5) πόσου ἐωνήθη ἡ ἀσπὶς ἥδε; τὴν ἐμὴν ἀσπίδα δραχμῶν δέκα ἐπριάμην. μήποτε οὕτως κακὰς ἀσπίδας τοσαύτης τιμῆς πριώμεθα. (6) ἐπίσταμαι τὸν ῥήτορα, καίπερ τὸν θησαυρὸν τοῖς παισὶ δόντα, τὰ βιβλία πᾶσι τοῖς πολίταις δόντα ἵνα σταθείη ἐν τῇ ἀγορᾷ καὶ ὠνηθείη καὶ πωληθείη. (7) οὐδὲ ἴσμεν ὁποῖος ἄνθρωπος τὰ ἑαυτοῦ τέκνα φάγοι ἄν. (8) τὴν κλίνην στήσασα, παρὰ τῇ θύρᾳ εἱστήκη βοῶσα τῷ ἀνδρὶ κατὰ τῆς κλίμακος ἰέναι. (9) ταῦτα τὰ ζῷα τῷ βασιλεῖ ἐδόθη ἵνα περὶ αὐτοῦ στῇ (10) τοσόνδε σῖτον πριαμένη, οὐκ ἐπίσταμαι ὅπως αὐτὸν ἐδόμεθα.

14. Check your answers against **13**. in the exercises for Lesson 46.

Lesson 47

1. Check your answers against Groton, pp. 330–331.

2. Check your answers against Groton, pp. 331–333.

3.
    (1) τίθησι(ν), ἔθηκα, τεθήκασι(ν), τιθῶμεν;
    (2) ἵησι(ν), ἧκα, εἷκασι(ν), ἰῶμεν;
    (3) θές, θέτε, θείη ἄν, θήσει, ἐτέθησαν
    (4) ἕς, ἕτε, εἵη ἄν, ἥσει, εἵθησαν
    (5) τὴν ἀσπίδα ἐπὶ τὸ τεῖχος θείς, βιβλίον ἵει ὁ στρατιώτης.
    (6) εἶπέν μοι ἡ γυνὴ θεῖναι τὸ βιβλίον ἐπὶ τὴν κλίμακα.
    (7) βιβλία μὴ ὦσιν. τὰ βιβλία ἐπὶ τὴν κλίμακα θέντων.
    (8) ἐκ τοῦ ἄστεως εἷθμεν ἄν, εἰ τὰς ἁμάξας ἐν τῇ ἀγορᾷ μὴ ἔθεμεν.
    (9) εἰ γὰρ τὰ παιδία διὰ τῆς θύρας μὴ ἵειτε.
    (10) λίθους εἷμεν ἵνα τοὺς πολεμίους ἐν κινδύνῳ θῶμεν.

4. Check your answers against Groton §274.

5.
    (1) ἵημι, ἥσω, ἧκα, εἷκα, εἷμαι, εἵθην
    (2) κεῖμαι, κείσομαι, _____, _____, _____,

_____
    (3) ἠμί, _____, _____, _____, _____,

_____
    (4) δύναμαι, δυνήσομαι, _____, _____, δεδύνημαι, ἐδυνήθην
    (5) τίθημι, θήσω, ἔθηκα, τέθηκα, τέθημαι, ἔθησαν

6. It is found only in the first and third person singular in the present and imperfect indicative active. Those forms are:

	Present	**Imperfect**
First	ἠμί	ἦν
Third	ἠσί(ν)	ἦ

7. μεθίημι, ἀφίημι, παρίημι

8.
δύναμαι	δυνάμεθα
δύνασαι	δύνασθε
δύναται	δύνανται

9. (1) ἐδυνάμεθα, ἦν δ᾽ ἐγώ, κεῖσθαι ἐπὶ ταῖς κλίναις ταῖς καλαῖς. (2) εἴπερ οἱ γονεῖς σ᾽ ἔθεσαν ὑπὸ δένδρῳ ἵνα ἀποθάνοις, ὦνερ τυφλέ, τί οὐ δύνασαι σεαυτὸν ἀφιέναι. (3) ποῦ, ἦ δ᾽ ὅς, κεῖνται αἱ ἀσπίδες; εἶπον οὖν αὐτῷ ὡς αὐτὰς εἰς τὴν τριήρη θεῖναι. (4) καίπερ ὢν δυνατὸς ὁ βασιλεύς, ἆρα δύναται ἡ δύναμις αὐτοῦ μηχανήσασθαι ὅπως ὑπὸ πάντων φιληθήσεται καὶ τιμηθήσεται; (5) τί ἄρα δύνασαι ποιῆσαι, ὦ δέσποινα; ἐάνπερ αἱ θεράπαιναι τὰ φυτὰ ἐπὶ τὴν οἰκίαν τιθῶσιν, καὶ μὴ ὑπὸ δένδρῳ, ἀποθανεῖται δὴ τὰ φυτά. (6) ἔντων τοίνυν τὰ φυτὰ κατὰ τῆς οἰκίας ἵνα αὐτὰ ὑπὸ δένδρῳ θῶμεν. (7) ἆρα κείσονται ἄνθρωποι σοφοὶ καὶ σώφρονες μετὰ ζῴων; ἐὰν τὸν βίον σχολῇ ἄγειν βούλωνται, ἐπὶ κλίναις ἐν οἰκίαις κείσθων. (8) κῦμά ἐστι φόβου μὴ θῇ ὁ στρατηγὸς τὴν στρατιὰν εἰς μέγαν κίνδυνον. (9) τὸν φόβον ἐκ τῆς ψυχῆς θές, ἦν δ᾽ ἐγὼ κείμενος, καὶ τὰς λυπὰς ἕς, ὦ οἰκέτα, σὺ γὰρ ἀπὸ τοῦ δεσπότου μεθείθης. (10) σὺν τοῖς πρυτάνεσιν ἑστῶτες, τοῖς ἄρχουσι τοὺς νόμους πολλούς τε καὶ ἀγαθοὺς θεῖσι, δῶρα πολλὰ ἔδομεν.

10. Check your answers against **9.** in the exercises for Lesson 47.

Lesson 48

1. It belongs to an altogether different class of –μι verbs. The other –μι verbs studied to this point are considered to belong to the "root class" of –μι verbs, i.e., to that class of verbs to whose root the personal endings are directly attached. δείκνυμι belongs to a class of –μι verbs to whose root the syllable –νυ– is attached before attaching the personal endings. The practical impact of this is that the only forms in which δείκνυμι shows itself to be a –μι verb are: present indicative, imperative, participle, and infinitive; and imperfect indicative. Otherwise, δείκνυμι is formed as a regular –ω verb.

2. (a) δείκνυμι, δείξω, ἔδειξα, δέδειχα, δέδειγμαι, ἐδείχθην.
   (b) (1)–(3) See Groton §277.

(4)	δειχθείην	δειχθείημεν
	δειχθείης	δειχθείητε
	δειχθείη	δειχθείησαν
(5)	δεικνύωμαι	δεικνυώμεθα
	δεικνύῃ	δεικνύησθε
	δεικνύηται	δεικνύωνται

   (6) δεικνύναι, δείκνυσθαι, δείξειν, δείξεσθαι, δεῖξαι, δείξασθαι, δεδειχέναι, δέδειχθαι, δειχθῆναι.

(7)	δεικνύς,	δεικνύντος
	δεικνῦσα,	δεικνύσης
	δεικνύν,	δεικνύντος
	δεικνύμενος,	δεικνυμένου
	δεικνυμένη,	δεικνυμένης
	δεικνύμενον,	δεικνυμέμου

3. (1) τὸ βιβλίον ἐδείκνυ. (2) τὸ βιβλίον δεικνύντων. (3) τὸ βιβλίον δεικνύω; (4) τὸ βιβλίον δεικνύοι ἄν. (5) εἰ γὰρ δεικνύοιντο. (6) τὰ βιβλία δεικνύς, ἐκέλευσεν ὁ πρύτανις αὐτὰ λυθῆναι. (7) τὰ βιβλία δείκνυσο.

4. It differs from the standard root class of –μι verbs in that its formation is based upon the paradigm of –ω verbs, and is not impacted by any vowel contraction as is found in the root class.

5. ἀνοίγνυμι, ἀποδείκνυμι

6. See Groton §278.

7. (1) εἰ γὰρ ταῦτα τὰ βιβλία ἐν τῇ ἀγορᾷ ἐδείχθη. or ὤφελε τὰ βιβλία ταῦτα ἐν τῇ ἀγορᾷ δειχθῆναι. (2) εἰ γὰρ ταῦτα τὰ βιβλία ἐν τῇ ἀγορᾷ ἐδείκνυτο. or ὤφελε τὰ βιβλία ταῦτα ἐν τῇ ἀγορᾷ δείκνυσθαι. (3) εἰ γὰρ ταῦτα τὰ βιβλία ἐν τῇ ἀγορᾷ δεικνύοιντο. (4) εἴθε σῖτον βελτίω ἐφάγομεν. or ὠφέλομεν σῖτον βελτίω φαγεῖν. (5) εἴθε σῖτον βελτίω ἠσθίομεν. or ὠφέλομεν σῖτον βελτίω ἐσθίειν. (6) εἴθε σῖτον βελτίονα φάγοιμεν.

8. See Groton §279.

9. (1) We wish to know what kind of animal humankind is. (2) Prove whether the account is true. (3) Say whence the orator came. (4) Ask the general on account of what the war started. (5) Don't be amazed at how much food the triremes are able to carry.

10. (1) εὗρον τοὺς θεοὺς ἐκ ποίου γένους γεννηθεῖησαν. (2) ἀνήγγειλεν ὁ κῆρυξ τοὺς στρατιώτας ὁπόσοι ἀποθάνοιεν. (3) ἠπιστήθη τοὺς ῥήτορας ὅποι τὴν πόλιν ἄγοιεν. (4) οἶδας τὰ ἱμάτια πόσα δέκα ὀβολῶν ἐωνήθη; (5) ἐπύθοντο τὸν Σωκράτη οὕστινας διαφθείραι.

11. (1) ὤφελεν εὑρεῖν τὸν θησαυρὸν ὅπου κεῖται. (2) ἀπόδεικνυ εἰ οἷός τ᾽ εἶ, ὦ σοφὲ φιλόσοφε, πῶς ἔξεστιν ὁμολογεῖν τοὺς θεοὺς τοῖς ἀνθρώποις ὁμοίους εἶναι. (3) τοῦ πολλὰ μαθεῖν ἕνεκα ὠφέλομεν ζητῆσαι τὴν ἀλήθειαν ἐν πᾶσιν. (4) ἔστω ὁ κύων ἡμῖν πᾶσι παράδειγμα. μήποτε ἐπιμελώμεθα τοῦ σίτου οὕτως ὥστε αὐτὸν παρὰ τῶν ἐχθρῶν ζητεῖν. (5) πάνυ τοι ὁμολογῶ σοί, ὦ Σώκρατες, ἦν δ᾽ ἐγώ, τῇ δ᾽ ἀληθείᾳ οἰόμεθα ὡς ἐποιήθη ὁ κόσμος παραδείγματί τινι; (6) ἡμεῖς μὲν γένος ἡλίου, ἔφασεν ὁ βασιλεύς, καὶ πάντας τοὺς ἡμῖν μὴ ὁμολογοῦντας νικήσομεν. (7) τῶν λόγων τῷ ῥήτορι δειχθέντων, ἦρξαν οἱ πολλοὶ νομίζειν κακόν τι μέγα πραχθῆναι. (8) τότε μὲν αὐτὸν ἄνδρα κακὸν ἐνόμισαν, νῦν δὲ θαυμάζουσιν αὐτὸν ὁποῖός ἐστιν. (9) δεικνύωμεν τὰς οἰκίας τοῖς ξένοις ἵνα βούλωνται κληθῆναι ἐπὶ τὸ δεῖπνον. (10) ἐμηχανησάμεθα ὅπως παύσοιτο ὁ οἰκέτης κλέπτων ἀφ᾽ ἡμῶν τὸν θησαυρόν.

12. Check your answers against **11.** in the exercises for Lesson 48.

Lesson 49

1. βαίνω, βήσομαι, ἔβην, βέβηκα, βέβημαι, ἐβήθην
   γιγνώσκω, γνώσομαι, ἔγνων, ἔγνωκα, ἔγνωσμαι, ἐγνώσθην

2. (1) 3rd pl., aor. act. ind.
   (2) fut. mid. inf.
   (3) 2nd s., aor. act. opt.
   (4) 3rd s., aor. act. imptv.
   (5) masc./neut. dat. s., aor. act. ptcpl.
   (6) 3rd pl., fut. pass. ind.
   (7) 1st pl., aor. act. opt.
   (8) 1st s., aor. act. subj.
   (9) 2nd pl., aor. act. subj. or imptv.
   (10) 3rd s., pf. mid./pass. ind.
   (11) 1st pl., pf. act. ind.
   (12) 1st s., plpf. act. ind.
   (13) 2nd s., aor. act. subj.
   (14) 3rd s., fut. act. opt.
   (15) 2nd pl., plpf. mid./pass. ind.
   (16) 1st pl., impf. act. ind.
   (17) 1st pl., aor. act. ind.
   (18) 3rd pl., aor. act. imptv.
   (19) fem. dat. pl., aor. act. ptcpl.
   (20) masc./neut. dat. pl., aor. act. ptcpl.
   (21) 3rd pl., pres. act. subj.
   (22) 3rd pl., aor. act. opt.
   (23) aor. act. inf.
   (24) aor. pass. inf.

3. (1) aor. pass. inf.
   (2) aor. act. inf.
   (3) 3rd pl., aor. act. opt.
   (4) 3rd pl., pres. act. subj.
   (5) masc./neut dat. pl., aor. act. ptcpl.
   (6) fem. dat. pl., aor. act. ptcpl.
   (7) 3rd pl., aor. act. imptv.
   (8) 1st pl., aor. act. ind.
   (9) 1st pl., impf. act. ind.
   (10) 2nd pl., pf. or plpf. mid./pass. ind.
   (11) 3rd s., fut. mid./pass. opt
   (12) 2nd s., aor. act. subj.
   (13) 1st s., plpf. act. ind
   (14) 1st pl., pf. act. ind.
   (15) 3rd s., pf. mid./pass. ind.
   (16) 2nd pl., aor. act. subj. or imptv.
   (17) 1st s., aor. act. subj.
   (18) 1st pl., aor. act. opt.
   (19) 3rd pl., fut. pass. ind.
   (20) masc./neut. dat. s., aor. act. ptcpl.
   (21) 3rd s., aor. act. imptv.
   (22) 2nd s., aor. act. opt.
   (23) fut. mid. inf.
   (24) 3rd pl., aor. act. ind.

4. (1) εἰ γὰρ τοῦτ᾽ ἔγνω. (2) εἰ γὰρ τοῦτ᾽ ἐγιγνώσκομεν. (3) εἴθε τοῦτο γνοῖεν. (4) εἰς τὴν ἀγορὰν ἔβημεν. (5) εἰς τὴν ἀγορὰν βαῖτε ἄν. (6) βῶ εἰς τὴν ἀγοράν.

5. (1) –θεν; (2) –δε, –ζε, or –σε; (3) –ι, –θι, or –σι(ν).

6.
	(1)	thither	(7)	thither
	(2)	at home	(8)	to Athens
	(3)	here	(9)	from home
	(4)	from Athens	(10)	at another place
	(5)	at the same place	(11)	thence
	(6)	to another place	(12)	to the same place

7. (1) ἱμάτια καλὰ Ἀθήνησιν ἐπριάμεθα. (2) ποῖ βαίνεις; βαίνω οἴκαδε. (3) δεῦρο ἀφικόμεθα ἄλλοθεν. (4) πῶς λέγειν δύνασαι ὅτι ὁμόθεν ἔβης; (5) οἱ γονεῖς μου ἐκεῖ ἑστήκασιν ὑπὸ τούτῳ τῷ δένδρῳ. (6) πότ᾽ ἐνθένδ᾽ εἶ;

8. See Groton §284.

9. (1) τοῦ ἡμετέρου οἴκου μέμνησαι; μέμνημαι ὡς κακῶς ἐπάθομεν ὑπὸ τῶν γονέων. (2) ποῦ αἱ Ἀθῆναι; πῶς ἔξεστιν Ἀθήναζε βῆναι; (3) τῶν τειχῶν ἤδη πεσόντων, ἡ πόλις δὴ πεσοῦται. (4) πότερον τῇ ἀληθείᾳ, ὦ πάτερ καὶ μῆτερ, ἀλλήλους ἀγαπᾶτε ἢ μόνον προσποιεῖσθε ἀλλήλους φιλεῖν. (5) γνόντες τὸν στρατηγὸν οὐ δυνησόμενον τοὺς στρατιώτας τῆς πατρίδος μνῆσαι, ἐπιστολὰς ἔπεμψαν αὐτοῖς οἱ ἄρχοντες. (6) ἕκαστος Ἀθήνησι πολλοὺς ὀβολοὺς πρὸς τῶν τῶν Ἀθηναίων συμμάχων ἔλαβεν. (7) μία μὲν θεράπαινα εἰς τὸν οἶκον ἔβη, ἡ δ᾽ ἑτέρα οὐκ ἔγνω ποῖ βῇ. (8) ἆρ᾽ ὁ οἶκός σου μέγας; ὁ ἡμέτερος ὁμός ἐστιν, καίπερ τῶν γονέων ἀποθανόντων. (9) δῶρα πολλὰ παρ᾽ ἀλλήλων ἔλαβον, ἀλλήλους πολλάκις ἐπὶ τὸ δεῖπνον καλέσαντες. (10) ἆρα μὴ ὁρᾷς τὸν ἥλιον; εἰ οὖν τυφλὸς τοὺς ὀφθαλμούς; οὐ μέντοι μέμνησαί μου; ἀληθῶς παλαίτατος τῇ ἡλικίᾳ ἐγένου.

10. Check your answers against **9.** in the exercises for Lesson 49.

Lesson 50

1. The redundant μή is sometimes used following a verb of hindering and in connexion with the infinitive that follows it. If the verb of hindering is negated, it may be followed by a redundant μὴ οὐ in connexion with the infinitive that follows it.

2. Cautious assertions with μή can be found either with the indicative (showing the speaker thinks the assertion to be true), or with the subjunctive (showing the speaker thinks the assertion may turn out to be true). Cautious denials with μὴ οὐ using the indicative indicate the speaker is speaking of something he thinks not true. When used in the subjunctive, they indicate the speaker is speaking of something he thinks may not be true.

3. οὐ μή followed either by the subjunctive or by the future indicative may indicate either (a) emphatic denial or (b) an urgent prohibition. Urgent prohibitions may also use ὅπως μή + future indicative.

4. (1) The guard is on guard against the shields being stolen. (2) Thou shalt not drink the water! (3) [I think that] the general might be hindered. (4) They shall not escape her notice in running. (5) [I suspect] they won't escape her notice in running. (6) Why do you prevent me from harming the horses? (7) They did not prevent the enemy from destroying the city. (8) [I think that] the servant is running through the plain. (9) The servant shall not run through the plain. (10) Thou shalt not run through the plain. (11) [I suspect that] you mightn't run through the plain.

5. Attraction is a phenomenon in which the case of a relative pronoun or adverb is attracted into the case or form of its antecedent, and out of the case demanded by its use in the relative clause. Often when the antecedent is a demonstrative, the attracted relative "bumps" the demonstrative out of the sentence.

6. (1) Many gifts were given to the citizens whom the king chose. δῶρα πολλὰ ἐδόθη τοῖς πολίταις οὓς εἷλεν ὁ βασιλεύς. (2) I am standing in that place whither I fled from Athens. ἕστηκα ἐκεῖ οἷ ἔφυγον ἀπὸ τῶν Ἀθηνῶν. (3) What do you think about the things which the philosopher was saying? τί νομίζεις περὶ τούτων ἃ ἔλεγεν ὁ φιλόσοφος; (4) Do they remember the things said which have escaped even the wise? ἆρα μέμνηνται τῶν εἰρημένων ἃ

ἔλαθε καὶ τοὺς σοφούς; (5) I wish to go to that place from which I fled. ἐθέλω βῆναι ἐκεῖσε ὅθεν ἔφυγον. (6) Do you know those whom you met in the marketplace? ἆρα γιγνώσκετε τούτους ὧν ἐτύχετε ἐν τῇ ἀγορᾷ;

7. See Groton §291.

8. See Groton §292.

9. (1) πολλάκις ἐκωλύθην ὑπὸ τοῦ στρατηγοῦ τοῦ μὴ τοῖς πολεμίοις προσβαλεῖν. (2) μέχρι τοῦ δείπνου, πίωμεν ἵνα ἡμᾶς αἱ λῦπαι λάθωσιν. (3) πότε τῷ ἄστει τεύξεται τοῦτο τὸ κακόν; ἐὰν τυγχάνει τὸ ἄστυ εὔδαιμον ὄν, τὸν μέγαν θησαυρὸν ἀφαιρήσει ἡ τύχη. (4) ψευδὲς ἡ τύχη. ἕως ἄρχῃ ἡ τύχη, βίῳ χαλεπῷ οἱ ἄνθρωποι χρήσονται. (5) πινέτω ὁ χορός· πληττέσθω τὸ πέδιον τῷ ποδί τῷ ἐλευθέρῳ· ἀκουέτω τὰ ὄρη τὴν τῆς χαρᾶς φωνήν. (6) αὕτη ἡ σοφία τὸν νοῦν τὸν καὶ τῶν ἀρίστων φιλοσόφων ἔλαθεν. (7) τοὺς πρυτάνεας οὐκ ἐλάθομεν πολέμιοι τῆς πόλεως γενόμενοι. (8) ᾐσθόμην τὸν ἵππον πλεῖον ὕδωρ πιόντα, ὁ δ' ἄλλος ἵππος τὸν στρατηγὸν ἔλαθεν πλεῖον πίνων. (9) ἆρ᾽, ὦ φιλόσοφε σοφέ, τῇ ἀληθείᾳ ὁ κόσμος ἄρχεται μεγάλῳ νοΐ, τῇ μοίρᾳ, ἢ μόνον τῇ τύχῃ; (10) μή μοι ψευδῆ εἰπέ, ἦν δ' ἐγώ, ἀλλ' εἰπέ μοι λόγον ἀληθῆν περὶ οὗ ἔτυχέν σοι.

10. Check your answers against **9**. in the exercises for Lesson 50.